Neo-Socialist Property Rights

Cover photo: *A solitary tree and the tower crane.* This photo was taken by the author.

Neo-Socialist Property Rights

The Predicament of Housing Ownership in China

Ho Cheuk-Yuet

LEXINGTON BOOKS
Lanham • Boulder • New York • London

Published by Lexington Books
An imprint of The Rowman & Littlefield Publishing Group, Inc.
4501 Forbes Boulevard, Suite 200, Lanham, Maryland 20706
www.rowman.com

Unit A, Whitacre Mews, 26-34 Stannary Street, London SE11 4AB

British Library Cataloguing in Publication Information Available

Library of Congress Cataloging-in-Publication Data

Ho, Cheuk-Yuet.
Neo-socialist property rights : the predicament of housing ownership in China / Cheuk-Yuet Ho.
pages cm
Includes bibliographical references and index.
ISBN 978-1-4985-0683-0 (cloth : alk. paper) -- ISBN 978-1-4985-0684-7 (electronic)
1. Home ownership--China. 2. Home ownership--Political aspects--China. 3. Housing policy--China.
4. Right of property--China. I. Title.
HD7287.82.C6H6 2015
333.33'80951--dc23
2015018550

∞™ The paper used in this publication meets the minimum requirements of American National Standard for Information Sciences Permanence of Paper for Printed Library Materials, ANSI/NISO Z39.48-1992.

Printed in the United States of America

For my mother and Yuen Wah.

Contents

List of Figures

Glossary of Chinese Terms

anlao fenpei (按劳分配): Allocation by work
anxu fenpei (按需分配): Allocation by need
baqi (霸气): Mighty bearing
chai (拆): Demolition
chaiqian (拆迁): Demolition and relocation
chaiqianhu (拆迁户): Evictee
changhong (唱红): Red singing
dahei (打黑): Black purging
dangzhongyang (党中央): The Party's central leadership
danwei (单位): Workplace, work unit
daobazi (刀把子): Knife handle; a metaphor of the law enforcement and judiciary organizations
dengjia jiaohuan (等价交换): Parity exchange
dingxing (定性): Determining the nature
dingzihu (钉子户): Nail householder
fangnu (房奴): House slave; property owners who borrow heavily to finance their purchase
fangzi (房子): Housing property
gequ suosu (各取所需): To each according to his need
gongtong fuyu (共同富裕): Common prosperity, getting rich together
guanxi (关系): Relationship network, relatedness
guapai (挂牌): Invitation for bidding
guojin mintui (国进民退): State-advance, civic-retreat
hukou (户口): Household registration
jiaodai (交代): Accountability
jiedao (街道): Sub-district
kaifashang (开发商): Real estate developer
kexuefazhan fuminxingyu (科学发展 富民兴渝): Scientific development for the prosperity of both the people and Chongqing
minjian (民间): A realm of people-to-people relationships separate from the formal bureaucratic channels
neisheng waiwang (内圣外王): The exercise of perfect self-cultivation and benevolent governance
nongchuanfei (农转非): Change of household status from agricultural to non-agricultural
paimai (拍卖): Public auction
quanli (权力): Power, authority
quanli (权利): Rights and interests

renmin (人民): People, commoners
RENMINBI (人民币): Chinese currency
renquan (人权): Human rights, people's power
shangfang (上访): Petition to the higher authorities
shehuizhuyi hexieshehui (社会主义和谐社会): Socialist harmonious society
shehuizhuyi hexin jiazhiguan (社会主义核心价值观): Socialist core values
shequ (社区): Community residents' committee
weiwen (维稳): Maintenance of stability
yifa zhiguo (依法治国): Rule of law
zhaobiao (招标): Tender
zouguochang (走过场): To do something perfunctorily

Acknowledgments

My deepest gratitude goes to my interlocutors in Chongqing for their indispensable help and enthusiastic support, and, of course, to my PhD supervisor, Harri Englund, for his patient guidance and invaluable advice. I also benefited greatly from the comprehensive reviews and thorough critiques of my dissertation, provided by Frank Pieke and David Sneath, to whom I am most deeply grateful.

In China, I am immensely indebted to Guo Xi, Joe Fan, and Guo Qi for their instrumental roles in referring contacts for my field work, and Tang Zifeng, Liao Kun, Liao Chenghong, Patsy Yu, and Yang Hong for their generous hospitality in making Chongqing feel like home for me. The extensive loop of relationships built up there was indeed referred all the way by Pan Jianping in Shanghai, Arnold Chan and Ball Wong in Hong Kong, Zhang Ningxiang in Shenzhen, He Jian at Southwest University, and Xu Bo at Chongqing University, to whom I am extremely thankful.

My sincere appreciation is extended to Ran Xueyu, Gao Minyi, and Yang Ling, who provided me with essential, impressive research assistance in the field. Special thanks also go to Lian Weijun, Liu Yan, Yang Huanyuan, Wang Xu, and Yan Xin for their kind assistance with research matters, Susie Casson and Hazel Ho for their painstaking proofreading support, Tu Jiong for her resourceful help in locating reference materials, and Nikolay Mintchev for his intellectual inspiration.

I am extremely grateful for the invaluable experience and knowledge that I gained from the many superb social anthropology seminars and classes at University of Cambridge I attended. I also wish to thank the members of the PhD Committee for their guidance and other staff members of the Division for their support. At the Chinese University of Hong Kong, I wish to acknowledge my appreciation of Tan Chee-Beng, Gordon Mathews, and Wu

Keping, who inspired and supported my further studies in the field of anthropology, despite my advanced age. I am also grateful to Amy King, Francinia Williams, Kayla Riddleberger, and an anonymous reviewer for Lexington Books. Portions and different versions of chapters 2 and 3 appeared in *Asian Anthropology* (Ho 2013) and *Critique of Anthropology* (Ho 2013) as gold open access articles. I thank the editors and reviewers of these journals for their constructive comments and suggestions.

Last but not least, I must express my thanks for the warm companionship of Hoi Pok and Pui Pui, although they may not have been particularly excited about my research topic, as well as the friends and relatives who had come all the way to visit me at Cambridge and Chongqing to lift me out of a thousand days of solitude.

No government or foundation money was used in the research, writing, or publication of this book.

Chapter One

Introduction

From Vice to the Virtue of Owning Private Property

Ubiquitous urban housing ownership has emerged together with a pervasive yet particularized rights discourse and practice in the barely two decades since the 1990s. Chinese people are indeed witnessing and experiencing an astonishing formation and proliferation of a new property regime under the auspices of the party-state. Paradoxically, the ruling Communist Party of China (CPC) has never ceased to proclaim that China is a "socialist country," albeit acknowledging that it is still in the primary stage of socialism. Nonetheless, by negating the past cardinal principle of the ownership of private property as the root of all evil, the new property regime may, by chance, reformulate the meaning of citizenship and well-being, and in so doing germinate a new conception of values and rights.

Shortly after I had settled into my field site in the Chongqing Municipality in July 2011, coincidentally, the Supreme People's Court in Beijing released two instructions in relation to housing demolition and property ownership, indicating the social repercussions of my research topic for housing, real estate investment, and property rights.

On August 12, 2011, a judiciary interpretation of the "Marriage Law" was released on how to divide housing property in cases of divorce. It directs that a house bought by parents for a newlywed son or daughter would be their child's sole property unless otherwise specified, and that if the husband or wife made the down payment for the marital home, then he or she shall own it.[1] Officials stated that the goal of this interpretation was to protect personal property rights more equitably, but it also indicated that a commodity economy's principles were encroaching on family relations and private life. As one commentator noted, the judicial interpretation had "effectively turned a gift into a lease of sorts" and clearly departed from the "Marriage Law's" guiding principle (Chang Ping 2011). As such, house purchase and gifting have become not only a critical financial decision but also a value determinant of intimate relationships. Moreover, the following month, on September 8, 2011, in unusual recognition of the proliferation of forced evictions, the Supreme People's Court posted an emergency notice on its website, urging law enforcement personnel to cease demolition work immediately if they encountered radical resistance.[2] The notice candidly admits that:

> In recent years, notorious incidents have happened during the course of land expropriation and house demolition. Resistance is known to include suicide by self-immolation and jumping from rooftops, self-inflicted harm, as well as setting fire to gas tanks, spraying gasoline, throwing bricks, and organizing mass assaults against demolition workers. There have also been inappropriate uses of weapons by judiciary police causing deaths and causalities.

This account basically confirmed what many members of the domestic media and international human rights advocates had been reporting for years. Still, this revelation highlighted concerns that local judiciary bodies had been dragged into realizing the notorious work of forced eviction and thereby compromised their supposedly impartial role. The emergency notice requires that all courts stringently vet executive applications for forced eviction and warns that, in the event of misconduct, the abusive use of coercive action, and the reckless deployment of a judiciary police force, leading to notorious consequences, both the court leadership and officials in charge will be held personally accountable. However, the notice was removed from the website a mere day later, after extensive coverage by the media, which is indicative of probable internal disagreement within the judiciary or between different government organs, or concerns that it might incite even more instances of fierce public resistance to forced evictions.

The Supreme Court's judicial interventions, in addressing housing demolition and the sharing of marital property, genuinely reflect the public's deep concern. Astoundingly, private property rights have become a preeminent value proposition, blossoming into a variety of reactions, such as euphoria, lust, and fear, in contemporary Chinese society. Since the 1990s, various anthropologists have explored the changing shape of China's state-society relations and raised the question as to whether a hybrid of a market economy, private property rights, and authoritarian politics represents an oxymoronic anomaly or a historical synthesis that is unfamiliar to the conventional political models. Mayfair Yang (1994) formulates a tripartite scheme of social relationships to examine the case for constructing a civil society amid the state's monopolization of resource redistribution power. Hill Gates (1996) and Robert Weller (1999) map out the latent seeds for change embedded in the very cultural fabric of Chinese society. Gates concludes that the chance to achieve justice and human social formation is predicated on China's kinship-based, petty-capitalist mode of production, as opposed to the powerful state tributary mode of production; whereas Weller asserts that informal social associations represent the crucial cultural resource for forming alternate civilities. In reality, however, such an imagined civil or alternate society simply cannot exist in the shadow of the party-state. Aihwa Ong and Li Zhang (2008) point out that the state and the private sphere are indeed engaged in the co-production of practices, values, and solutions, which in combination produce a paradoxical coexistence of micro-freedoms with illimitable political power. Based on the notion of an existing socialism, Frank Pieke (2009) also explains how the Party has successfully reinvigorated itself and put its rule on an increasingly solid footing materially, organizationally, and ideologically. All in all, an ambivalent situation has been emerging, epitomized by the complex issues surrounding housing, as private homeownership in China reconfigures the urban space, ways of life, definitions of class, and governance. These issues present a fertile ethnographic setting for analysis and constitute the theoretical landscape for the focus of my inquiry.

The proliferation of forced evictions, real property investment, and rights defense is a legacy of the dramatic land and housing reforms that have been implemented since 1988, which have given rise to an intertwined functioning of state and market powers and alleged rampant corruption. Real property has become a principal source of wealth creation and social discontent over the widening wealth disparity, with the local authorities performing a dual role in land expropriation and the approval of real estate development. Economist Yasheng Huang (2008) warns that land grabs have become an endemic problem; geographer You-tien Hsing (2010) argues that land is shaping the restructuring of state power; and anthropologist Li Zhang claims that a new urban geography of class is emerging, with a heightened consciousness regarding property ownership. The Chinese government's property policy lacks transparency and is characterized by inconsistencies often between the central and local governments; thus, it is very difficult for ordinary investors to conduct risk evaluation to mitigate extreme loss. The state control is principally threefold in nature: the monopolized distribution of land, the provision of credit, and the administering of purchase restrictions and pricing. The government's power is all-embracing, spanning from the upstream supply of land resources and control over the production of property assets to the downstream elicitation of demand and surveillance of market activities. A basic understanding of the development and structure of the housing sector offers a critical vantage point from which one can apprehend the state-market relationship.

China's land leasehold market was formally established in 1988, when land ownership was separated from land-use rights. Thereafter, land-use rights could be transferred by tender, open auction, or negotiation; and private and state-owned real estate companies were granted permission to develop housing properties for sale in the market. The People's Republic of China's (PRC) Constitution stipulates that urban land belongs to the state and rural land to the collectives, yet the state retains the ultimate claim over all land. Municipal governments have authority over land-use rights transfer, such as expropriating land for building housing projects, industrial zones, commercial complexes, highways, and so forth, in the name of the public good. By the 2000s, income from land sales and property transactions had become vital, accounting variously for 30 to 70 percent of the local governments' annual revenue.[3] The soaring land values caused by economic growth and housing demand further accelerated the pace of urban renewal and outward expansion. This development frenzy is also attributable to the Party cadre's responsibility system, which rewards a "single-minded focus on GDP growth" (Heimer 2006, 134), with real estate being an effective way to boost economic performance by creating a multiplying demand for labor, materials, electricity, and transportation.

Prior to the 1990s, most urban quarters were provided by the state through the workplace. In 1998, the government resolved to phase out welfare housing by 2003, by subsidizing workers who wished to purchase their own home. The status of the work unit was crucial in determining the overall endowment of resources. Important state enterprises and government departments typically had access to an abundant supply of housing units for sale at a discounted price. Well-situated work units would also occupy precious plots of land for lucrative subsequent redevelopment. Apart from Shenzhen, Guangzhou, Shanghai, and Beijing, the majority of cities have only witnessed a more mature housing market since the early 2000s, after the ending of welfare housing provision. Many localities have introduced accommodative policies for activating real estate development and some have even provided additional incentives by entitling buyers to local urban household status. Broadly speaking, the past decade has witnessed a three-stage uptrend: 2000–2004, 2005–2007, and 2008–2010. During each of the downturns in 2005 and 2008, property prices immediately recovered and surpassed the previous peak levels. Overall, average residential prices more than tripled. This explains homeowners' skepticism about the efficacy of the government's extended round of clampdowns circa 2011–2014. As my research was in progress, property prices regained a solid momentum, after tailing off very modestly.[4]

The experience of 2008 was particularly painful for investors, who had trusted the government's determination to cool down the manic speculation. The eruption of the American real estate-driven financial crisis led to central banks worldwide embarking on "quantitative easing" (QE) by purchasing financial assets from the market, with a view to preventing a global systemic meltdown. In the midst of the subsequent economic slowdown and appalling corporate credit crunch, the Chinese government launched its own RMB4-trillion (US$635 billion) stimulus package and drastically reversed its credit tightening policy. Much of the money had found its way into investment in infrastructure and housing demand, thus averting an across-the-board collapse of the real estate industry. Various local governments also sanctioned an immediate relaxation on property purchase conditions, mortgage rates, and taxation to entice buyers to return to the market. Not only in China, a liquidity-driven real estate boom was also triggered in many other countries, camouflaging investment hazards and sowing the seeds for yet another asset bubble. However, the economic recovery induced by QE proved to be fragile and further QE was necessary to sustain its effect (Joyce et al. 2012). In the third quarter of 2012, against the backdrop of the European sovereign-debt crisis, the U.S. Federal Reserve announced a further round of QE and, in China, another economic dip prompted many localities to relaunch their own fiscal stimulus programs.

From April 2010, Beijing embarked on a nationwide clampdown on property speculation again through purchase restrictions, higher mortgage interest rates, and the introduction of a real estate tax. However, these measures had little effect on the prices. On July 7 and September 1, 2012, Premier Wen Jiabao repeatedly proclaimed that the government should "pre-set and fine-tune its policies in a more aggressive manner."[5] However, the efficacy of the state's discretionary policy move is questionable, given that land sales, housing and infrastructure construction, and property transactions in the aggregate have become a major impetus to the overall economy. In 2012, total land sales income in all localities dropped by 13 percent compared to the previous year, to RMB2,700 billion, so the local authorities had every incentive to hope for a real estate revival; then, by 2013, unsurprisingly, land sales income rebounded by 45 percent to reach a historic record of RMB3,100 billion.[6] My current aim is not to analyze the results of the central government's tug-of-war with the local authorities but, rather, my principal concern is the issue of the state's painstaking involvement in and even control of the real estate market on both the supply and demand sides. The extent and nature of such micromanagement and mediation affects ordinary people's broader cultural conception of their property ownership possibilities vis-à-vis the party-state. My informants like to use the metaphor of the government's dual role as both referee and player to indicate this inherent conflict of interest. Scholars of housing studies Ya Ping Wang et al. (2012) regard such interventions as necessary for market progress but nonetheless concur that swift government interventions play an important role in housing market performance. As mentioned, China's statist approach is closely related to the pervasive influence of the 2008 global financial crisis. This has fostered an inseparable relationship between the domestic property market and the distant yet immediate force of financial globalization. China's property market is at a crossroads, after running at full steam for a decade, and its socioeconomic impacts are yet to be comprehended critically.

Moreover, the concomitant phasing out of welfare housing and liquidity inflow due to monetary easing in the aftermath of the global financial crisis engendered solid structural housing and cyclical investment demands, as well as a rampant increase in housing prices across China. These, in turn, triggered the proliferation of housing demolition, orchestrated by collusion between the local governments and property developers. When a building structure is designated to be demolished, a circle containing the awful, big character *chai* (demolish) will be painted on the walls. Examining this widespread phenomenon, Adam Chau states that "a one-character message issued by institutions of power is to be read and understood as an explicit command not to be resisted" (2008, 206). According to a report by the Chinese Academy of Social Sciences (Chen Guangjin 2012), out of an estimated 100,000 "mass incidents" (protests) caused by social contradictions annually, half are related to land expropriation and forced eviction. A report by Amnesty International (2012) points out that forced eviction has become a routine occurrence and represents a gross violation of China's international human rights obligations on an enormous scale.

In accordance with the PRC Constitution, "The state may in the public interest take over land for its use in accordance with the law" (Article 10) and "The state protects by law the right of citizens to inherit private property" (Article 13). In the routine conflicts arising from demolition, however, contradictions between the rights of the property owners and of the state were not equitably addressed until the long overdue endorsement of the "Property Rights Law" on March 16, 2007, by the National People's Congress. The law is formulated with a view to "giving full effect to the meaning of property, protecting the obligee's property ownership rights" (Article 1). The law is designed to provide a legal framework governing evictions and it is significant that it places public and private property rights on an equal footing, but legal experts Gebhard Rehm and Hinrich Julius (2009) assert, on closer analysis, that the property rights law does not strengthen the rights of the owner compared with the previous legal position, because it neither clarifies the requirements for expropriation nor standardizes the levels of compensation. Such clarification would have to wait until January 2011, when the State Council adopted the "Regulations on the Expropriation of and Compensation for Houses on State-owned Land," which prohibits violent and coercive evictions, and stipulates that demolition compensation must be based on market value. Noticeably, in the actual protection of people's rights, constitutional and legislative provisions represent a mere formality; it is the executive regulations (nonetheless subject to certain degree of local government discretion) that really matter.

On March 19, 2007, by coincidence three days after the adoption of the Property Rights Law, the People's Court of Jiunongbo District, Chongqing, decreed that the last household in an area slated for commercial redevelopment would have to be vacated within three days. This incident was widely reported by the domestic and international media, along with striking pictures of a two-story house standing in the middle of a vast, excavated building site, popularly referred as the "most vibrant nail house." House demolition and relocation are referred to as *chaiqian*, and evictees as *chaiqianhu*. When evictees defy government orders to vacate their residence, they become known as *dingzihu* (nail householders), a term that vividly evokes the image of nails sticking out of wood that cannot be pounded down with a hammer (see Figure 1.1). In the end, the occupants accepted the district government's revised offer of generous compensation. Thereafter, the image of this Chongqing "nail house" has become the national icon for counter-demolition. In August 2010, a free online game, entitled "The Nail householders vs. the Demolition Team," was released and became an instant hit. The game was said to be "the latest example of how demolition is bleeding into Chinese pop culture."[7] In this game, a female character throws sandals at encroaching attackers, and a potbellied man drops dynamite from the roof. In the real world, the struggle is far less even-handed but no less fierce. Refusing to leave, residents will throw rocks and Molotov cocktails, and even set themselves on fire using gasoline. Some of these scenes have been broadcast on the official news channels and captured live on Internet portals. Amnesty International (2012) documented forty-one cases of self-immolation related to forced eviction between 2009 and 2011.

During my field work in Chongqing, as the central government had pressed on in cultivating a "socialist harmonious society,"[8] forced evictions were a regular practice but no longer as frequent and violent as had been the case in previous years. The local authorities also exercised extra caution ahead of senior-level personnel reshufflings. Moreover, the abrupt dismissal of Bo Xilai as Municipal Party Secretary, in March 2012, placed a drastic brake on government activities that had the potential to stir up social discontent. While the basic economic logic of demolition and counter-demolition remained very much intact, an extraordinary moment of suspense had been created, with many evictees thus building up a sense of anticipation about bargaining. This situation meant that I was less likely to witness a forced eviction. The flip side was I had more time to listen to the evictees and gain an understanding of their rationales and bargaining tactics, which provided a more complete account of the practices of demolition and counter-demolition.

This book is an ethnographic account of urban dwellers' desire for housing ownership and how their acquiring and defending of their property rights reshape the state-property-family relationality in the context of neo-socialist

Figure 1.1. A "Nail House" in Chongqing. This photo was taken by the author.

China. It defines neo-socialism as a synthesis of orthodox socialist and new market moralities and practices in their ideological, political, and economic underpinnings. My ultimate concern is whether the economic ethos pertaining to the ubiquitous phenomena of individual property rights in the past two decades may harness a broader rights discourse or, conversely, impede the emergence of universal rights ethics. In so doing, I take the connection between property rights practice and the broader human rights discourse as both a working hypothesis and a historical question. In this ethnography, I explore the situation of runaway property prices as a conjoint consequence of domestic housing privatization and global monetary relaxation, and how these constitute a source of great wealth for many yet dispossession for others. I have discovered a changing meaning of property relations, which is embedded in a discourse of rights, apparently individualized yet intricately tied to the re-emerging family values that could be interpreted as a counter-current to the legacy of a communist utopia of a propertyless, classless, and selfless society. I aim to expound the peculiar roles of the party-state and its symbiotic relations with the housing market in engendering a hitherto unseen real estate boom, as well as the consequential, pervasive phenomena of forced evictions and the perceived "risklessness" of investing in real property. The issue of how evictees and investors conceive of, and factor in, the logic and parameters of need, desire, right, and risk in their agency shall be depicted by way of ethnographic observation. My objective is to shed light on the complexity and ambivalence within the social production of rights, grounded in empirical studies of the practices of housing demolition and property investment.

In recent years, a growing number of China-based legal scholars and sociologists have enquired into the sensitive topic of demolition and forced eviction (Bi Xiangyang 2006; Feng Yujun 2004; Peng Xiaobing and Zheng Rongjuan 2010; Shi Yunqing 2007; Xu Mingyue and Huang Dongbin 2010). From overseas, historian Qin Shao (2013) has contributed a detailed ethnographic account of grassroots resistance to demolition and relocation in Shanghai, based on an investigation into the interaction between the residents, government, courts, developers, media, and other agencies in dealing with the conflict. The political scientist Jonathan Bach (2010) has examined how peasants have become landlords in Shenzhen's urban villages by building extra-legal premises and their subsequent bargaining for compensation, while Steve Hess (2010) has surveyed the general situation of China's land-rights-based protests. In the field of anthropology, however, the research interest appears scant, with the noticeable exception of Li Zhang's exemplary study of the large-scale demolition of a rural-urban migrant community on the outskirts of Beijing (2001) and overview of urban housing demolition (2004), as well as Matthew Erie's (2012) discussion of new media's role and limitation in effecting evictees' resistance against forced evictions by producing alternative discourse on law. On property owners' defense of their rights, there is also a growing body of studies that has brought attention to how they organize themselves to counter pressure from cohorts of property developers, estate managers, housing authorities, and court officials by means of localized protests, a refusal to pay management fees, petitions to the various levels of the administration, lengthy litigation, and even violent confrontation (Chen Peng 2010; Guan Bing 2010; Guo Yuhua and Shen Yuan 2012; Jiang 2013; Read 2003, 2008; Tomba 2005; Wang et al. 2013; Zhang Lei 2005; Zhang 2010; Zhu Jiangang 2011; Zhuang Wenjia 2011). Resident owners' resistance mainly concerns property developers' unlawful use of the public areas and estate management companies' malpractices. These protest activities typically entail extensive organization and are of long duration, from several months to a few years, but, in the end, like the evictees' struggle against forced evictions, tend to prove unsuccessful.

Moreover, anthropologists who have researched China's housing topics have been concerned primarily with the consumption aspect and have rarely focused on the other side of urban housing demolition and investment. Investment and consumption are indeed *not* two strictly incompatible or ambivalent categories but, rather, dialectic concepts and concrete practices that constitute the duality of property buying, ownership, dwelling, and selling. Meanwhile, momentous property investment by real estate developers and the Chinese public, on the back of fully fledged bank lending and the policy support of local governments, have co-engineered waves of property price spirals, exacerbating the greed and need for urban demolition to make way for lucrative redevelopment projects. This book thus aims to contribute to an overlooked but important topic. I also suggest that these situations and observations should be understood in the broader context of the formidable economic reforms post-1979 and post-1992, respectively, upon which a neo-socialist state is formed.

DEFINING NEO-SOCIALISM AS THE CHINA ALTERNATIVE

In the preamble of the PRC Constitution, it is declared categorically that Chinese people of all ethnic groups will continue to adhere to the "people's democratic dictatorship" and the "socialist road;" and that the nation's basic task is to concentrate its efforts on socialist modernization along the road of "socialism with Chinese characteristics," while acknowledging that China is still in the primary stage of socialism.[9] At the ideological level, the Party vows that realizing communism and achieving "common prosperity" are its highest ideals and ultimate goals.[10] As substantive proof of the party-state's political will and/but pragmatic policy goal, on November 12, 2013, at the close of the third Plenary Session of the 18th CPC Central Committee, a reform blueprint was unveiled that calls for a "decisive role of the market" in resource allocation, but proclaims that "China will stick to the dominant role of public ownership, playing the leading role of the state-owned economy, while encouraging, supporting, and guiding the non-public sector."[11] Hence, it is counter-intuitive when, from time to time, many (if not most) scholars, including anthropologists, insist on referring to China as "post-socialism" or as an example of "late socialism."

Of course, China is no longer the same socialist state that it was between the 1950s and 1970s, as the principal welfare provisions in healthcare and housing, and job security have been phased out. I consider it essentially neo-socialist due to its unconventional agglomeration between a market and property rights logic and the Leninist party-state power structure, combined and complete with an untarnished goal of socialism. The state retains formidable influence through proactive policy management, as well as public ownership and senior management control in strategic enterprises—a mix of private-state economy. Essentially, there is no such thing as a segregated economy but a *political economy*, one imbued at every point with one-party politics and state policies, even in the business and welfare arenas.[12] Taken together, these distinctive characteristics differentiate it substantively from all the ex-Soviet states and constitute a China alternative to radical postsocialist transformation. Without doubt, China remains a socialist country, albeit more appropriately and accurately described as "reform socialist" (Hann and Hart

2011, 137) or what I call "actually existing neo-socialist." In the aftermath of the 1989–1991 political turmoil across most communist regimes, China had followed a political-economic path that differed vastly from that of others. It had taken advantage of earlier successes in establishing a rural household responsibility system to boost agricultural production and an open-door policy to promote foreign trade and investments since 1979. It continued to overhaul its mammoth state enterprises and substantiated the role of market forces and private property rights to incorporate the coastal economies into the global labor force. China's prudent market reforms have proved more robust and sustainable than those of all of the postsocialist regimes during their equivalent transition period.[13] In the ensuing two decades, China has continued its hyper-growth strategy, transforming itself into the world's second-largest economy. In retrospect, the late paramount leader Deng Xiaoping's "southern tour" to the coastal regions in 1992 marked a definitive break with Mao Zedong's ideological legacy. Deng's stern warnings against the regressive policy inclinations within the Party subsequently engendered unprecedented privatization mania and nationwide "development zone fever" (Hsing 2010, 98).[14] People are asked to exercise "choice" in everyday life and adopt individual responsibility as their dominant economic ethos. In the aftermath of the 2008 global financial crisis, China's economic resilience further distinguishes itself from the Western liberal model of market economy.

The Chinese reformist path has proved a politically contested, historically contingent by-product of policy rather than strategic designs and a well-planned model. Its transformation does not accord with a typically dichotomized, abrupt transition to an industrial society or a sudden abandonment of a command economy (Davies and Wang Feng 2009), whereas its state enterprise shareholding system reform is considered consistently gradualist and the entire process characterized as "privatizing by groping for stepping stones to cross the river" (Ma 2010, 6). Michael Burawoy and Katherine Verdery (1999) attribute that policy emanating from the center always encounters resistance, which reverberates back as unintended consequences. Frances Pine and Sue Bridger (1998) also argue that, because of the wide diversity between individual countries and even between the communities and regions within each country, arising from the specificities of local history, cultural experience, the environment, and the landscape, as well as the economic position of each at the precise moment of change, their particular paths toward a free market economy and civil society have differed, despite the uniformity of experience created by the principles of centralized distribution and a command economy. Hence, we should not conceive of the various postsocialist trajectories as unilineal or multilineal processes of transition to a predetermined endpoint but, rather, avoid mistaking a historically contingent private property form as universal, natural, and neutral (Humphrey and Verdery 2004). It is thus more useful to analyze China's unique pathway as a transformational rather than a transitional process. In the realm of politics, China's approach also differs sharply from that of the ex-Soviet trajectories. Multiparty polity is deemed absolutely out of the question by the communist leadership, and any singularly conceived image of capitalism also fails to capture the full picture of the party-state's monopolization of resource redistributive power in a market economy. Concerning this agglomeration, Mayfair Yang (1994) warned that a nonmarket, non-transparent technique of power, *guanxi*, might proliferate, which would compromise the construction of a social order that would work for the public good. Surprisingly, China's mainstream statist approach, combined with rampant systemic corruption, has failed to result in a floundering economy. On the contrary, after three decades of partial reform (economic but apolitical), its economy has fared far better than that of most industrialized and developing countries in the world. This complex oscillation between state resource monopolization and a market mechanism is hitherto unseen, un-conceptualized, and uncharted. It is certainly not a mode of conventional socialism as we know it, but also *not* definitively un-socialist.

Moreover, from the ruling Party's native point of view (*emic* perspective), this mode of governance surely constitutes a viable form of socialism. By my own reckoning, the real world offers no such thing as prototypical Marxism, but only socialism as lived. I concur with Frank Pieke's (2009) framing of "an anthropology of neosocialist rule," by approaching socialism ethnographically as it is lived and reproduced every day. As Pieke puts it, China's current trajectory of neo-socialist development combines many contradictory elements, such as the reaffirmation of the Leninist organizational discipline, creation of a modern governmental bureaucracy, and neoliberal marketization but, most imperatively, it seems to be steering a steady forward course, so far. Alternatively, Andrew Kipnis (2008) advocated a postsocialist anthropology for China as a critical theoretical stance, offering a theory of hope so as to revisit the failures of actually existing socialism in order to move on to different ways of theorizing social relations. Kipnis wants to go beyond other postsocialist analysts' mere descriptions of a set of historical circumstances, by recognizing a complex field of continuities and discontinuities between abuses of power in the Maoist and post-Mao periods, respectively. I share his perspective but believe that, while problematizing the holistic use of neoliberalism as leaving no possibility for the theorization of change (Kipnis 2007), his positing of China as postsocialist paradoxically risks making too broad a claim regarding the actual possibility of change. I suggest neo-socialist anthropology as a more forthright descriptor that captures the essence of continuity but is no less cogent in explicating dynamism and contradictions.[15] Implicit is the goal of objectively and critically examining both the party-state's solid achievements and crippling deficiencies at present, while not abandoning reflexivity on the past calamities inflicted on the people. The idea of neo-socialism also captures the possibility of both advancement and disjuncture on its future trajectory.

Lastly, while postsocialism has been customarily employed to signify both a macro and a historical context, numerous social scientists also invoke the term "neoliberal" to describe a wide range of economic and cultural practices in the everyday life of Chinese people, as if "neoliberalization" is a global, universal transformative process that has also triumphed over the party-state's ideological vigor and political dominance. Commonly, neoliberalism is located and analyzed in the context of and/or in conjunction with postsocialism. For instance, Lisa Rofel's (2007) ethnographic project aimed to bring together questions of desire, sexuality, political subjectivity, postsocialism, liberal politics, and transnational capitalism with its "neoliberal inflections." Rofel claims that neoliberalism in China is "a *national* project about global reordering" (20; original emphasis), while Lisa Hoffman (2010) explores "late-socialist neoliberalism" in China and how these new ways of doing things have shaped the global city spaces and urban professional subjects. Scholars of housing studies Ya Ping Wang et al. (2012) meanwhile lumped China's new housing regime under the neoliberal housing policy reform; while geographer David Harvey (2005) even used the holistic but rather hollow term "neoliberalism with Chinese characteristics" to describe the mix of authoritarianism and neoliberal elements. It is somewhat of a relief that certain anthropologists, while invoking and endorsing neoliberalism as an analytical concept, invariably take cautious note of its inherent "temporal contingencies, ambivalences, and uncertainties" and "contingent, diverse, and yet interrelated nature." Aihwa Ong has indeed inspiringly advocated the study of neoliberalism not as a culture or a structure but as "mobile calculative techniques of governing" that can be decontextualized from their original sources and recontextualized in constellations of mutually constitutive and contingent relationships (2006, 13). Nonetheless, the pervasive usage of neoliberalism as an encompassing global order and prescriptive model in almost any context, as Donald Nonini (2008) correctly cautions, risks this term being used to refer to almost any disparate process associated with capitalism and implies the universalization of a neoliberal governance.[16] Similarly, Kipnis (2007) cogently warns against reifying neoliberalism as a holistic context of contemporary human action, and warns fellow anthropologists against succumbing to the temptation to posit a social whole when connecting social actions observed ethnographically with larger, generalized social forces.

Analytically speaking, I also find it difficult to come to terms with the rationale and usefulness of employing the overarching typology of neoliberalism to understand China's complex and incidental socioeconomic development—if they are not conceived as either imported ready-made from a paradigmatic neoliberal state or strategically implanted by the Chinese government based on normative principles, neither of which, of course, is true. Moreover, if neoliberal forms are so diverse, dynamic, and mutating, do the benefits of inventing and invoking such an analytical bracket for empirical and comparative analysis outweigh the potential shortcomings due to its lack of clarity and specificity? The main thrust of my study is to delineate any new form(s) of socioeconomic development and explore their meanings and implications as an integral part of a particularistic regime of governance. Hence, the purported original sources of certain "decontextualized-recontextualized" elements or techniques of governance (cf. Ong 2006) of a putative neoliberalism do not appear the most relevant aspects or even necessary for this study. Instead, the use of neo-socialism facilitates a more focused, nuanced analysis of the apparent and latent cohesiveness and/or contradictions of an important, emergent political regime, without conforming to the customary, stereotypical expositions.

Regardless, assuming that a neoliberal economism exists but is mixed with (post)socialist party-state politics then, conceivably, the situation may be conveniently coined a hybrid. However, such a description again implies the existence of presupposed, generalized models as universal benchmarks, which is anthropologically problematic. Moreover, the term "hybridity," as Henrietta Moore (2011) reckons, seems an imprecise formulation that offers little insight or understanding into how or why these specific differences should be generated. The image of a hybrid offers no more clarification than that straightforwardly conveyed by the constituent parameters themselves; I thus suggest that the notion of a "synthesis in the making" captures more effectively the essence of what is happening and connotes a sense of something emerging, of open possibility. The China model, specifically, has been more a product of contingent trial and error than of a farsighted, ingenious design, functioning more as an unintended consequence and survival mode borne out of social chaos and human despair than a historical inevitability and universal paradigm. As Pieke neatly puts it, the irony of neo-socialism is precisely that it has fully incorporated the neoliberal reinvention of the economy and society in its recipe for China's future modernity. Let it suffice to acknowledge that Chinese neo-socialism is a historic and sociocultural process of synthesis, defying intellectual stereotypes and ideological prejudices, yet seemingly providing a functioning alternative to both radical socialist and presupposed neoliberal logic and governance, albeit it is too early to render a verdict on whether it promises the ultimate triumph of humankind's wellbeing.

FIELD WORK IN A NEO-SOCIALIST PARADIGM

I conducted field work between July 2011 and June 2012 in the Chongqing Municipality, with brief return visits in September 2012, January 2013, and September 2013. I chose Chongqing because of its bustling urban development and exemplary representation of China's neo-socialist governance upon the appointment of Bo Xilai as its Municipal Party Secretary in 2007. When my field work began, the municipality had embarked on controversial ideological campaigns to resurrect the communist ideal and pursue an economic development path that endorsed proactive governmental involvement. While short-lived as a political movement, Bo Xilai's policies and aspirations actually portrayed what socialist governance in the new era might look like in its extreme form, and provided a most unusual backdrop for my enquiry into the neo-socialist property regime.

Chongqing is located in the southwestern hinterland of China, at the confluence of the Yangtze and Jialing rivers. Of the resident population, 74 percent live outside the city proper, as the majority of the municipality lies in a suburban/rural area. Chongqing's administrative status was elevated to the equivalent of a province in March 1997, from a mere provincial city of Sichuan, and has been designated a pilot area for rural-urban integration. It is now the most important industrial and commercial center in the upper reaches of the Yangtze. But for most of Chinese history, Chongqing was largely a military fortress and modest administrative district, constrained by mountain terrain and little commercial activity, and so it remains relatively backward in terms of social and cultural development (cf. Kui Yingtao 1991; Lin Chengxi 1994; Zhou Yong 1989). A watershed event occurred in 1891, when Chongqing was designated the first inland commercial port open to foreigners, thereby linking the southwestern region with the rest of the world. In 1929, Chongqing was officially established as a city and has since become more significant in China's modern history. During much of the eight-year War of Resistance against the Japanese in 1937–1945, Chongqing became China's wartime capital and was later designated as the Provisional Capital, owing to its location deep inland, protected by its mountainous landscape. A large number of mining, manufacturing, and weapons enterprises were set up to provide logistical support for the war. There was also the large-scale relocation of colleges and universities from other parts of China. Chongqing was instantly transformed into the nation's tripartite capital of economics, culture, and politics, and also played a crucial role in the history of China's communist revolution. During the War of Resistance, i.e. before the Chinese Civil War, the city was home to the Southern Bureau of the Communist Party of China's Central Committee (CPCCC), housed at 52 Red Crag Village. The Communist revolutionary discourse was subsequently referred to as the Red Crag Culture to glorify Chongqing's historical status. After China's victory in the War of Resistance, in August, 1945, Chairman Mao Zedong of the Communist Party arrived in Chongqing for a peace summit with Generalissimo Chiang Kai-shek of the Nationalist Party under U.S. mediation but, after the Nationalist government reinstated Nanjing as the capital in 1946, Chongqing resumed its junior municipal status. In 1954, it was further reshuffled as a city under the jurisdiction of the Sichuan provincial government.

The eventful history during the 1930s and 1940s served as the basis for a government-orchestrated cultural movement in the 2010s to relearn the Chongqing "Red Crag revolutionary and patriotic spirit." This revived red culture also gave rise to a historical backdrop of pride and a vigorous ideological impetus for Chongqing to enter into a new era of economic development, with an emphasis on the more equitable distribution of wealth rather than mere wealth creation per se. Since Bo Xilai was appointed Chongqing party secretary, replacing Wang Yang, who was transferred to lead the affluent Guangdong Province, Bo Xilai and Wang Yang, as well as Chongqing and Guangdong, have become entangled in an ideological and strategic debate over how best to develop a sustainable and equitable socialist economy. While Chongqing aspires to attain a more just distribution of the fruits of development, Guangdong maintains that the pressing task remains the "baking of a bigger cake for all to share." Bo Xilai's approach has been reframed as a unique endeavor, pioneered by Chongqing (see Figure 1.2). Having settled there, he launched two controversial campaigns, "black purging" (*dahei*) and "red singing" (*changhong*), to combat gang activities and street crime, and re-energize people's enthusiasm for the communist past under Mao Zedong.

Black purging refers to a furious law enforcement campaign (see Figure 1.3). In China, eliminating gang activity is not a simple police effort; success requires the removal of the criminal syndicates' ubiquitous protection provided by corrupt officials. During the ten-month clampdown, more than 3,300 people, including businessmen, gang members, and police officers, were arrested. Hailed by some as the most effective anti–gang activity campaign in the nation, Bo Xilai's offensive was also accused of sanctioning unlawful acts against suspects, persecuting his political opponents, and confiscating the wealth of private entrepreneurs.[17] Red singing, meanwhile, was launched to encourage local people to sing patriotic and revolutionary songs, and study and recite Marxist and Maoist classics, in an effort to restore some of the beliefs and values of Mao Zedong's era. The campaign was epitomized by a concert held in June 2010, to celebrate the Party's ninetieth anniversary. Red singing was the symbolic starting point for a comprehensive ideological campaign of red culture. For instance, Party cadre members were required to spend a week every year living, eating, and laboring with peasants. Local college students were encouraged to spend time in the rural areas, with the objective of "developing the red and professional builders of and successors for the socialist ideal." According to Su Wei (2010), at the Municipal Party School, red singing is more significant than black purging, and Bo Xilai's resurrection of Maoist thought's moral appeal could counterbalance the proliferating selfishness that accompanies the burgeoning market economy. However, very few of the Chongqingers I met had ever participated in red singing, and many were skeptical as to what purpose such a campaign could serve in an exceedingly materialistic world.

Nevertheless, the red singing and black purging movements constituted an integrated and aggressive approach of governance, commonly termed the "Chongqing model."[18] Chongqing was praised for performing impressively, against the backdrop of the global financial crisis, with its domestically driven and government-coordinated approach, in contrast to the export-led, mar-

Figure 1.2. The "City Dream" of Chongqingers. This photo was taken by the author.

Figure 1.3. "Black Purging"—A Police Patrol Station. This photo was taken by the author.

ket-driven coastal economies. In 2009, the municipal government started to contemplate a massive public rental housing project, which calls for the building of forty million square meters of floor space by 2020 to accommodate 650,000 households or two million people, targeting peasant workers, new college graduates, and residents with limited per capita living space. The government aims to set up a dual-track property market to provide basic housing for the needy while allowing more freedom for the commodity housing market, paving the way for aggressive housing demolition and redevelopment programs. Then, in January 2011, a Chinese book entitled *The Chongqing Model* was published (Su Wei et al. 2011), providing by far the most systematic account of this ideological paradigm. The model aims to develop a sustainable and moral economy with the optimal use of market efficiency, guided by the superior standard of socialist morality. The ultimate objective is to uphold the Party's governing legitimacy and the well-being and dignity of the people. In short, the Chongqing model has become a catchphrase, with rising popularity among the media and left-wing academics.[19]

The project of constructing a genuine Chongqing approach or model reached a climax in July 2011, when the Municipal Party Committee passed an important resolution on reducing the "three disparities": between rich and poor, between urban and rural, and between regions. It advanced a "common prosperity" among the people and aspired to solve the daunting issue of sharing the fruits of economic success more equitably, thereby exemplifying the ideological content of the Chongqing model.[20] A specific policy target was to reduce the urban-to-rural income ratio from 3.3:1 as of 2010 to 2.5:1 by 2015 (Gini Coefficient down from 0.43 to 0.35). An earlier OECD report (2007) on Chongqing pointed out several policy ambiguities in the role of market mechanisms vis-à-vis state intervention and in the approach taken to address territorial disparity but, by 2011, the municipal government had opted for an unambiguous, statist approach to tackling territorial disparity. On January 9, 2012, the *People's Daily*, the Party's flagship newspaper, carried a front-page article on Chongqing's drive toward "common prosperity."[21] Quoting President Hu Jintao's keynote remark at the Party's ninetieth anniversary celebration, that the Party must "walk the road of common prosperity unrelentingly," the article appears to endorse Chongqing's ideological paradigm. By late March 2012, however, when the revamped municipal leadership convened its first meeting, the motto was replaced by "scientific development for the prosperity of both the people and Chongqing" (*kexuefazhan fuminxingyu*), with a subdued emphasis on egalitarianism.[22]

Chongqing's approach to governance and economic development cannot be totally attributed to Bo Xilai himself. Much of the mainstream statist approach and reliance on state enterprises have been due to Chongqing's slowness to embark on economic reform and late elevation in administrative status to fulfil the central government's designated socioeconomic objectives. The following insight from a deputy of the Chongqing National People's Congress is worth noting, as he called this social and economic rationale a new "state-advance, civic-retreat" (*guojin mintui*) approach, in contrast to the perception of a broad-based "retreat of the state and advance of the role of market" in China. The municipal government channeled public resources to embark on strategic development initiatives and held controlling stakes in enterprises in the strategic sectors, as opposed to the coastal provinces' largely market- and private-sector-driven model. The deputy, himself an entrepreneur, argued that this model suited China better, as private enterprises' profit-driven behaviors may be inconsistent with the common goals of society; whereas the state enterprises were better able to anchor social stability by means of participating in and controlling the market. He reckoned that most people did not have a fair share of the explosive wealth, and hence there was a need to re-emphasize ideological education and the government's role in engineering an affordable housing market to avoid the risk of real estate meltdown and social instability.

Nonetheless, I frequently encountered informants who bitterly disputed the government's romantic policy discourse and the rosy pictures of narrowing wealth inequality, and rejected the possibility of a real choice between "common prosperity" and the market mechanism. A graduate who had recently returned from overseas engaged in a cynical reading of the government's drive for "common prosperity":

> This is actually a policy of obscurantism. There'll always be gap in wealth unless you return to the Mao era's absolutely equitable society. In those days, everybody, including the Party cadre, was poor. Now, the wealthiest people are the communists and their cohorts who control natural resources and real estate. Just think, who has the power to share the wealth; who is entitled to share most of the wealth?

Another man in his mid-twentiess, whose father oversaw the housing demolition at one of my field sites, commented:

> Here is the reality. Income inequality is a matter of fact; this is the only way forward. In this society, no one would care for you; every individual must strive to improve his well-being. Perhaps the government should clear the structural barriers that impede free competition, like the privileged class of "red offspring" [descendants of the senior Communist cadre]. But can it be done? Honestly?

A senior expatriate with an international real estate company in Chongqing spelled out an inherent contradiction in the policy objective:

> All over the world, income inequality could only worsen during the high-speed phase of economic development. It's not a moral judgment of whether income inequality is bad; the real question is, how can the municipal government claim to be able to achieve hyper growth yet attain a narrowing Gini Coefficient?

Bo Xilai's movement-like style and political propaganda tactics were also criticized by Premier Wen Jiabao at a live press conference that was broadcast worldwide, warning that "such historical tragedies as the Cultural Revolution may happen again."[23] In March 2012, the day after Wen Jiabao's thinly veiled criticism, Bo Xilai was abruptly dismissed.[24] Shortly after Bo Xilai's downfall and arrest, the *People's Daily* condemned him for damaging the cause and image of the Party and the state, and his serious disciplinary violations were said to date back to 1992.[25] He was later sentenced to life imprisonment for bribery, embezzlement, and the abuse of power, and was deprived of political rights for life at the Jinan Intermediate People's Court in Shandong Province.[26] Most of the people I spoke to expressed a keen interest in what was happening but, in the absence of facts, they all depended on hearsay (for example, via the immensely popular micro blogs) and speculation. Whether they liked Bo Xilai or not, everyone was forced to accept the reality as given, with no questions asked publicly, even though the gossip raged like wildfire. They felt neither sorry nor jubilant, but dismayed. This is a surreal world in which people can enjoy the most luxurious consumptive lifestyle and access the latest information from all over the world, but have no idea of the whereabouts of a once powerful leader, who was flamboyantly championing the orthodox Communist ideal of "common prosperity" to the whole nation barely a month previously. For the vast majority of ordinary people, the truth remains forever a myth. How could anybody predict that the self-proclaimed ideological heir of Mao Zedong, who rose through the communist ranks for two decades, would suddenly become a traitor to the people?

Nevertheless, such was the complete crumbling of Bo Xilai's legacy and his idealized socialist project, but does this mean that Bo Xilai and Chongqing's socioeconomic approach, or what I consider an exemplary of Chinese neo-socialism, truly contravenes and represents a rupture from the mainstream principle and approach of the central government? On the ideological front, "common prosperity" has always been a stated objective of the Party and hallmark of the Communist ideal, not subject to challenge by any power faction. Regardless, almost each and every one of my Chongqing informants do not see that wealth and income inequality in contemporary China practically has any immediate prospect of improving, never mind how often the "common prosperity" paradigm is invoked in the Party propaganda, or even if it never is. Thus, the issue of whether the most pressing task at present should be a fairer distribution or the "baking of a bigger cake," I reckon, is more a matter of difference in rhetorical priority than a definite trade-off between two incompatible roads. Moreover, as discussed in chapter 6, the defining socialist redistributive function is far from being taken over by the market's integrative role, as China at large remains very much a gigantic allocative monopoly. Hence, both Chongqing and Guangdong are, arguably, merely oscillating along a continuum of the bigger China model. On the contrary, the Bo Xilai fiasco highlights and illuminates exactly how the absolute but opaque power structure of the Party-state has remained intact, overshadowing China's historic transformation into the world's leading economy, a mega magnet for foreign investment, and a mammoth factory for satisfying global consumption. In a nutshell, the eventful development and debates that unfolded in Chongqing actually serve to contextualize and signify the essence of China's neo-socialism, albeit in a dramatic and probably exaggerated fashion.

PROPERTY, RIGHTS, AND ANTHROPOLOGY

This book focuses principally on two theoretical realms: *property* and *rights*, a duo whose connectivity sounds trivial but has rarely been employed as the main focus of enquiry within anthropology. In everyday usage, property is understood as the possession of physical or intangible entities, which produce streams of income or services and bring "economic value" (Fisher 1930). Individuals or institutions are said to possess property rights over these entities when they establish control over them. These "productive" properties play a crucial role in production, exchange, and consumption, and thus have an important bearing on analyses of the economic and political orders of society. However, the referents of property need not be restricted to purely utilitarian, productive, or material confines; there are cultural objects and artifacts that do not yield immediate income or benefit, but are deemed precious pieces of property and an important storage of wealth due to their rarity and embedded aesthetic or cultural value. In addition, many examples of cultural and natural heritage (like cathedrals, temples, monuments, rain forests, and rock formations) are priceless properties, owned collectively by public institutions or states. Although they are not possessed by any individual and there are practically no transactions or market value related to them, these "unproductive" properties belong to all members of society and constitute an important, integral part of the broader sociocultural landscape.

Traditionally, anthropologists have been concerned with the broader dimensions of property: as relations between persons mediated through things (Humphrey and Verdery 2004, 1), as rights that entail relationships (Goody 1998, 201), as a communications technology (Strathern and Hirsch 2004, 11), or as an encompassing covering term (von Benda-Beckmann et al. 2006, 15). In this regard, rights are only one aspect of the holistic concept of property and Alan Macfarlane (1998) pinpoints the deep difference between the anthropological perspective, which sees property as a relation between persons and things, and those who see property in the thing itself. Chris Hann (1998) also reminds us that the ground for the later anthropological usage and emphasis of social relations was laid in Henry Maine's representation of property as "a bundle of rights" in the late nineteenth century, whereby the right to use a particular thing might not coincide with the right to bequeath it to others or sell it to a stranger. This view is similar to some institutional economists' approach to the closer specification of property rights, which essentially separates, although does not completely dissociate, possession from outright ownership of a piece of property. This understanding and approach is particularly relevant and important for analyzing the various cases of postsocialist property regime change, in which a multiple form of changing rights has been discovered.

In socialist China, property ownership in the cities had been tolerated until the late 1950s, when a radical privatization and collectivization program was hastily instituted, which was in contrast to the prevalence of the private ownership of residential property in some Eastern European countries throughout the Communist era. Still, Chinese urbanites by then enjoyed effective, secure possession of their residences for use, though legally they did not own them. In recent decades, however, ordinary people have come to understand and engender relations of right via their experience of possession and counter-dispossession of housing property vis-à-vis the activities of the local states and various groups who maintain vested interests in establishing control over such rights. Hence, property, possession, and ownership always constitute a dynamic relationship and a robust field of research for understanding socioeconomic change. Of course, housing property may not be the most important aspect of rights, but the pervasiveness of private housing property ownership positions it as a robust field of contestation and a fertile ground for the empirical study of rights. Whether or not this gives rise to an abstract concept of rights as an ethical concern raises a deeper question, subject to ethnographic verification.

Unlike the notion of natural rights as embedded in the Western tradition, the idea of rights is hardly a common affinity for the Chinese. Political scientist Elizabeth Perry (2008) points out that the Chinese term for human rights (*renquan*) actually bears the possible meaning of "people's power," and cautions against assuming that the invocation of rights bears a close affinity to Anglo-American conceptions of human rights and civil society. It appears that, until the mid-nineteenth century, there was no single Chinese term corresponding to the English term "rights," notwithstanding the ample discussion of privileges and powers in ancient philosophy; and that Confucian thinkers actually stress "reciprocal responsibilities" rather than correlative rights and duties (Angle and Svensson 2001, xiii). Instead, tracing the philosophical origins since the Song Dynasty, Stephen Angle (2002) argues that China has been the site of a robust, coherent, and distinctive discourse about rights, made up of China-centered concepts—foremost of which are power, interests, and benefits. In a sense, "rights" as conceived by the Chinese throughout history do not coincide exactly with the Western concept of natural rights, and something may have been "lost in translation" when the latter was first introduced and transmitted to China, mainly through Japan. Indeed, all too often in my field work, people conflate rights (*quanli* 权利) with power and authority (*quanli* 权力), because the two compound terms are pronounced exactly the same and are only distinguished in writing by their second syllable—*li*. Typically, the first thing that came into my informants' minds when asked about "quan" is power rather than rights. Common rhetoric and vernacular idioms noted at the field sites are: "Only the Party has power, we people don't" and "when one has power, one has rights." To confuse the situation even further, the second character, *li*, in the Chinese term for rights actually means benefits or interests. Thus, confusion over rights, power, and interests is all too frequent in the ethnographic field. One sunny afternoon, I was touring a demolition field, from which the majority of households had been evicted, and asked some of the remaining evictees casually about their views on human rights in China. One elderly evictee came forward and said, "This society is only concerned with money, not law; when you don't have the rule of law, you don't have rights." The others nodded. This matches the notion that rights must first be problematized if we want to understand its nature and potential of "rootedness" in the soil of neo-socialist China, where power and money are the dominant overtones in everyday practice. Instead of tackling the problem of rights as a philosophical question, I treat it as an empirical one, framed in the perspective of property regime change as a potentiality, concomitantly enabled and constrained by neo-socialist governance and traditional family values. I interrogate the meaning of property and rights in my desire to understand them as metaphors and mediators of a new social order of relationality.

During the formative period of anthropology in the nineteenth century, property was employed as a core concept of the evolutionary perspective. It gradually lost its once dynamic central role and only began to regain momentum in the early 1990s.[27] Chris Hann and Keith Hart (2011) note that, for some anthropologists, the very concept of property is irreducibly Eurocentric and therefore inappropriate when studying other regions. For instance, in conceiving Melanesian persons as "dividual," who are frequently constructed as the plural and composite site of the relationships that produce them, Marilyn Strathern (1988) questions the assumption that there can be some independent determination of what a person's "rights" should be. It appears that, as there is no absolute distinction between subjects and objects as persons and the things they exchange, the Western notion of ownership or possession would seem incongruous with indigenous Melanesian precepts (Mosko 2000). However, while the Melanesian perspective carries weight in the debate of whether or not a property rights concept is universal, there is no sound theoretical basis for locating "Chinese persons" at the dividual/individual polarity either, and we should not assume indiscriminatingly property rights as an exclusive Western construct or a peculiar characteristic of capitalism. Indeed, historian Thomas Buoye (2000) demonstrates that the violent disputes in China over agricultural land in the eighteenth century were related to the trend toward privatization and the enforcement of property rights, driven by indigenously generated market forces, well before the economy's incorporation into the world capitalist system after the 1842 Opium War. Another historian, Bettine Birge (2002), also cites ancient records from the third century BCE to prove that wives not only owned private property, like cash, jewelry, land, and exquisite cosmetics, but could also take it with them out of a marriage. Birge argues that it was not until the Mongols' arrival (1271 CE) that Chinese marriage and property law became unequivocally patrilineal, depriving women of their property rights, although Chinese law and practice always purported to uphold principles of patrilineality.

It is perhaps also some anthropologists' sentimental aversion to topics related to money, the markets, and investment, considered "intrinsically anti-social" (Hart 2000, 206), and their "instinctive mistrust of liberal thought" (Englund 2013, 249) that have impeded ethnographic interest in this arena. Socialist property in particular is not a topic with a wide anthropological literature (Verdery 2004) but the dismantling of the Soviet bloc has led to a pressing need to understand the broader processes and deeper relations pertinent to property regime change. Following Hann (1998), questions of political economy indeed engage both at the micro level with property relations, wherein people build up social identities through holding and using a variety of things, and at the macro level with issues of political power and control over the distributions of things. In addition, Strathern (1999) holds that emergent forms of intellectual property signify new possibilities for corporeality or bodily integration, while Eric Hirsch (2010) attributes the dominance of neoliberal ideology since the 1980s as having given rise to an intensification of contests over diverse property forms. In a nutshell, a dynamic of societal forces, technology, and cultural concepts incidentally have combined to stimulate renewed anthropological inquiries. The nexus of person-thing-relations is challenged, becoming complexly situational and contingent upon the identifiability and separation of persons and things obtained ethnographically, and it is important to answer Hann's call to re-embed the moral aspects of property in the examination of practical economic outcomes, paying attention to both cultural sense and power relations.

Moreover, following the two systemic collapses (and resilient recovery) of the global financial markets in the late 1990s and 2000s, a new breed of ethnographic research, focused on finance, investment, and risk, is emerging (for example, Ho 2009; Miyazaki 2013; Ortiz 2013; Ouroussoff 2010; Riles 2011; Tett 2009; Zaloom 2006). Intertwining these is a new reading of the intrinsic nature of financial assets, and how these and the practice of financial professionals intricately overwhelm everybody's ordinary lives—both those near and far from the heartland of financial operations. The 2008 U.S. "financial dislocation," triggered by the complex (and disguised) web of financial innovation instruments, was indeed rooted in the housing property bubble and excessive credit (Marshall 2009). The resulting financial crisis shook the once-naïve belief in global financial governance, awakening people throughout the world to the risky nature of real property. People are now alerted to a knowledge that, aside from its tangible sense of materiality and relationality, a housing asset actually reflects a complex web of connectivity, causality, and risk, commonly going unnoticed or undetected. In light of these developments, a study on how the private property rights of housing are intertwined with the forces of economic regime change and the flow of financial capital offers a fresh, multipronged perspective for the anthropological enterprise at large.

My discussion of China also adds a useful comparative perspective to the recent literature on postsocialism, published in the aftermath of the ex-Soviet bloc's demise. Even though China is definitively not characteristically post-socialist, its reform shares numerous features and challenges endemic to casting off the socialist/communist legacy. Apart from individual monographs, several edited volumes covering a wide range of topics have shed light on the profound relational changes and impacts on societies weathering the changes wrought by postsocialism, such as the survival strategies of ordinary people (Bridger and Pine 1998), unintended consequences of change brought about locally (Burawoy and Verdery 1999), contradictions, paradoxes, and ambiguities in urban contexts (Berdahl et al. 2000), social relations and life-worlds of postsocialist citizens (Hann 2002), and confrontations, ambiguities, and compromises concerning the introduction of market activities (Mandel and Humphrey 2002). Two central consensual views have emerged from this literature. First, postsocialist states appear to follow diverse trajectories and unpredicted directions; hence the notion of "transition" is critically questioned (Hann and Hart 2011; Humphrey and Mandel 2002; Pine and Bridger 1998). Second, there are important continuities between socialist and postsocialist societies; for example, the principle that shaped the relations between the Soviet people and the authoritative discourse had continued to play a central role in shaping the activities of the last Soviet generation and that drawing a sharp line between the two periods violates the complex flow of memory, community, family, politics, and culture in which people live (Berdahl 2000; Lampland 2000; Yurchak 2006). Hence, we must caution against the risk of perceiving a singular, paradigmatic shift in post-reform institutional arrangements, particularly in the case of China, where the state power and institutional arrangements down to the very grassroots level have not been ruptured in any substantive or final sense. In real estate, for instance, the state maintains its key roles as land owner and referee of distributive justice in housing commoditization.

My study of homeownership in relation to rights defense in particular contributes to the understanding of the "embeddedness" of real estate in party-state governance.[28] China's unique neo-socialist model should be understood as a distinct alternative and important comparative perspective vis-à-vis the broad stroke of postsocialist regimes. In this regard, I enquire how housing and property rights are encountered, embodied, and contested by evictees vis-à-vis the state and developers; and how values, meanings, and affects are conceived by investors as being mediated by the market for an "abstraction of things" for which they may have little or no affection. In contrast to treating housing consumption as a source for constructing a collective identity (Fleischer 2010; Tomba 2005; Zhang 2010), property investment appears to engender individual-based possessive rights, and a new form of citizenship as practice and identity rather than status. The same individualized contest is observed for evictees at large. Nonetheless, housing investors and evictees of the middle- and lower-income classes alike consider parental gifting as a crucial factor of their practice. Hence, I raise the question of whether the agency of China's propertied and dispossessed urbanites alike leans toward an individualized strategy or whether the traditional family values are being reimagined to anchor a new web of social-familial relationships. Either way, the implications for a broad-based conception of rights can be profound.

RIGHTS, NEEDS, DESIRES, AND INTERESTS

The topic of human rights was not quite taboo during private conversations at my field site, but rarely aroused much interest, other than brief, sarcastic remarks. Some said that they are a "good" thing, but are dubious about their applicability and efficacy, not seeing them as a realistic outcome. During both my field work and subsequent writing up, moreover, I was questioned by my informants and academics alike about why I linked property rights with human rights as a research topic or hypothesis. In my own reckoning, in the Western liberal tradition, property rights have been a prerequisite, integral part of the human rights concept. Thus, one of my crucial research questions asks whether property rights may also become and constitute a formative element in China's own emergent human rights regime, or whether and why Europe and China may be following different historic pathways.

Tracing the roots of human rights from the eighteenth century to the 1948 United Nations' Declaration, historian Lynn Hunt (2007) notes that there is an inherent claim of self-evidence, which she argues relies ultimately on the embodied ideas of *empathy* and *autonomy*. For Hunt, empathy requires "a leap of faith," to imagine that someone else is like you (2007, 32). At present human rights advocate Michael Ignatieff likewise advocates the idea of moral reciprocity to avoid human suffering as a "minimalist conception of shared human capacities" (2001, 88). In this respect, it is particularly probing to interrogate why there is an apparent lack of empathy or moral reciprocity in contemporary Chinese society. If true, this might suffocate the formation of a universal rights ethic and/or cultivate an indigenous rights practice very different from that of the Western tradition, which indeed may be only one historically specific way of conceptualizing the relations of entitlement and obligation (Cowan et al. 2001). As for the concept of autonomy, when French political elites first conceived of citizens with full human rights in the late eighteenth century, landed subjects were considered foremost in qualifying as *people* capable of moral autonomy by virtue of their independent status. John Locke was instrumental in this socio-political breakthrough due to his argument that the primary rights of life and liberty entailed a natural right to property. However, even though Americans were similarly influenced by liberal traditions, the 1776 Declaration contains no reference to property among the inalienable rights of man. Historian Peter Garnsey argues that this omission was deliberate and significant, claiming that "slaves and Indians might provide sufficient explanation" (2007, 224). The implication is obvious; namely, that the scope of property and who is entitled to owning it (thus resulting in autonomy as a citizenry) is situationally engendered, more as a matter of interests and politics than justice.

It follows that the issue of property has always been a controversial yet crucial constituent of the human rights genealogy since the concept's very inception in European history. In modern times, economist Armen Alchian (2008) proclaims that property rights are human rights, because they restrain the balance of power from shifting toward behavior of which the political authorities approve. Libertarian Murray Rothbard (1998) even goes so far as to claim that human rights lose their absoluteness and clarity and become fuzzy and vulnerable when property rights are not employed as the standard. On the contrary, philosopher Henry Rosemont (1998) criticizes the Western rights-based framework for precisely the same reason that a legal system that is protective of individual property rights serves to perpetuate wealth, power, and privilege. Accordingly, a study of the sociocultural transformation of property rights' moral content has profound implications for the broader question of human rights. It should be useful to ask why Europe and China, both premised similarly on the importance of property rights at one point, seem to follow strikingly different trajectories. Moreover, the proliferation of property rights in contemporary China stems from the epochal housing reform and thus is entangled with housing rights, part of the socioeconomic and cultural rights that are fully embraced by most socialist and capitalist welfare states. In the course of protecting the property rights of middle-class owners and evictees affected by housing demolition, concerns over the rule of law and violence commonly loom large. In this regard my study of property investment and counter-dispossession should be taken seriously as an integral and indispensable part of the human rights discussion at large. Among Ellen Messer's (1993) suggestions about how ethnography contributes to the formulation of better cross-cultural understanding of local human rights concepts, two are particularly relevant to my focus of state-property-family relationships: how the notion of personhood creates categories of privileged or underprivileged; and how social relationships of reciprocity advance our understanding of the alternative forms that social bridges take.

An empirical approach to rights study also underlines the impossibility of a one-size-fits-all perspective. For instance, in exploring how "individual freedoms" are invoked to represent rights in Malawi, Harri Englund (2006) discovers that the establishment of a human rights regime appeared to be perpetually unfinished, because the poor were ironically given little else to work with other than abstract notions. In the Malawian context, citizens' experiences of exploitation and inequality in their everyday life were overshadowed by an elitist discourse that assumed a highly particular content and marginalized other grounds for making claims. Englund thus speaks of an attempt to "unchain the minds of those who became the prisoners of a specific kind of freedom" (2006, 201). In the case of China, precisely the opposite was observed, whereby evictees were practicing within a domain of government-initiated property rights but without an abstract notion of human rights narration to incorporate, neither given by human rights translators nor allowed by the party-state. Moreover, as I have recounted, in many cases, it was not even clear that the agents were embracing a principle of rights in their perceived practice of rights. In a sense, local cadres and demolition personnel act as both mediator and translator, with their own particularistic interpretation and discursive use of rights, desires, and interests as a tool for eliding many evictees' need-based rights claims. It appears, rather ironically though, that it is the very notion of rights which needs to be problematized, in order to unchain the minds of those who have become the prisoners of a specific kind of rights.

Variously, in her review of the female inheritance movement in Hong Kong, Sally Merry (2006) finds it unnecessary for rural women to have a deep commitment to human rights to make them work because of the active involvement of "transnational elites." Starting from grievances against kin, the village women's initial inheritance claim was translated into a language and perspective of rights to gender equality that the legislature and reporters could hear and understand effectively. Merry thus considers this an example of human rights made vernacular as the centerpiece of a local protest, with a limited commitment to this vision by the claimants themselves. This is again rather different from the situation in Malawi, where human rights translators are said to have played a dubious role. In contrast, the cases of Hong Kong and Chongqing are similar in the sense that the agents are not necessarily animated by a belief in or discourse of rights; but the presence or absence of translators makes a huge difference to how the agents' vocabulary and social representations are rephrased and recast, and how their actions are strategized.

Hence, nothing is self-evident; while the contrasts are sharp and ostensible, the Malawian, Hong Kong, and Chongqing cases in conjunction highlight the importance of context in understanding how a culture of rights actually or perceptibly germinates and what form it takes in each particular situation. Ultimately, however, it also remains unclear whether the agents in Chongqing, Hong Kong, or Malawi may have a more solid, "indigenous" culture of rights in development, either now or in the future. The presence of "external" agents and translators is a double-edged sword that may help in mediating and facilitating human rights applications, but at the same time may also serve to distort or compromise the natural dynamics and potentiality for change and evolvement. One thing is certain though: culture is inescapable in the contextualization of social relations and ethical practices. Thus, as Cowan et al. (2001) note, the correlated issues of culture and rights should be addressed explicitly, to enable a stronger grounding for the conversation between theory and practice. This ethnography represents a cogent attempt to engage in a particular neo-socialist context in its emergent moment of rights, and aims to offer a useful comparative perspective.

In the everyday narratives I encountered, I noticed two binary pairs of vocabularies of which the informants make regular use. On the one hand, rights and needs are invoked by the investors and evictees themselves as a value and reason justifying their demands and endeavors. On the other hand, property agents and demolition personnel attribute their counterparts' behavior to sheer boundless desires and self-interest. While rights and needs appear to connote a sense of morality and normativity, desires and self-interest could be used by the authorities to discredit their real motive, with the outright dismissal of their claims of needs and rights being mere disguises of unlimited wants and bargaining tactics. From another perspective, needs and desires arguably are ethnographically observable or inferable, while interests and rights are analytical constructs that necessitate abstract conceptualization.[29] Hence, ethnography that aims to explore how interests define and how rights are grounded in needs/desires is a complex but potentially fruitful pursuit. It is with these objectives and caveats in mind that I attempt to employ these concepts in this book: to address the primacy of needs and rights respectively as a defining feature of communism and neo-socialist governance; to illustrate how the contrasting notions of needs and desires have been contested by evictees and evictors; to explore how the pursuit of property rights is animated by desires, in contrast to a defense of housing rights informed by needs; and to highlight the possible contradictions between rights as interests and rights as a moral principle that trumps interests.

Also, during my literature review for this research, I noticed that anthropologists seem to be far more drawn toward desire than need as an analytical focus. Ethnographic works that invoke the image of desire are numerous, covering a wide range of topics, while need is rarely mentioned or only incorporated implicitly in anthropological discussion, if addressed at all. Intuitively, the concept of need sounds unproblematic, objective, natural, universal, innate, and static, and analytically more physiological and materialistic than sociocultural. For instance, in his discussion on desire and demand for commodity consumption, Arjun Appadurai mentions in passing that need is, by nature, "assumed to be fixed," while desire is "infinite and transcultural" (1986, 29). Thus, perhaps, the notion of need is not considered sufficiently fluid or interesting for field study and analytical dissemination. In contrast, desire is constantly connected with expressiveness, hope, freedom, and subjectivity. For instance, Rofel (2007) uses the term desire to gloss a wide range of aspirations, needs, and longings, arguing that central to the meanings and practices of becoming a transnational citizen-subject in China is the historical and cultural constitution of desire. As Moore puts it, desire is both personal and relational; and "when we desire something, we are hopeful" (2011, 29); perhaps it is this mode of reflexivity that renders anthropologists willing to embrace desire as both an interesting subject and robust idea for inquiry.

However, this mechanistic interpretation needs not be true, even from the Marxian perspective. According to Marshall Sahlins, in Marx's early, humanist interpretation of man's dialectic transformation of the world and himself in the process of satisfying his needs, "man develops a historical nature which determines for him the character of living nature and the spiritual as well as the political character of society" (1976, 127). It was only in the "second moment" of Marx's materialist theory that the practical experience of men becomes "untranscendable," with the mediation between men and nature amounting to the rational and material logic of effective production to satisfy abstract and ahistorical human needs. As critiqued by Sahlins, it is indeed a fateful differentiation of cultural components into the material and social aspects—as if the former were referable to the satisfaction of needs by the exploitation of nature, and the latter to problems surrounding the relations between men. Instead, need, as a driver of human activity, is imperatively linked to social relationality and cultural processes, as the social specification of both needs and purpose is always stressed; and I argue that needs should be resynthesized into sociocultural analysis particularly in a neo-socialist context.

In this respect, philosopher Garrett Thomson's (1987) elucidation on need, desire, and interest represents a useful framework for my analysis. Initially, it is crucial to differentiate instrumental needs from normative or fundamental needs: the former being the need for something for a particular purpose, which may not say anything about the value of that purpose, and the latter being one's practical necessities that relate to overall quality of life, with a clear connotation of value attached to the needs in question. Agents may not even be aware of what is fundamentally needed, yet such normative need claims "have an accent of importance and this accent is often used to demand as of right" (Thomson 1987, 11). As for desire, it pertains to the motivation of action, and the element of choice is essential to many forms of desire. Need is a justificatory reason or value; whereas desire explains intentional action and is belief-dependent. Moreover, any account of need must involve a characterization of harm, which should be regarded as a type of deprivation (rather than a state of mind, unlike desire). The notion of interest in turn is introduced as the reason for and root of desire, as well as a frame for defining what fundamental needs are by virtue of determining which types of activities and experiences we are deprived of when we are harmed. While desire is belief-dependent, interest is an objectified attribute. Desire can be instrumental and particular, but interest explains intrinsic desire non-instrumentally and is essentially non-particular. In summary, the interest is the reason for desire, while the desire is the reason for action. Thus understood, notions of need and desire as conceived and grounded in counter-dispossessions (demolition) and active possessions (investing) of property offer a prism for understanding the emergent manifestation of interest as a generalized representation of a new propertied class. Another philosopher, Bill Wringe (2005), notes that the vocabulary of needs carries with it "implications of urgency which talk of preferences cannot" and a class of human needs (for example, food and shelter) exists whose satisfaction is necessary as a precondition for pursuing any goal at all; because of their central moral significance, human beings have a *right* to their satisfaction. Philosopher David Braybrooke (2005) likewise considers that the concept of needs is familiar to all, intuitively understandable, in contradistinction to, for example, the notion of "utilities," which is too refined and problematical, or "capabilities," which could extend far beyond the provisions of basic needs and so risk diminishing the force of the appeal to needs.

Yet the paradox of need claims is that, when one's basic needs, such as clean water and fresh air, are satisfied, the result may be barely noticeable and, essentially, their satisfaction serves no role as a motivating factor. As Thomson puts it, needs are "passive dispositions to suffer certain harms because of certain lacks" (1987, 100); only when certain indispensable needs, say, safe shelter and clean drinking water, are lacking, does one feel miserable and become agitated. Hence, it is probing and potentially fruitful, when trying to discover and verify why and how informants may invoke and employ needs and rights claims, variously or tactically to justify and rationalize their causes and practices. I aim also to inquire whether the manifestation of interests could either assist or obstruct the advent of a rights-based ethos.

ORGANIZATION OF THE BOOK

Throughout this book, the notion of neo-socialism constitutes an indispensable context that structures and informs the re-emergence of private property rights in tandem with the pervasive phenomena of house demolition and property investment. And owing to the inherent sensitivity of demolition work and rights defense, all names of places, people, and companies are kept anonymous, with pseudonyms used where necessary. Chapters 2 and 4 feature mainly the narratives of housing evictees and investors, parallel to chapters 3 and 5, that account for their actual encounters and interactions. I approach the analysis of actions in chapters 3 and 5 through the nonrepresentational theories of "practice" and "affect," in juxtaposition with the discussion of "rights" in relation to the representational entities of "need," "desire," and "risk."

In chapters 2 and 3, I depict the life stories, narratives, and encounters of home evictees. Chapter 2 deals specifically with radical evictees' rationales and subjectivities with regard to resisting demolition and eviction, as expressed in the dual notions of "rights" and "needs." I address needs' primacy as a defining feature of Communism and explore the tension between the vernacular claim of needs and the state-endorsed claim of rights, a tension with significant implications concerning China's neo-socialist governance and legitimacy. Chapter 3 details the process of demolition lobbying and micro-power bargaining relationships between the evictees and the frontline demolition personnel. It illustrates their strategies and how the contrasting notions of "needs" and "desires" have been routinely but variously contested. The notion of an "economics of rights interpretation" is introduced to reflect how a needs claim is concealed by a rights claim in the demolition field, as the logic of needs is buried in desire talk.

In chapters 4 and 5, I investigate how urban households have evolved into "investing citizens" and how the pursuit of property rights is animated by a desire for material gain and family well-being, in contrast to a defense of housing rights animated by needs. Chapter 4 depicts the broader context of Chongqing's statist housing market and explores the meaning of investment for Chongqingers from three dimensions: first, the pursuit of the right to possession as a *desire* for material gain and personal security; second, the duality of real estate possession as *investment* and consumption; and, third, a new paradigm of *risk* emerging from the new economic ethos. My ethnographic cases clearly point to a new form of urban citizenship emerging from the practice of investing in housing property and the endorsement of private property rights as an imperative principle for achieving well-being. Chapter 5 examines in detail how housing owners defend their perceived infringement of property rights through limited resistance and explores how "desire" enters as a critical driver for investors' practice. I also caution against deducing a broad-stroke causality between property rights and the formation of rights consciousness.

Chapter 6 is a synthesis of my ethnographic observations on active possession and counter-dispossession. I show that a new tripartite relationality has emerged among the state, property, and family, giving rise to new notions of meaning and value. This chapter illustrates how housing property acts as a formidable mediator of social relationships in the broader context of Chinese privatization and global financialization. Chapter 7 picks up the threads of the discussion of "needs," "desires," "rights," and "interests" in relation to forced eviction, investment, renewed family centrality, and the resurrection of the cultural tradition. I discuss how evictees' and owners' value(s) are situated between their own family perimeter and the broader cultural and political context of a neo-socialist property regime, still under the pervasive influence of Confucian thought and values. I suggest that a revived interest in Confucianism by the Party and the resurrecting emphasis on family values in Chinese society may not mean the same thing in their official and vernacular disseminations.

In chapter 8, I conclude by highlighting the potential and ambivalence of the concept of "rights" as a broad-based, penetrating ethos. I suggest that the ubiquitous pursuit and defense of individualized private property rights by both investing citizens and demolition bargainers at once cements a platform for securing peoples' interests and nurturing their rights consciousness, yet at the same time reinforces and accentuates an ambivalence of the values and moralities inherent in the tripartite realm of the state-property-family.

NOTES

1. See www.focus.cn (Wang Yu and Li Jing 2011).
2. See *Chongqing Times* (2011).
3. In 2012, income from land use rights transfer (before real estate taxes and charges) amounted to 42 percent of Chongqing's overall public financial and government fund revenues; as for other major localities such as Tianjin and Sichuan, the ratios were 32 percent and 35 percent respectively. Source: Ministry of Finance (2013).
4. By December 2013, housing prices in one hundred large cities averaged a 12 percent year-on-year increase, of which Shenzhen, Guangzhou, Nanjing, and Beijing soared over 20 percent; with Chongqing also rebounding by 11 percent. See *China Index Academy* (2014).
5. See *Xinhua News* (2012).
6. See *The People's Daily* (Liang Qian and Wang Zheng 2013) and wallstreetcn.com (Ruo Li 2014).
7. See *China Real Time Report* (Ye and Ashbum 2010).
8. The idea was first put forward by the 16th Communist Party of China Central Committee (CPCCC) at its fourth Plenary Session in September 2004. Then, in October 2006, the sixth Plenary Session of CPCCC passed the Resolution on "Major Issues Regarding the Building of a Harmonious Socialist Society," which identifies the general requirements of such efforts as "democracy and the rule of law, equity and justice, honesty and fraternity, vigor and vitality, stability and order, and harmony between man and nature." See *Xinhua News* (2006; 2007).
9. The People's Republic of China's Constitution; adopted March 14, 2004.
10. General Program, Constitution of the Communist Party of China; adopted November 14, 2012.
11. See *Xinhua News* (2013a).
12. For instance, political scientist Jane Duckett (2011) points out that, between 1978 and 2002, the state's retreat from healthcare has been swift and thorough, leading to the collapse of the (rural) cooperative medical system and erosion of medical provisions through (urban) workplace insurance. Notwithstanding the tendency to explain this transformation as a by-product of economic reform, she reckons it is best explained by ideological change and political struggles among stakeholders in the health policy arena.
13. The bulk of the new regimes saw their economies collapse immediately after the "shock therapy" (Kotz 2000; Kingston-Mann 2006; World Bank 1996), arguably attributable to a disjuncture between private property and economic performance (Caskie 2000; Kingston-Mann 2006; Sneath 2004; Visser 2006). By contrast, China's development is described as a "partial, phased-in" experiment (World Bank 1996, 142), but its GDP recorded an 8 percent compound annual growth during the early transitional phase between 1978 and 1983. The sharp difference

does not necessarily undermine the cardinal principle of private property theory but suggests that something more substantive was at work, and Kingston-Mann suggests it is time for a more inclusive and balanced study of the potential agents of change (2006).

14. During the tour from January 18 through February 21, 1992, Deng criticized those who harbored doubts about the reform. Declaring that a market economy did not equate with capitalism, he called on leaders to break free of ideological strictures and boldly adopt measures associated with capitalism (Wong and Zheng Yongnian 2001).

15. Dominic Boyer observes that, currently "anthropology sees neoliberalism everywhere" in the world, but actually there are a lot of political ideas, cultural practices, and social institutions that would be better described as "neosocialist" out there in abundance already, for examples, in China and Venezuela, in green politics, and anti-free-trade (2010, un-paginated).

16. This author grew up in the ex-British colony of Hong Kong in the 1970s, where and when the defining features of neoliberalism—market principles of discipline, efficiency, and competitiveness, and self-governance—had long been the norm, well before Margaret Thatcher's smashing of the U.K. welfare state and the advent of Reaganism and Thatcherism, for that matter. Thus I find it difficult to appreciate the relevance and added value of inventing the term neoliberalism as a sweeping descriptor of characteristics that are actually, and plainly, associated with capitalism as we have lived to know it for a long time.

17. The most ironic was that the officer-in-charge of black purging, Wang Lijun, had himself fled to the U.S. Consulate in Chengdu for fear of his own safety, a fiasco which led to Bo Xilai's dismissal. Wang was later sentenced to fifteen years in jail for defection, abuse of power, and bribe taking. Nonetheless, black purging remains the most remembered policy of the Bo Xilai era for many Chongqingers, because of the substantial improvement of law and order.

18. The term "Chongqing model" was initially used by the Hong Kong–based Chinese magazine *Yazhou Zhoukan* in February 2009 to describe the municipal government's governing vision and policy initiatives. *Yazhou Zhoukan* (Ji Shiming 2009) published several articles to patronize Chongqing in pioneering a moral alternative and sustainable model for development. But after Bo Xilai's downfall, on April 13, 2012, the magazine reversed its position with severe criticism of his approach, and on May 25, 2012, it printed a long article in elaborate praise of Guangdong's pro-market economy approach (Guo Zhongxiao 2012).

19. For instance, Huang Zongzhi (2011) praised that the Chongqing model represents a "Third Hand" other than the market capitalism and command socialism and a bold attempt at prioritizing social equality and public interests; while Cui Zhiyuan (2011) stated that Chongqing was on its way to re-vitalizing the relationship between the Party and the people.

20. See *Chongqing Morning Post* (2011, A02).

21. See *People's Daily* (Wang Jianxin et al. 2012, 1).

22. The new slogan adheres to the central government's party line by emphasizing the objectivity of economic development as opposed to Bo Xilai's aggressive short-term investment drive. It also differs critically from Bo Xilai's egalitarian discourse of prioritizing distribution over growth by emphasizing prosperity for the collective good. See *Chongqing Daily* (Chongqing Daily Editorial 2012).

23. See Reuters (Buckley and Blanchard 2012).

24. Widely regarded as one of China's most dramatic political purges and serious power struggles since 1989, Bo Xilai's abrupt downfall is also attributable to his ideological confrontation and power struggle with the mainstream reformist faction. See *BBC* (Grammaticas 2012) and *Reuters* (Buckley 2012).

25. See *People's Daily Online* (People's Daily Commentator 2012).

26. See *People's Daily Online* (2012) and *People's Daily Online* (2013).

27. Lewis Henry Morgan postulated that property mars the commencement of civilization and that a critical knowledge of its evolution embodies the "most remarkable portion of the mental history of mankind" ([1877] 2006, 43). Edward Tylor also envisaged an evolutionary theory of property holding in relation to the state, and he once remarked that an anthropologist can see land communism's disadvantages "have been found to outweigh its advantages, so that it tends to fall out of use" (Opler 1968, 6).

28. Even within the Lockean tradition, first among the characteristics of property is its embeddedness in state law, authority, and sovereignty (Geisler 2006). John Gledhill (2004) also speaks of demystifying the notion of neutral market forces not embedded in specific power relations.

29. In philosophy, Patricia Springborg (1981) notes that from Aristotle to Hegel and the existentialists, a long line of philosophers has put the emphasis on the concept of desire as "being in some way symptomatic of the human condition." Hegel made the connection between "needs" as a defining category of the social and economic realms and "desires" as signifying human objectification and motivations. For a Hegelian subject, Judith Butler notes, "it is always the desire-for-reflection, the pursuit of identity in what appears to be different" (1987, 7). In Marxism, rather, human needs are an ultimate value criterion; Marx's concept of needs is said to derive from Hegel's concept of desire, to express an awareness of the limits and finitude of human existence (Springborg 1981, 99).

Chapter Two

Exit, or Evict

Re-Grounding Rights in Needs

> "Leading the squad were a few dozen men all dressed in black, without any badges or identifying signs on their clothing. They arrived suddenly after 9am, when we were out. But this time, there was nothing they could take away; they simply tore down the whole building." —Mr. and Mrs. Cao

During my field work on house counter-demolition, many eyewitnesses described forced evictions led by "people in black," who had "dressed up" mere minutes before entering the demolition zone. As both the neighborhood residents and demolition personnel stated, forced evictions typically occurred in the morning when the dwellers were away, with the authorities probably being tipped off by scouts. Commonly, at least 100 people participated, including representatives from: the court; the housing bureau; the urban administration; the police, fire, and medical services; and the sub-district and community residents' committee, with each of the participants receiving an allowance of some RMB200 (about US$32).[1] The sub-district's and community residents' committee's involvement was primarily to maintain social harmony by facilitating communication with the evictees but, in practice, their staff also provided useful neighborhood intelligence to enable the demolition company to lobby evictees to accept the terms of compensation.

The forced eviction of Mr. and Mrs. Cao was one of the more bizarre cases I encountered, as they had been evicted more than once. Their comment at the start of this chapter was made in September 2012, during an interview with them two years after their first eviction. At that time, the demolition team had knocked a few big holes into their apartment's living room and bedroom floor, and disconnected the water and electricity supply, yet the Caos refused to budge; instead, they placed wooden planks and bricks over the holes, tapped into the electrical power lines, and fetched water from other households, all the while continuing to live in the structure until their second eviction. Mr. Cao had traveled to Beijing, China's capital, 2,000 km away, four times to petition the higher authorities. They informed me: "The local government is too corrupt. I want the Party's central leadership (*dang zhongyang*) to listen to the voice of the people. They may send us back, but at the least the local officials will feel the pressure."

The Caos' situation may seem dramatic but nonetheless reflects a distinctive culture of counter demolition and *shangfang* (petitions to the higher authorities to seek redress).[2] While petition is not new in the history of the People's Republic, in recent years, demolition and eviction-(*chaiqian*) related disputes have become the single most prominent feature of a culture of open petitions and social protest. Take for example the so-called "6.19 incident," which was a public protest that took place on June 19, 2012, in Chongqing but was not reported by the press at all. A local source informed me that dozens of evictees had gathered before the venue of the 4th Congress of the Party's Chongqing Municipal Committee, dressed in white (a sign of grief), and carrying white banners, condemning the unfairness of their forced eviction. The protesters, having failed to break through the police cordon and enter the venue, were detained within minutes. Photos and videos were taken by the police and relayed electronically to the sub-district and community resident committee offices for identification. The respective local cadres then rushed to the scene to escort their "subjects" back to the neighborhood for "education" and surveillance, customarily called *weiwen* (the maintenance of stability). The local cadres were then ordered to "demobilize" the activists. One grassroots official told me that, usually working as a team of three, with one member for the sub-district, community, and local police offices respectively, the *weiwen* task unit speaks to the activists or takes up position outside their apartment twenty-four hours a day. Activists are prohibited from leaving their district of residence. If, for instance, they board a bus and attempt to cross the river by bridge, the task force can assume a negative intention and call for police reinforcement to stop the vehicle and arrest the activists, even though they have not broken the law in any way.[3] While *weiwen* applies to all sorts of social discontent and illegal activities, protests against forced eviction constitute the most provocative challenge.

NAIL HOUSEHOLDERS' CLAIM TO NEEDS AND RIGHTS

In chapter 1, I explain that a combination of dramatic changes in government housing policy and the sharp property price spirals sparked the prevalence and intensity of this social discontent and precarious everyday resistance but, after all, nail households only represent a minority of those affected, which begs the question: are there any particular situations that characterize resistant nail householders? In this chapter, I aim to expose certain nail householders' counter-demolition and counter-dispossession experiences to gain a better understanding of their rationales, as expressed in the dual notions of "rights," as employed by the state's proxies, and of "needs," implicit in the nail householders' narratives. I address needs' primacy as a defining feature of communism, and explore the tension between the vernacular claim of needs and the state-endorsed claim of rights, a tension with significant implications concerning China's neo-socialist governance and legitimacy.

Notwithstanding the nail householders' common rhetoric of social injustice, it is ironic that the process is characterized by individuals' struggle—one finds no collective struggle. Framed and defined by the official discourse as a commercial dispute over property rights, the evictees' demands based on housing needs are not regarded by the authorities as a legitimate basis for deliberation or negotiation, but are customarily dismissed by demolition personnel as a mere manifestation of the evictees' limitless greed. However, evictees continue to narrate their family's housing needs as the justification for their demands and defiance against demolition and forced eviction. Accordingly, I suggest that the claim of *needs* actually represents a moral imperative for nail householders' self-rationalization and maintenance of morale, forming an inescapable foundation for conceiving the claim of *rights*. I argue that *needs* are not a common category like *desires* or *interests*, which are invoked habitually to explain choice and agency. Rather, needs are a latent force to be uncovered only occasionally and situationally to justify a dramatic scheme of actions, such as those witnessed and evidenced in the demolition field. In contrast, the equally normative but more provocative vocabulary of rights is often thought to encourage those designated as rights-holders to "take an active role in securing the performance of such obligations as they take to be owed" (Wringe 2005, 187). Nonetheless, based on my ethnographic observations, I suggest that the two normative terms, *rights* and *needs*, are hardly mutually exclusive but instead constitute, at times, a formidable alliance and, at other times, an ambivalent polarity that permeates resistance practices. In the following, I will discuss nail householders' experiences and vicissitudes, particularly those of the Lin and Gu families, representing two equally defiant attitudinal poles. The Lin family experienced disbelief and despair at their eviction. Mr. Gu, in contrast, remained high-spiritedly defiant and anticipatory regarding the eventual showdown. The Lin and Gu families' accounts will sketch out the practice of counter-dispossession in an era of private-property rights.

One cold, damp, misty morning in early January 2012, I surveyed the Gaoshan house-demolition region.[4] It had once been a bustling hillside area, hosting more than one thousand households, of which several dozen still refused to relocate. The dwellings there tended to be six- to eight-story apartment blocks, built previously by state enterprises, plus some dozen two-story brick houses built by inhabitants who had moved to the area one or two decades ago. Most of the structures had been vacated, with some having been demolished by private contractors. Broken concrete was lying about, and rusted iron bars were exposed here and there, poking through the demolished walls and punched-out ceilings. On clear days, one could see across the valley to the river. The nail householders whom I spoke with in this now-desolate neighborhood recounted how pleasant the environment had been previously, with trees, mountains, river views, fresh air, and tea shops. Several high-rise buildings were being built near the riverbank, on land reclaimed from relocated residents. On that site, I photographed a bare tree standing against the backdrop of a towering construction crane, a symbolic contrast between the bare nail houses and the bustling construction for progress and profit (see cover photo). A couple of months earlier, the developer had started pre-selling at RMB18,000 per square meter, a record for Chongqing's high-rises and four times the amount of the local residents' compensation. Judging by the building progress, in a year or so, the building work could extend to the site on which I wandered, implying that final demolition and evictions lay ahead in the not-too-distant future.

I chose the area of Gaoshan as my field site because different phases of demolition have occurred there simultaneously. This enabled me to inquire about and compare policy changes and their various impacts on the evictees. Gaoshan is situated on the southern side of the Yangtze River and is one of the nine administrative sub-districts of the Peninsula District (a pseudonym). According to some elders, Gaoshan developed much earlier than many other city districts, with many medium-sized industrial enterprises being located there. For a long time, the area was a popular choice for rural-city migrants and households affected by demolition in some suburban area. In the mid-1990s, as the enterprise reform gathered speed, there were mass layoffs, with a devastating neighborhood impact. In 2003, the municipal government decided to gear up the redevelopment of Gaoshan. Several years ago, a large property consortium acquired development rights over a 300,000m^2 riverside site, with a planned construction of 1.3 million m^2 of floor area for residential use. The developers advertised that the project was intended "to achieve a riverside city complex status and to become a landmark of Chongqing." This project required the clearance of almost 200,000m^2 of existing houses, with the first few phases of resettlement work beginning immediately after the land was granted. In the latter phase, with which this chapter is concerned, more than 90 percent of the residents had already left their home, leaving the remainder to accept final offers or face eviction.

In the developer's exhibition hall, I saw a three-dimensional model depicting the project's luxurious layout. Within ten years, this artistic vision would be turned into a real, glamorous estate for the wealthy. The nail householders had also been transformed: their neighborhood had become a site for luxurious redevelopment and a place for protesting against what they saw as unfair treatment, and for contesting their newly conceived rights.

RIGHTS OF HOUSING OR RIGHTS OF OWNERSHIP

In most cities in the developing world, urban renewal and the demolition of existing slums are common practice, often forming a complicated housing strategy and controversial public policy. Other than the question of who (government or private sector agents) will take the initiative in orchestrating the planning, funding, and execution, how the affected dwellers are compensated is an exceedingly sensitive issue and arduous task. There are three principal options regarding urban renewal: outright slum clearance and the resettlement of dwellers, slum improvement, and slum redevelopment (Mukhija 2003). Under slum clearance, slums or deteriorating buildings are demolished, with the dwellers resettled in alternative locations either as tenants or title holders, and the potential appreciation in the land value of the vacated site largely accrues to the developer, be it public or private. Under slum improvement, dwellers receive a legal title to their property from the state as an incentive to invest in the residential compound. Under slum redevelopment, dwellers receive a new house in exchange for their old one; they may hold the legal title to the house also but must endure the inconvenience of temporary displacement and the financial risk associated with redevelopment. Under these different approaches, it is important to understand whether dwellers are *invited* to participate and protect their living and property rights, or are simply *drafted* to comply with the government directive and denied any entitlement to their housing rights as citizens or fair compensation for their property rights.

In China, between 2006 and 2011, clearance and reconstruction work on urban and township slums commenced that would benefit 10 million households, but left at least a further 12 million households to be resettled.[5] Given that urban renewal had become a "pretext" for commercialized residential projects (Shao 2013, 9), the number of to-be-affected evictee households was hardly determinable. The policy aimed to ensure the basic resettlement of dwellers, but the problematic quality of resettlement houses and the difficulties associated with land resumption remained major stumbling blocks. Urban renewal across all cities has predominantly adopted a singular approach of demolition and relocation, with slum improvement and redevelopment options being very infrequently pursued.[6] In the prosperous city of Shenzhen, Jonathan Bach (2010) came across a very rare case of business cooperation with government blessing between the developer and the villagers residing in the urban periphery, attributable to the village's prime location and villagers' collective-based bargaining power. In Chongqing, each district government retained a certain degree of autonomy with regards to demolition compensation and eviction arrangements, although they were all subject to the various laws, regulations, and policy directives as promulgated by the central and municipal authorities. The district governments typically played a proactive role in both site clearance and the earmarking of redevelopment projects for private or state-owned developers to participate for profit but, as property prices skyrocketed, this approach has inevitably encountered stern resistance.

In Mumbai, India, urban planner Vinit Mukhija (2003) has studied a case of slum redevelopment, which demonstrates the pivotal role of the state in creating and distributing land values and shows how the government managed new opportunities, revised the development regulations, and resolved social conflict due to the increased land values. At first glance, this appears identical to China's statist approach, but Mukhija discovers a poor implementation speed for the projects, notwithstanding the slum-dwellers' enthusiasm and the government's market-friendly policies. This is in sharp contrast to the China model's lightning speed of demolition and reconstruction, attributable to the clearly delineated property rights reverting to the state and local officials' direct intervention in the process of land resumption. At Gaoshan, for example, the redevelopment site had been sold off to a developer for an agreed lump sum; thus, the district government bore all the urgency to deliver the site to schedule. Elsewhere in the world, "extra-legal" property proliferation at the city outskirts is not unusual, representing both a daunting challenge and a contentious political issue. In Almaty, Kazakhstan, for instance, the explosive growth of informal settlements in the aftermath of socialism is said to represent a shadow economy in its own right, fueled by the rapid inflation of real estate prices in the mid-2000s. Kazakhstan has embarked on a campaign for eradicating squatters by the simultaneous means of eviction and discretionary formalization of property rights, driven by a "need" for the land occupied by the squatter dwellings, generated by the rise of the speculative market in the midst of a housing credit bubble. In his final analysis, Saulesh Yessenova deems that the Kazakhstan government was unsuccessful in actually formalizing squatters' rights, because of concern about enticing "land invasion," and failed in its aim to enable all of Almaty's residents either to improve their housing conditions or become homeowners (2010, 41). Conversely, James Holston (2008) discovered in São Paulo, Brazil's urban periphery, pervasive, concomitant processes of illegal occupation and the legalization of illegal homeownership. In the very different setting of minimally fettered capitalist dynamics in Hong Kong, the formalization of property rights has never been pursued in an attempt to regulate illegally occupied spaces, with the officials registering and tolerating the structures rather than their occupants. Rather, as Alan Smart demonstrates, it was "eligibility for rehousing" that was the stated policy (2001, 34). Even toward the eventual phasing out of squatter areas, when most of the occupants no longer received resettlement arrangement officially, in practice, homeless people in Hong Kong were offered places in transit centers (however unpleasant and inconvenient) pending temporary housing.

In sharp contrast, urban dwellers in China are under the stringent control of the housing bureaus and the police; large-scale, unauthorized occupation of public land is unthinkable. Urban demolition principally involves land resumption for real estate redevelopment or public work construction over the existing legal structure, including shanty houses built on leased government land that date back a few decades. According to the "Regulation on Chongqing's Urban Housing Demolition and Relocation," only title holders and contracted users of public housing are considered legitimate targets for compensation. The tenants of private property are entitled only to compensation from their landlord. Ironically, even this minor provision of tenant protection was omitted in the 2011 "Method on Chongqing's Expropriation of and Compensation for Houses on State-owned Land," which is an administrative act replacing the regulation governing demolition work. In comparing the experiences of urban renewal in Shanghai and Mumbai that have invariably destabilized residents' rights to housing in an unequal manner, sociologists Liza Weinstein and Xuefei Ren (2009) also note that Mumbai's housing rights regime has been more deeply contested, as the major laws and regulations guiding Shanghai's urban renewal favor the interest of local governments and private investors over those of the people, thus paving the way for mass demolition and evictions.

In Gaoshan, many inhabitants are the former employees of state enterprises, residing in apartment units which they own. There are also many others who moved to the neighborhood a long time ago, building their own single-story bungalow on land leased from the district government. Most of them subsequently enlarged the structures by building an additional story or extension to accommodate their expanding family but failed to register these additions with the authorities. Such modifications have led to major disputes, because demolition settlement was offered principally on the basis of property rights rather than housing needs. Government policy failed to pay heed to how many people or families occupy the same dwelling (for instance, a householder who lives with his adult children and their families would all be counted as one household). Strictly speaking, the compensation arrangement was not a "formalization process," because the authorities officially only recognized the status of "legal" dwellings, defined as building structures that were properly registered and authorized. However, in practice, the demolition company has the discretion to decide whether or not certain public spaces or even illegal structures can be included within the measurement of the legitimate floor area for compensation, albeit partially, hence representing de facto "add on" formalization features. This "practice of discretion" was a frequent cause for complaint among disadvantaged evictees without legal recourse, implying the existence of corruption and unfair treatment. To add to this confusion, although rural migrant tenants who lacked urban household status were not entitled to resettlement, in practice, cash payments of up to many thousand RENMINBI were offered to expedite the clearance work. In any case, the resettlement policy in principle merely recognized property entitlement and rights rather than housing needs and rights.

The Cao family, mentioned above, and the Pu family had lived in the neighborhood for several decades. Both Mr. Cao and Mr. Pu were former employees of a local tobacco enterprise, but similarly only the tenants rather than the owners of their apartments. At the height of the welfare housing purchases, the tobacco company did not offer to sell the units to its staff; instead, tenants were offered a housing allowance. Many used the money to buy private housing from the market, and were thus more amenable to accepting the compensation terms, as they already had alternative accommodation. In the case of the Pu family, however, Mr. Pu had passed away in 1995, so his widow lost her housing allowance. In 2009, she was offered RMB30,000 in compensation for the demolition, with the bulk of the cash being taken by the enterprise which still owned the apartment. Mrs. Pu refused to move out and petitioned Beijing. The difference between the Pu and Cao families is that Mr. Cao received the housing allowance back then failed to purchase his own apartment. Mrs. Pu also insisted on living in her "demolished" apartment; she was the only inhabitant in the apartment block and had kept two fierce guard dogs to scare off the thieves who frequented the vicinity.

The situations of the Cao and Pu families were quite unusual, as they did not have legal possession of their dwelling. Though their history and reason for resistance may differ, they demonstrated clearly that it was the ownership rights rather than the dwelling needs and rights which were recognized and addressed by the demolition authorities. Moreover, it was exactly because of their lack of property rights that the Cao and Pu families were evicted much earlier than many other owner-nail householders, who allegedly had a legitimate ground for disputing the unfair compensation offered to them. Mrs. Pu and the Cao family repeatedly accused the demolishers of having "no conscience," but simultaneously added that, because they were poor, they needed vigilantly to continue fighting. When it comes to their experience of demolition and petition, however, their views coincided with those of other nail householders, with or without property rights.

CLOSE ENCOUNTER OF THE HARSH KIND

In the Peninsula District, demolition projects were carried out by the official convener *Dafa* (a pseudonym), a company registered by the district government to undertake co-redevelopment with property developers. Most of Dafa's employees were allegedly either former employees of or well-connected with the district housing bureau. Dafa then appointed demolition companies, which could be either commercially or government-run, to conduct field investigations and home visits, and to persuade and bargain.

During 2007 and 2009, a contract responsibility arrangement was widely endorsed whereby demolition companies were given a lump sum by the demolition convener to embark on their own projects. In the absence of explicit guidelines or transparent criteria on how the compensation was to be derived and enacted, these companies enjoyed great flexibility in extracting all possible benefits by squeezing evictees. This was probably the darkest time in the history of China's urban housing demolition, as property prices soared and developers became frenetic about expediting construction work. Widespread cases of notorious evictions and desperate resistance occurred during that time. Legal scholars Xu Mingyue and Huang Dongbin say that demolition is not fundamentally a legal concept; the local state's active participation in demolition and eviction on behalf of commercial interests has led to the exploitation of private property rights and "an alienation of the nature of house demolition laws" (2010, 90). Sociologists Fang Yaomei and Wang Bintuan (2006) also note that the unfair compensation structure of urban demolition had given rise to systemic risk and soaring numbers of petitions. On January 21, 2011, the State Council promulgated the "Regulation on the Expropriation of and Compensation for Houses on State-owned Land," which stipulated the abolishment of forced demolition by executive order. Pursuant to this, the much criticized "Administrative Regulations on Urban Housing Demolition and Relocation" and its variants in different localities were repealed. As such, the phrase *housing demolition* was supposedly discarded in favor of *housing expropriation*. However, demolition projects approved prior to the regulation's effective date remain subject to the previous guidelines. In practice, *chaiqian* remained the catchphrase in widespread use; and forced eviction remained inevitable for diehard nail householders. In the following, I present a few examples of forced eviction.

"We're in Debt, They're in Wealth."

Ms. Zhen had accompanied her husband to hospital for a health check one morning in December, 2010, when Dafa mobilized a team to dismantle her house. The workers confiscated her clothes, food, wage payment card, and, worst of all, her son's exam certificates and computer. Zhen stated that, after that incident, her son lost interest in studying and dropped out of school. The Zhen family then rented an apartment, financed through borrowing. She stated that the government should never have sold the land while it was still inhabited; now, the developer had paid for the land cost, and Dafa was able to take advantage of this to enrich themselves at the expense of the evictees. Zheng later went to Beijing to petition the Ministry of Housing and Urban-Rural Development. She stated that an official spent half an hour with her and remarked that her demand was not excessive, before phoning Chongqing's Housing Bureau to dispatch people immediately to escort her back to Chongqing. However, Ms. Zhen's problem remained unsolved; instead, she claimed that Nanfa once threatened to arrest her for involvement in "triad activities."

"My House Is More Important than My Life."

Ms. Li, in her late twenties, lived with her family of eight; they demanded compensation for three apartments. In December, 2010, at 11 a.m., some two hundred people stormed her home while her mother was away. Li and her uncle were at home at that time; the demolition workers first struck her uncle on his neck to drag him out, then tried to use a stretcher and ropes to tie her up. Li smashed a bedside mirror and threatened to slash her wrist with a shard of the glass. The workers backed off, seeing that she was bleeding and had lost control. During the three-hour standoff, the workers tore down the courtyard and seized their housing certificate as well as their chickens and ducks. On her way home, Li's mother was taken to the demolition office and forced to sign a compensation contract, under threat that her daughter would be arrested if she failed to comply. Dafa then claimed that they had conducted legal demolition based on the contract. Refusing to vacate, Ms. Li went to Beijing and posted her petition on the Internet. "If the contract my mother was forced to sign is legal, they could request court authorization; why don't they? If they return, I'll sacrifice myself to protect my house, for my house is more important than my life," Li said, showing me the scar on her wrist.

"They Owe Me the Lives of My Husband and My Dogs."

In June 2008, sixty-year-old Mrs. Wen had just completed rebuilding the family's two-story house when she received a demolition notice. She was told that her old home was an endangered structure and thus must be demolished. Her husband, a retired, disabled Korean War veteran, was living in a nursing home when the forced eviction happened, during which their two dogs were killed. "They're like the bloody Japanese entering the village, burning, killing, and robbing everything; what a disgrace to the Party. Is this a government for *renmin* (people) or for RENMINBI!" Upon learning of the demolition, Mr. Wen became gravely ill and, shortly afterward, died. Mrs. Wen's two sons-in-law also left their wives once the house was razed to the ground without any compensation. Distressed, Mrs. Wen went to Beijing six times to petition to the authorities, all to no avail. From April, 2011, onward, she lived in a tent near her demolished house (see Figure 2.1). Outside her tent, a large cardboard sign stated in red letters, "This house has not been sold: defend the dignity of the law, support legal *chaiqian*, protest against violent *chaiqian*."

THE AMBIVALENCE BETWEEN NEEDS AND RIGHTS

Ms. Lin, in her late-fifties, was a retired factory worker, who lived with her older sister and her younger brother's family in a compound that had been built in the 1980s by her parents. Their dwelling consisted of two brick-built houses and a small courtyard, measuring 110m² in area. Attached to the house was a vacated, partially destroyed, seven-story building. The Lin family first settled in the area in the 1950s, when Ms. Lin was five years old. In

Figure 2.1. Mrs. Wen, a Nail Householder, Fighting On. This photo was taken by the author.

the 1980s, as the family increased in size, her parents leased a piece of land from the government to build a single-story bungalow measuring 55m^2. Later, when her eldest brother married, the family built an additional floor but chose not to register this with the government to avoid paying tax. Even by the time her parents passed away, twenty years ago, no family member had altered the deed to change the title or registered the second floor.

The demolition company deemed that the additional area was uncertified, while the courtyard area belonged to the state; thus, both areas were excluded from the compensation assessment. The family was furious about this, as they claimed they had been paying land use tax for the courtyard also until the early 2000s. They had kept the tax receipts elsewhere in case someone broke in to seize the evidence. Ms. Lin recalled that, on one occasion, the demolition company sent a truckload of people to threaten them, but her family had nothing to fear, as she felt they "had a reason. . . . It is not us who wish to relocate, how can you force us to sell? And we should not be burdened by becoming house slaves for the rest of our lives!" The term "house slaves" (*fangnu*) refers to the demolition company's suggestion that the Lin family should take out a loan to pay RMB200,000, if they wanted three apartments but lacked the means to buy them. Ms. Lin depended upon her pension and social security benefits, whereas her younger brother's job paid RMB1,800 per month.[7] "We don't have any valuables as collateral; who'll lend money to poor families? And we also don't want to be looked down upon because we borrow the money," stated Mr. Lin. His daughter, thirteen-year-old Ah May, stated most of her former schoolmates had moved out of the district. She feared a forced eviction, as she had witnessed a few such cases, yet reflected that "I'm a Chinese citizen; the government should take care of our housing right."

The Lin family's situation was actually very complicated. After their parents passed away, the house's title was not transferred to the offspring, and each family member now wanted a share of the estate. When negotiations started, the demolition company had offered a 96m^2 apartment for the three resident households. In response, the Lins demanded one one-bedroom and two two-bedroom units for the three households who were still residing there, plus cash for the other five family members. The Lin family's inherent logic was that the three residing households had practical housing needs that the government should meet, while the property rights of the compound per se should also be compensated for fairly. This package was rejected outright by Dafa. In early 2011, a public hearing was held, at which time a court representative stated that, unless the family could afford to pay the difference in valuation, they should not demand three apartments. Thereafter, they received a court order to vacate.

The Lin family stressed that they were not unreasonable people but then insisted that they could not care less whether their demand complied with the laws or policies, stating: "We won't budge until our problem is resolved, no alternative." But, one morning, Ms. Lin suddenly summoned me because of a forced eviction that was happening not far from her house. By the time I arrived, it was over, leaving the householders to pick out their personal belongings from the ruins. A woman living opposite to the demolished house told me that, at about 9:30 a.m., some one hundred people had suddenly turned up and cordoned off the area. The householders happened to be away, so the workers immediately broke in and smashed the two-story building structure with hammers. Ms. Lin was anxious that the team might return that afternoon. I commented that, apparently, demolition rarely takes place in the afternoon, joking that she should be safe for now. Obviously, Ms. Lin was in a constant state of "temporal instability," that Erik Harms (2013) similarly noted among housing evictees in Ho Chi Minh City, Vietnam, that makes it difficult for people to plan for the future and leads evictees to see themselves as oppressed by endless waiting. However, as chapter 3 demonstrates, in Chongqing's urban demolition, as much as in Ho Chi Minh City, a few evictees do exhibit remarkable resilience in the face of enforced "temporality of eviction" (Harms 2013, 347), by virtue of their economic resources or tacit knowledge of the demolition practices.

A few weeks later, the demolition company invited the Lin family to attend another meeting. Ms. Lin was adamant that relocation was the last thing her family wanted, yet felt unsure about whether or not they should compromise. The following is a debriefing of what transpired:

> That morning, Ms. Lin, her elder sister, Mr. Lin, the family's eldest son and the widows of her two older brothers attended the meeting. On the other side were a manager from the demolition office, a court representative, and two executives from the demolition company. The manager stated that the company's offer has been made in consideration of the family's certified rights and living conditions, adding that the family's demand was equivalent to four times their legitimate living area. The court representative urged them to accept the terms. Ms. Lin's sister pleaded that, "There're ill people and we are poor." The manager explained that "Compensation is based on the principle of parity exchange (*dengjia jiaohuan*), but your demand is based on allocation by need (*anxu fenpei*), a principle which doesn't work anywhere." The Lin family challenged the basis of such "parity": "How much floor area could be built on the reclaimed land and for how much will the new houses be sold?!" The quarrel lasted ninety minutes, without the parties reaching agreement.

The two contrasting principles of "allocation by need" and "parity exchange," as quoted, vividly summarize the essential contradictions over demolition—two contrasting rationales based on welfare need and market transaction price.[8] Several weeks later, Ms. Lin told me that she was having discussions with the company "in good faith." She showed signs of a misconceived hope that something might emerge from the bargaining process. Shortly afterward, one morning in July 2012, while everybody was out, the demolition team finally arrived without notice. By the time the Lin family members had rushed back, it was all over. Their compound had been leveled by a bulldozer, leaving only rubble. They were sent to stay, without cost, in a nearby hostel with a few other evictees, but had no idea where their belongings had been taken. Without a kitchen, the evictees could not cook for themselves, so eating out became an additional financial burden for them. After their eviction, they no longer obstructed the construction work, so no one from the demolition company ever contacted them again and the Lins did not know whether the original offer had been rescinded or not. When I saw Ms. Lin, she said that she had become depressed through worry and helplessness. She kept murmuring, "I'll go to Beijing; what kind of society is this?"

The various members of the Lin family had displayed striking consistency in terms of their ambivalence between the notions of needs and rights in justifying their resettlement demands and rationalizing their expectations. For them, their need was adequate ground for constituting an ethical disposition of justice to engage in bargaining. They may have possessed papers which they believed proved their home's legal status but soon realized that these were of no practical value. Their housing need did not constitute a legal right per se in reality. Unconvinced, they knew what they wanted but did not know how to achieve it. Despite their knowledge of, and anxiety about, forced eviction, strangely, they remained ill-prepared for the inevitable course of events. Unlike other nail householders, who were prepared for a hard fight, the Lin family's mind-set of concrete needs had yet to shift into a proactive, strategizing mode.

TEN THOUSAND YEARS IS TOO LONG FOR THE CLAIM OF NEEDS

I first met Mr. Gu on a cold, winter afternoon. He was sitting with a few neighbors around a campfire in front of his two-story nail house. Facing the grand property construction project, he enjoyed a terrific river view and bore witness to the concomitant rise of luxurious residential buildings and the dismantling of houses in his neighborhood. With most of the surrounding houses vacated and partially demolished, Gu's compound had become a conspicuous nail house. Now in his early sixties, he lived with his mother, his second wife, and younger son. "I just want a shelter to live in; I'm not greedy; just compensate me with one of those apartments being built," said Gu. Strangely, he was the only nail householder to mention the idea of a direct exchange in the same place, even though it sounded reasonable to me but he was only joking, as he admitted that the newly built high-rises in front of him were far more expensive than his own dwelling.

Inside his dark, congested house, and sometimes in the open space outside, Mr. Gu told me his story several times. He had been married twice; before his first wife passed away, in the 1980s, he had had a few temporary jobs. After that, he became a monk in a monastery, as it was a stable "job," but, later, his income could not keep pace with inflation, so he abandoned his religious vocation after ten years. He moved to Gaoshan to care for his aging aunt, who owned three small houses there, acquired before the 1949 revolution. Grateful for his kindness, Mr. Gu's aunt left him a house in her will. Regarding his religious belief, this is what he has to say:

> I used to be a true believer; now, I'm only an actor. Occasionally, I help out at the temple fair for money; by dressing up, I'm a monk again. The head of Lohan Temple got that post by paying a bribe of four million RENMINBI. How could a monk have so much money? It's all "incense money" from donations. Being a monk is like being a communist: so much grand talk about doing good things. Buddhism learners are like three-year-old children; they actually understand nothing. I advise people to buy medicine or sweets for elderly people in the nursing home, instead of donating money to the corrupt temples.

Gu's house covered more than $100m^2$, including the upper floor and part of the kitchen that had been illegally added, but only $45m^2$ was recorded on the official document to avoid paying additional taxation. The Gu family lived on social security benefits of some RMB700 per month. His married elder son worked in Beijing. He wanted two $80m^2$ apartments as compensation, the additional one for his elder son's family, plus a refurbishment allowance (which is not a standard item of compensation). No deal had been reached and, feeling frustrated, two years ago, he had teamed up with ten neighbors to take a petition to Beijing. On the train, they suspected that the conductor only checked their tickets and not those of any other passengers, so they decided to get off early at Zhengzhou, noting: "We adopted Chairman Mao's tactics of guerrilla warfare, boarding a bus to Tianjin before heading for Beijing." After handing their petition to the State Bureau for Letters and Calls, which is responsible for receiving suggestions, opinions, and questions from the public for the consideration of the Party and State Council, they went sightseeing in Tiananmen Square; there, they were intercepted by the police and repatriated to Chongqing by escorts sent by the municipal government.

Mr. Gu said that first-time petitioners were normally held for five days but, because he had caused a disturbance at the police station, he was detained for more than a month. He was still proud of his act and appeared fearless, despite his hardship and punishment. It is understood that, for each petition, the sub-district office will be fined and reprimanded, and the demolition convener will bear the transport costs of the returnees and official escorts. Thus, petitioning was not at all viewed as a welcome incident for the local authorities. Gu showed me a bag full of documents and newspaper clippings pertaining to the general policies of demolition and relocation that he had collected. He said that he understood these well, but still the demolition people insisted that his household had not followed the standard procedure: "The fact is, each household is subjected to a different set of procedures." Pulling out a notebook recording his neighbors' terms of compensation, Gu claimed that most of the settled families were well-off and could afford to pay extra for better, bigger replacement apartments, "or else they must have paid bribes." If no deal was reached, Gu said he would make and detonate a bomb, if his house was demolished by force, "Black powder is easy to make: just mix potassium nitrate, sulfur, and charcoal powder. I'd exchange my own life for at least two of theirs." He said that it would make the news and force the government to satisfy their needs and compensation demands: "The only way to counter the government's barbarism is with primitive violence."

Mr. Gu differed from Ms. Lin in that he had moved far beyond yearning for justice and lamenting the social unfairness of the world to form a deeper comprehension of the concept of human equality and socialist egalitarianism. If Ms. Lin were poorly prepared for her eventual fate, then Mr. Gu could be described as overprepared for it. When Gu joked that he was employing Chairman Mao's legendary guerrilla warfare tactics, he was probably also thinking about a line from Mao's classic poem that "Ten thousand years are too long, seize the day, seize the hour."[9] Yet time was not really on Gu's side, as his forced eviction was drawing closer, day by day; he could see demolition and rubble encroaching ever nearer to his courtyard (see Figure 2.2). For Gu, deliberating on his needs and dissemination of his cause patiently was pointless, as only stern resistance had any practical meaning. Gu took his needs claim for granted but it meant virtually nothing in light of the logic of the demolition policy. His agitation seemed to have been fueled by a self-acclaimed righteousness in defending his dwelling and the legitimacy of demanding compensation, grounded in his knowledge of demolition malpractices.

Gu's concrete needs had transformed into an abstract sense of rights that drove his actions. His rhetoric was filled with irony and sarcasm, yet his logic was not devoid of sense. His threats were probably empty, but whether a "black powder explosive" actually existed did not matter. The world rolls on, and Gu may merely have aspired to a moment of truth and perhaps, as well, a fleeting desire for revenge. From his rubble-encircled brick house, Mr. Gu stood witness to the bustling construction site before him—day in, day out—as the once-gorgeous scenery receded into memory. At Gaoshan, a

Figure 2.2. Mr. Gu Tending to His "Field" on Borrowed Time. This photo was taken by the author.

sense of tension and anxiety existed amid the "tumbling" and "rising" buildings in the landscape. When the inevitable eviction became increasingly imminent, a vibrant subjectivity and distinctive kind of consciousness was mapped—that people did not want to leave but must; that people wanted to exit but were disempowered to do so. Sherry Ortner (2006), in reference to Clifford Geertz, has pinpointed the centrality of "anxiety" in the analysis of the subjectivity of the human condition, stressing subjectivity's relations to the changing and subtle forms of power that saturate everyday life, through experiences of ties, space, and work. At Gaoshan, we observed no lack of history, power, tension, and anxiety, as all were at once convoluted to produce a subjectivity of needs and rights through everyday life and contestation, and Gaoshan itself was becoming a landscape that once existed, remembered but *unbelonged to*.

RECLAIMING THE MORAL IMPERATIVE OF NEEDS

In summary, we see that, in everyday life, many people are often inclined to conflate the notion of needs with that of rights. The demolition company enforces property rights verification and compensation as the overriding criteria, imposing them upon evictees, who in turn have no alternative but to adopt the same principles and vocabulary to inform and legitimize their counter-dispossession actions. The housing need of evictees has become elusive, although it is exactly such need that intrinsically empowers people's resistance. As Alan Smart sees it: "To decide why a practice continues in a particular time and place, we need to ask questions such as whether it is legitimate in the eyes of practitioners or administrators, for the squatters themselves may see a great deal of legitimacy in their continued occupation" (2001, 41). Indeed, nail householders' responses to forced evictions are characteristically out of the ordinary (the majority of evictees had chosen to compromise and leave), which must require strong reasons for their justification. Only through deliberation of basic needs as rights are nail households able to reflect on their conduct. It follows that, despite the partial dismissal of their proclaimed rights by the official policies, the nail householders refuse to accept the denial of their need-based rights. Their defiance is indeed animated by a conjoined discourse of needs and rights. Need claims, like right claims, are drivers of action, albeit largely and paradoxically overshadowed and subdued by rights claims engendered and imposed by the demolition authorities in the first place.

The random, contemptuous criticism and mockery of the Party cadres and communist ideals by many stubborn nail householders and vigorous petitioners represent an experiential account of and personal testimony to the social reality. In the cities, most of the welfare provision, including housing, healthcare, and job security, has been rescinded since the turn of the century. The elements formerly considered basic needs, which had been provided for by the socialist state, are now largely a matter of personal and household responsibility to be fulfilled in the domain of the market. This epochal change is intrinsic in the governing logic of the official policy regarding demolition work and is also reflected in the evictees' own rhetoric in contesting demolition by means of negotiating property ownership rights. Only a small minority of evictees, those in the nail households, are resisting vigorously on the back of a robust claim of needs and an emergent claim of rights grounded in needs. However, the might of such a needs-based claim has been dissipated precipitously, compromised not only by expressions of wants tuned to the proliferation of private property rights, but also by calamitous abuses of its use historically.

As Katherine Verdery (1996) illustrates, socialism rests on a claim to satisfy people's basic needs in keeping with socialist egalitarianism, and at the center of both the Communist Party's official ideology and its efforts to secure popular support lies a claim that the Party would take care of everyone's needs by collecting the total social product and then making available whatever people needed. Thus, many who grew up under a communist regime no doubt remember this old socialist slogan: "From each according to his ability, to each according to his need." In reality, this Marxian maxim and socialist vision have never been employed in either policy or practice, but rather dangled as utopian rhetoric to sway millions of Chinese people to embrace communism and obey the Party.[10]

Philosopher Agnes Heller argues that "social need" is indeed a positive value category: it is the need of humans for communism, the need of what may be termed "socialised man" (1974, 70). Political scientist Patricia Springborg (1981) even suggests that it was Marx who first used the terms "needs" to refer to the whole range of peculiarly human powers and potentialities: capacities for thinking, acting, willing, loving, enjoying, suffering, as needs. The importance of needs in the communism project, however, lies more in a materialistic sense than in ontological functions—of acting as the motor of progress in historical materialism that culminates in an account of the development of the forces and relations of production as a "dialectic of needs" (Springborg 1981, 101). It is no exaggeration to claim that "needs" inform the analytical power of Marxism, and the promise to satisfy needs empowers the legitimacy of all the once-existent Marxian states. For instance, in examining the Hungarian postsocialist welfare state transformation through the "lens of social architectures of need," Lynne Haney finds that Hungarian women have contested the system by appealing to the prior maternalistic regime for a more responsive welfare structure and more participatory needs talk (1999, 178). Moreover, when the Mongolian Communist Party was re-elected by a staggering majority in 2001, Caroline Humphrey (2002b) viewed this outcome as the Mongolians' endorsement of its previous legitimacy of having provided for substantive "needs" during the socialist period.

Nonetheless, there has been a "disjuncture" of Marx's theorizing of the significance of needs, a polarity between needs in the sense of conditions for fulfilling or developing the essential qualities of human nature and needs conceived as necessary conditions of existence or physical drives (Seigel 1983, 513). Marx tended to abandon the first notion of needs in favor of the second. Marshall Sahlins explicates that, in the "first moment" of his materialist theory, the young Marx, a humanist, rejected the "interrelated reductions of knowledge to nature, society to technology, and production to need" (1976, 133); but then in the "second moment," the mature Marx, a scientist, purportedly turned away from a concern for human alienation in favor of the concrete analysis of history, and the symbolic determination of needs is theoretically "dissolved within the absolute objective action of their satisfaction" (1976, 140). It follows that human needs become abstract and ahistorical, and the wants and pleasures of people lose their origin in society. Hence, in their orthodox application of historical materialism as an actual political project, the ruling Communist Party everywhere considered needs as imputed attributes of an assumed, immutable human nature, and human needs as no longer historically and culturally determined. Need retained its historical significance, but had lost much of its fluid analytical power and sociocultural meaning; such is the legacy of Marxism.

However, as Mayfair Yang (1989) illustrates, under centralized state redistribution, experience has shown that needs only emerge through a "system of interpretation" derived from the larger social and political discourse, which may prioritize and legitimate certain needs, and may construct criteria for assigning certain individuals and groups with special rights to the satisfaction of needs. During the 1960s and 1970s, when class struggle in China had notoriously become the primary focus of socialist construction and everyday practice, the universal needs of ordinary people were pervasively and arbitrarily preempted by class-based, privileged-based rights, which was in breach of the basic tenet and grand promise of Marxism. It is said that, in the highest phase of communist society, there will be an abundance of goods to satisfy everybody's needs, such that no one needs to fall back on the claims of individual rights. Yet, prior to that, rights appropriately only belong to progressively revolutionary forces, as (re)interpreted by the frenetic who were in power in those dark, turbulent days. My own study also reveals how housing need has been engendered as a social phenomenon at a particular historic juncture, but the satisfaction of which is even more differentiating and discriminating as compared to past socialist welfare provisions. Hence, human needs are always a historical product, culturally and politically determined, but never a purely natural or biological attribute.

In China, scarcities and inequalities still abounded during the period of radical socialism. Nowadays, invoking the aforementioned socialist utopian statement of need invites ridicule from ordinary people, arousing bitter memories of an era of passionate excess and utopian non-sensibility. History has demonstrated, all too forcefully, such rhetoric as but a misevaluation of the social reality and a gross misjudgment of human nature. In the first place, the tenet blatantly overestimates the productive capability of a communist society organized by central planning and directed by the absolute concentration of power.[11] Second, it is flawed in that it overlooks the complex human propensity to expand the contours of need, be they genuine or artificial, compounded further in China by hitherto unseen efforts to alter human nature into a state of absolute altruism and to contain unworthy desires and even certain basic human needs.[12] A whole generation of people suffered, paying too high a price for such a social experiment, scarifying everything for a lost cause. As such, much of the otherwise moral imperative of needs in understanding and legitimizing human action is lost, both historically and politically.

The present and actual guiding principle of socialist distribution differs from that long-abandoned utopian rhetoric, as the PRC Constitution Article 6 stipulates: "The system of socialist public ownership supersedes the system of exploitation of man by man; it applies the principle of from each according to his ability, to each according to his work." The word "needs" does not appear throughout the constitution; instead, "rights," "duties," and "interests" predominate. Power and policy wax and wane; however, dismissing needs' relevance is unthinkable and untenable when attempting to read and analyze socialist China in its past and present forms. Indeed, the party-state has ceaselessly reiterated that the regime exists as a "socialist democracy" and "socialist market economy," and the Party's own constitution remains committed to catering to people's "needs," albeit vaguely: "The Party must . . . gradually eliminate poverty, achieve common prosperity, continuously meet the people's ever-growing material and cultural needs on the basis of the growth of production and social wealth."[13] Thus, there remains a possibility for neo-socialist China to embrace need-based claims, as need remains very much a cardinal principle for neo-socialist governance normatively, albeit relegated to an inferior position and in subordination to the ubiquitous claims of rights. It follows that a cogent diagnosis in reclaiming the significance of needs' due place is imperative for accurate ethnographic readings of how people assert and practice their rights in an era of property counter-dispossession. In the course of such a study, nonetheless, a sense of tension is readily and commonly discovered between the vernacular claim of needs and the state-endorsed claim of rights, which should be heeded for its implication concerning China's party-state legitimacy. It is critical to acquire a *neo-socialist sensibility* to avoid losing sight of the captivating notion of needs as an integral part of the socialist and neo-socialist moral discourse, albeit tempered substantively by the endorsement of market economics and private property rights. Notwithstanding, ironically, the moral imperative of needs claims may sometimes be inadvertently diluted and compromised by the evictees' own rights claims in their counter-demolition tactics and practice, as will be explored in the next chapter.

NOTES

1. The sub-district office (*jiedao*) is the lowest level of urban administration in Chinese cities, serving around 100,000–200,000 residents. Its officers-in-charge are appointed by the district government, while the rest of the staff tends to be three-year contract employees, hired locally. The community residents' committee, in turn, is set up by the sub-district office as a civic organization serving the interests of the masses in respect to community (*shequ*) civic affairs. Each community residents' committee serves up to 10,000 residents; its officers-in-charge are directly elected by the residents every three years, but their nominations are controlled by the sub-district office, and the community residents' committee has a de facto reporting line to the sub-district office.

2. According to Qin Shao (2008), the idea that aggrieved people can bring their complaints to higher authorities is rooted in ancient Chinese statecraft, whereby the benevolent, wise emperor would correct the wrongdoings of the lower-ranking officials and return justice to the people once they learned about their suffering. However, as the authorities that possess the power to resolve those issues are often the root cause of the complaints in the first place, the

system has become a trap that consumes enormous energy and resources of both the petitioner and the government without serving its stated purpose.

3. Sociologist Sun Liping (2013) condemns *weiwen* as serious infringement of civil rights and has created chronic opposition between the government and the masses.

4. Owing to the inherent sensitivity of demolition work, all names of places, people, and companies are kept anonymous, with pseudonyms used where necessary.

5. See *Xinhua News* (Du Yu 2012).

6. A notable exception of large-scale slum redevelopment took place in Liaoning Province, where the inhabitants were entitled to exchange their property rights and move back into the resettlement housing built on the original site. See *People's Daily* (Wang Wei 2012).

7. At the end of 2011, in the Peninsula District, the monthly allowance was around RMB400 for urban residents who lacked three things: working ability, income, and guardian care.

8. The translation of the Marxian axiom of "to each according to his need" into *anxu fenpei* (allocation by need) instead of *gequ suoxu* (to each according to his need) in China was dated back to 1958, which could have very different implications. Arguably, in different stages of the Chinese communist revolution, a certain degree of *anxu fenpei* had indeed been implemented; for instance, in the wartime Communist base at Yan'an during the 1930s and the period of strict allocation of basic necessities in the 1960s and 1970s. Hence, this translation may connote a sense of "continuity" between socialism and communism, as well as a sense of pragmatism in regard to what a communist society may look like. But at the same time, this interpretation may have substantively qualified the defining character of full communism and the ultimate promise communist society makes to all its members. See Yu Guangyuan (1978: 16).

9. From Chairman Mao's poem, "*Reply to Guo Moruo"—to the melody of "Manjianghong*," the lines, "*So many deeds cry out to be done; and always urgently. The world rolls on. Time presses. Ten thousand years are too long. Seize the day, seize the hour!*"

10. The phrase was first used by the French politician Louis Blanc in 1839 and popularized by Karl Marx in his 1875 *Critique of the Gotha Program*.

11. The Marxian socialist utopian's systemic fragility and brutality culminated in the 1957–1961 "Great Leap Forward," a forced industrialization and communalization program. Coinciding with a great famine, an estimated 30 million people starved or were tortured to death. Based on newly available archival data, Frank Dikötter (2010) puts the death toll at 45 million.

12. The idea of creating a selfless Socialist Man was dramatized by a 1963 propaganda campaign known as "Learn from Lei Feng" in the aftermath of the "Great Leap Forward." The otherwise unknown soldier Lei Feng, after his accidental death, was suddenly depicted and immortalized by the Party as a selfless, modest man who had been devoted to the Communist Party, Chairman Mao, and the people of China. In the official propaganda, Lei Feng continues to be an ideological icon to this day. See Liu Zhonghe and Zhou Ke (2012) on Lei Feng. Also see Lynteris (2012) for a less well-known case of the glorification of Norman Bethune, a Canadian medical volunteer who died in 1939 after serving under the Party's Eighth Army; Chairman Mao's praise for Bethune as a "spirit of absolute selflessness" subsequently was invoked and intriguingly reinterpreted to contend for the position of the true mode of constructing the socialist New Man.

13. General Principle, Constitution of Communist Party of China; amended and adopted November 14, 2012.

Chapter Three

Bargaining Demolition

When Needs and Desires Meet

> "The timing is just not right. The problem we face now is a consequence and legacy of the past unfairness, an unpleasant vicious circle. But it'll be equally chaotic and untenable if everybody is to be treated equitably; such is our social reality." —Manager Niu

This was how the manager of a demolition and relocation (*chaiqian*) company described the stagnant situation of urban demolition when I started my field work in mid-2011. The site was in a different situation from that described in chapter 2, with demolition work also starting much later. A combination of soaring property prices, experience of previous demolition malpractice, and the Party's resolve to create a "socialist harmonious society" were attributed to more stringent controls over how demolition work should be conducted. Demolition personnel were now operating in a far less favorable environment in their attempt to convince evictees to accept government compensation.

The *Chaiqianhu* (evictees) themselves were well-aware of the country's economic transformation, from the principle of socialist distribution based on part entitlement and part discretion to the new game of capitalist accumulation based partly on market mechanism and partly on statist control. The evictees invariably harbored a local belief based on previous inequitable cases of demolition, from which they developed a discursive, sarcastic reinterpretation of the official policy dissemination regarding the rules and terms of compensation. This underlines the belief that no such thing as a fair procedure or equitable compensation exists where a demolition settlement is concerned. The evictees understood their asymmetrical power position, but many were willing to take it to the limit, as the cost of being taken advantage of was too high for a whole family to bear. Through this perceived opportunity of a lifetime, wherein people's needs and desires became conflated and intermingled, vacating their premises too early could mean relinquishing too great a stake in a world of "first-mover disadvantage"—a reflection characteristic of the legacy of past unfairness and an absence of trust in the social system at large.

The evictees' forming of a righteous moral discourse along with formulating a defensive tactic pertaining to their homeownership resulted in a complex relationship, hitherto unseen, between the populace and the local state. Urban housing demolition became a mundane, everyday occurrence across every city in China after the welfare housing provisions were completely phased out in 2003. In this chapter, I explore the multifaceted interaction and micro-power bargaining relationships concerning the evictees and the frontline demolition personnel. I also provide a detailed, rare ethnographic record of the multivocal bargaining exchanges between the various agents.[1] In the course of presenting my data and analysis, I employ the framework of practice theory and discuss its analytical purchase and limitation. Moreover, the routine interactions between the evictees and demolition personnel reveal that the discernible tension and competing discursive statements, variously framed as *needs* and *desires*, are the rationale behind the evictees' stern attitudes and claim of *rights*. I shall raise the notion of the "economics of rights interpretation" to reflect on how a needs claim is concealed by a rights claim in the demolition field, as the logic of needs is buried in desire talk. Political scientist Elizabeth Perry (2008) characterizes the framing of protest in contemporary China as rules consciousness rather than rights consciousness, as rights are seen more as state-authorized channels to enhance national unity and prosperity than as naturally endowed protection against state intrusion. In contrast, in her ethnography on housing demolition in Shanghai, historian Qin Shao concludes that this duality is not necessarily contradictory, as evictees "play by the rules to secure their rights" (2013, 276). This rules-versus-rights binary and paradox is indeed a highly relevant question to my own study, as I discovered that evictees and evictors alike stick to the nominal official rules but contest vigorously the interpretation of rights, each in accordance with their tacit understanding of the actual norm of practicing demolition and the particular tactics of bending the rules of demolition bargaining and compensation.

DEMOLITION PRACTICE

In contrast to evictees who had moved out, most of my informants believed that they were subject to the improved policy protection enacted after 2011 and thus were more deliberate about engaging in prolonged bargaining and contestation. The home demolition social situation dovetails with practice theory's perspective to help us understand the mutual relationship and interaction between the socio-political reality's constraints and the agents' tactics and practices within a particular social field. In doing so, practice theory's strengths and shortcomings are unwittingly revealed and evaluated, with the representational categories of need and desire juxtaposed alongside. Nonetheless, I argue that such an analytical design expands and enriches our understanding of the concrete demolition practices from two vantage points, which are not necessarily incompatible.

In the present case, house demolition represents a secondary domain within a broader primary field of contesting private property rights. The central idea of such an approach is understood as the "duality of structure" (Giddens 1979, 255) and the "dialectical relationship" between the structure and the agents' dispositions (Bourdieu 1977, 84). Practice theorists emphasize bodily agency, intentionality, expressiveness and affective response, yet crucially insist that individual actions are shaped by social practices and the norms they embody (Rouse 2007; also see Postill 2010). My analysis highlights a situation in which constrained agency is significant and whereby routine distinctions are observed between rules and norms. The evictees' observed interactions with demolition personnel at my field site represent only one mode of action constituting a field of practice. Their knowing, presuming, gossiping, rationalizing, worrying, cursing, and ridiculing behaviors form interwoven mental and physical activities that function as manifold actions. The kind of practice being studied lasts from a few months to a few years; however, householders' decisions have long-term repercussions for the intergenerational relationships and well-being of the family members. The practice is locally situated according to both specific local policy and commercialized demolition teams' tactics, yet is also affected by nationwide housing policy and market conditions. While the practice is distanced in scope from the routine of everyday life, it has an enormous bearing on the totality of family life.

In his analysis of the French housing market, Pierre Bourdieu (2005) reckons that the forces of the field orient the dominant toward strategies whose end is the perpetuation or reinforcement of their domination. In the Bourdieuian paradigm, the asymmetric power relations between evictees and demolishers in the present case allow limited scope for social transformation (see Berard 2005; Ortner 2006; Rouse 2007). Two questions are of particular relevance to the present analysis: Who represents the state in the manifold asymmetrical power relations? And how can we discern the causal efficacy of the various actors' practices in reproducing or transforming the social structure? My study shows that the Party machinery needs not be conceived as a reified force but instead as a source of framing and enrichment for a mode of agency that is not necessarily heroic, as evictees scramble to defend their interests based on competitive claims to victimhood. Some of the Party cadres, equipped with an insider, insightful understanding of an intriguing political reality, demonstrated a greater capability to circumvent the hurdles and transcend the problems encountered, and viewing them as rare opportunities to enrich themselves. In this exceedingly dynamic field site, the state's representatives play shifting, competing roles that convey dynamic status, which challenges the common perception they are always at fault. In addition, their counterparts are not static in terms of either their identity or role. The agency, as depicted here, shifts and mutates, to the extent of obscuring my understanding of whether a structure is being reproduced or transformed in the conduct of house demolition by persuasion and threat, and counter-dispossession by discursive reinterpretations of the official policy. One thing is certain though: the majority of evictees and evictors alike are desirous agents, engaged in risky practices in a constant micro-power play and display. As I see it, their token rule-abiding and Party loyalty represent tactical gestures more than genuine beliefs.

The onsite office of the demolition company, Yidi, was situated on the ground floor of a run-down, two-story house.[2] A long red banner hanging outside the entrance stated in yellow characters: "Demolition for the people; demolition in accordance with the law; demolition under sunshine; demolition with harmony" (see Figure 3.1). The main office covered an area of about 150m^2; it was sparsely furnished with a couple of worn sofas, a few wooden tables, a personal computer, a printer, and a second-hand air-conditioner sitting on an uneven cement floor. Further inside was a larger room, used mainly for storage and holding public hearings. On the walls were posted various rules and regulations regarding "the urban demolition of endangered and old houses," as well as details of the demolition procedures and terms for compensation. Hanging on the walls were also colorful drawings of residential projects in the pipeline and a large whiteboard displaying the availability of apartment units; when a unit is taken, a red dot is stuck over it. However, since the day I arrived, the board was rarely updated; I was told that its purpose is merely to create the impression there is a good take-up rate by those who come in for a discussion. Yet, throughout my twelve-month observation period, there were usually only one or two visitors during the office's opening hours.

The demolition area in which I conducted my participant observation encompassed some three hundred households, managed by a convener, Dafa, a company under the district government registered for the purpose of undertaking co-redevelopment with property developers. Located on the second floor of the same building, Dafa was vested with the responsibility and authority to hold discussions with affected households and approve compensation. The overall onsite demolition and relocation office comprised both

Figure 3.1. The Front of the Demolition Office. This photo was taken by the author.

Dafa and its appointed demolition company, Yidi. Before negotiations began, Dafa would prepare a shortlist of property appraisers from which the evictees could choose, but some evictees told me that they had taken several hundred RENMINBI (RMB) from the bidding appraisers to choose them in return, as they cannot see what real difference between their choices anyway. The chosen appraiser then provided a supposedly independent valuation of the neighborhood's properties with reference to market prices. However, the evictees were generally cynical about the appraiser's impartiality. Initially, some households tried to organize collective action in their dealings with the demolition office, but these were soon banned and the whole process of bargaining became an emphatically individualized practice. Nonetheless, each individual evictee's rationale, arguments, rhetoric, and tactics, although not always completely reasonable or consistent, formed a complex, dynamic mode of interactions vis-à-vis the demolition personnel.

The onsite supervisor of Dafa was Mr. Gao, a man in his late forties, who was a no-nonsense quick thinker and persuasive talker. Privately, I was told that Gao owns a lot of property, including a townhouse that was also scheduled for demolition and compensation. Yidi's founder, Mr. Cen, was a private entrepreneur who established the company several years ago with the help of a relative with government connections. Cen would sometimes arrive at the office unannounced to check punctuality and give long speeches to his staff. The work had started in early 2011, but progress was slow. By July 2013, less than one-third of the households had consented to leave. During one crisis meeting initiated by Gao and Cen, the speakers took turns in blaming the poor progress on the work team's lack of experience and enthusiasm, as well as the tougher policy requirements. At the end of the meeting, few recommendations had been made and morale had not improved.

The territory for which Yidi was responsible comprised two areas. Site A had 150 households, mostly from the same rural village originally. Many of the ex-village cadres had resettled there and were the prime targets of the demolition office with whom they hope to strike agreements to establish examples for other ex-villagers. The remaining households also contained previous evictees from other districts; hence, all of the residents have had previous demolition experience. Site B included two twenty-year-old residential blocks occupied by the ex-employees of a state-owned pharmaceutical factory and one small residential/retail block developed by the owner ten years ago. The progress at Site B was much better, with a success ratio of 2:1 over Site A, probably because most of the residents of Site A had learned the tricks of hard bargaining, thereby making any negotiation efforts much more difficult. The occupants there resided in nine-story buildings, with barely any refurbishment to the outer walls or corridors. The principal standard units in the building had a gross floor area (GFA) of approximately 60 or 80m^2.[3] There were no elevators in the buildings; barren, dusky staircases complete with rusted iron railings lead the residents to each story's three units. Even in broad daylight, the corridors were dim, covered in rubbish and dust. Walking up to the top floors was particularly difficult for the elderly, not to mention in midsummer. That was perhaps why many evictees had requested a ground-floor apartment, despite their standard rhetoric of *not* being eager to move out.

The residential units were usually valued at around RMB280,000–380,000 (US$44,000–60,000), based on the appraiser's benchmarks of RMB4,840/m^2 GFA for residential property completed in the 1990s, and RMB4,730 for that completed in the 1980s. In accordance with the "Demolition Compensation and Resettlement Scheme" published by Dafa, if evictees contracted to vacate within the government's designated period, they would receive a special bonus of RMB10,000–30,000, a removal subsidy of RMB1,000–2,000, and a transition rental subsidy of RMB700–900 per month for households awaiting occupancy of their new homes. Additional protection was offered to needy households: a minimum floor area compensation of 35m^2 was guaranteed for families with two members and 45m^2 for those with three or more members. Compensation could be paid in kind or in cash. Evictees could opt for a replacement unit within a few kilometers of their present residence, based on a 1:1 ratio of unit area compensation, but these replacement apartments were still under construction, specifically for demolition resettlement. Thus, the evictees were not receptive toward these properties, which were of substandard quality. Regardless, the residents could request a larger unit and pay the difference in valuation. Typically, the replacement apartment was valued at a 5 to 10 percent discount of the evictees' home, so they could take a slight cut to gain a larger space. In reality, many people asked for two units with an aggregate floor area far exceeding the size of their present dwelling, without paying for the difference in market value.[4] Mr. Gao told me some even asked for three to four units plus a cash allowance. From what I learned, most of the completed cases involved a higher than 1:1 compensation ratio, but the evictees agreed to pay the difference. A completed residential complex's market price in the area was around RMB7,000/m^2; thus, apparently, it would make little sense to choose the cash option; but numerous informants told me that there was always flexibility, which meant that the final compensation substantially exceeded the stipulated ceiling, subject to Dafa's discretion. Privately, I was informed that the cash compensation actually started at RMB6,2000, reaching RMB9,000/m^2 for well-connected evictees by early 2013.

In successful cases, two separate contracts were signed. One contained a copy of the standard terms of agreement for evictees, while the other detailed their additional cash payment. The latter contract was withheld from signing evictees to prevent other evictees from learning the extent of the flexibility in individual cases, which was obviously unfair. Nonetheless, the gap between the benchmark figures and most of the evictees' demands remained largely between RMB100,000–200,000, that is, around 30 to 50 percent over the compensation benchmark. When asked how they justified their demand for two new apartments in return for their run-down property with inadequate facilities, the evictees typically answered, "It's you who want to demolish our home, not us who are asking to move away." Previously, in the case of evictees who wanted greater compensation, the demolition office would apply to the district house administration bureau for an executive order of forced eviction. An onsite public hearing would be held, with the evictees and Yidi each presenting their respective cases. Afterward, the house administration office would render a verdict, usually within three months. Once the decision on forced demolition had been made, households had fifteen days in which to comply. As public concern over forced evictions increased, however, from early 2011, executive forced eviction was abolished.[5] From then on, after the administrative verdict was delivered post-hearing, evictees were given three months in which to comply or appeal, after which the convener would file an application to the court for a judicial forced eviction, which could take a further three months. As the district government was poised for a major personnel reshuffle in October 2011, however, followed by the Communist Party's 18th Party Congress in November 2012, any sensitive actions that might jeopardize the social harmony and damage the local officials' career were not allowed to proceed. After the downfall of Secretary Bo Xilai in March 2012, the local authorities became even more cautious.

THE SITE OF SERIOUS BARGAINING

The demolition office run by Yidi had a staff of nine. It was headed by Manager Niu, a former factory worker, about forty years old, who joined Yidi two years ago. The majority of the team members were in their twenties or early thirties, and only one had received tertiary education. The team was responsible for the routine home visits, discussions, and subsequent documentation work. Niu and Gao remarked that the teammates were always to refer to themselves as demolition personnel, rather than representatives, to avoid any conspicuous connection with the government. As these people worked on the front line, I will refer to them as onsite demolition personnel (ODP). Most ODP had no prior experience in the profession. They got their job because of their relationship with Mr. Cen or someone from the house administration bureau. They were deeply conscious that their status differed from those who worked with Dafa upstairs, in terms of both economic well-being and discretionary power over the demolition work. ODP were paid a rather unenviable RMB1,800 per month, inclusive of allowances, an amount toward the low end of Chongqing's salary range.[6] Most ODP considered their job as temporary, due to their lack of qualifications for other jobs. They were entitled to a performance bonus, but this seemed a remote possibility, given the slow progress of the project. Indeed, shortly afterward, Mr. Cen decided to cut their monthly take-home pay. Demoralized, Manager Niu and three others resigned.

Director Hu from the local sub-district office and Secretary Yang from the community residents' committee also participated in the demolition efforts.[7] Both veteran Party members, Hu and Yang were longtime residents there who knew the neighborhood very well. Despite bearing fancy titles, however, they were not tenure civil servants but contract staff, representing and supporting the government to ensure social harmony at the grassroots level. Hu himself had served first in the community office for ten years before his appointment to the sub-district office. Their presence in the demolition office was to provide demographic intelligence on evictees and occasionally to attend home visits. Procedurally, they might witness deals struck between evictees and the demolition company, audit the efforts made by the ODP, and testify to the reasonableness of the subsequent application for forced eviction when necessary. Hu and Yang were government-hired, but both received a modest compensation from Yidi. In a sense, they were positioned midway in the relationship between Dafa/Yidi and the evictees, purporting to be neutral mediators but, in practice, they embodied the conflicting roles of protecting the masses' interests and facilitating the accomplishment of government tasks.

After a few months of home visits, the ODP had a good grasp of the demographic situation of the neighborhood. For each household, the ODP would pay at least two home visits to assess the situation. When I first joined their encounters, either at the office or in the evictees' homes, I almost felt that a fight was about to break out, as both sides customarily shouted loudly, insisting that the other side listen to them first. Frequently, all five persons spoke at the same time, rendering my memorized note-taking a daunting challenge. No one gave an inch; in the end, both sides urged the other to reconsider their position. From the ODP's viewpoint, they had little scope for maneuver, as any demand in excess of the standard compensation terms had to be reported to Mr. Gao for further deliberation. However, Gao repeatedly denied to me that he wielded such extensive discretionary power. On the one hand, he explained that, previously, there had been cases in which small apartments had been compensated with two units, "because some households built extra structures as their family size increased, we therefore exercise discretion on humanitarian grounds." On the other hand, he thought that the Yidi team was not fully conversant with explaining the government regulations and complained that its members lacked the kind of mighty bearing (*baqi*) necessary to achieve success. At an ODP review meeting, he advised that, notwithstanding the slogan about "harmonious demolition," such harmony was not without limit:

> You should explain to the *chaiqianhu* that the purpose of our demolition work is old-town redevelopment. Houses with outmoded facilities and antiquated infrastructures are not congruent with the modern urban image. Some may be of the view that we can't evict everybody by force. Tell them bluntly that their homes will be the first to be demolished! There're too many instances of cheating and pretense of ignorance; you can't be too accommodating. Show off your *baqi*; take a hardened approach if necessary.

Unlike interviewing the ODP or evictees separately, participant observation of the close encounters between them is rarely allowed and practiced, so I believe it is invaluable to present a few cases of the typical dialogue between them.

"Other People All Got Richer; Why Should I Be Poorer?"

A middle-aged woman visited the demolition office. Speaking in a high-pitched voice, she requested an 86 m^2, ready-made replacement nearby for her 63m^2 home.

ODP: Your request of $86m^2$ for $63m^2$, plus a renovation subsidy, means RMB100,000 over the government offer. If it were within our jurisdiction, we truly would have no reason to cause difficulty for you.

Evictee: If the replacement apartments already had three or four floors constructed, it would be acceptable, but, at present, the construction has not even commenced.

ODP: If you still feel disadvantaged, you could consider the cash option.

Evictee: No, I only want the house. I tell you, people who signed early on have special reasons for that; they have places to move to. In previous phases of demolition, some people got two-units-for-one compensation!

ODP: That's what you say. Can you show us the contract as proof?

Evictee: I tell you, you people must comply with Mayor Wang's policy speech regarding the 50 percent additional compensation!

ODP: Your interpretation is erroneous. This refers to the overall compensation ratio, but this doesn't mean that each household gets 50 percent more.

Evictee: Other people all got richer; why should I become poorer? No benefit, no deal!

"The Compensation Scheme Is Nonsense and Unfair."

Mr. Qiu led a home visit to the Liao family, an elderly couple in their seventies who lived on the sixth floor. The unit was rather run-down, minimally decorated, and equipped with an electric fan yet, despite the heat, it was not switched on. Opposite the Liao family was another household who had accepted the government compensation almost immediately when the scheme was offered. Mr. Liao wanted to stay in the same district and insisted that only an apples-to-apples compensation of an $80m^2$ unit in the same district, ready for occupation, would have any meaning for them. Qiu countered that, to achieve fair compensation, one must compare both the property valuation and the market price. They shouted at each other repeatedly, demanding to be allowed to finish talking. After half an hour, Mrs. Liao suddenly came out of her bedroom. Clearly deeply moved, she said that the compensation scheme was nonsense and unfair, and claimed to have heard that many others had received much better terms. [On our way back, Mr. Qiao remarked that, despite the outcome, the counter-offer from the Liao family was indeed "less outrageous" than many cases.]

"You're Dissenting Against Society."

The Zhu family's home on the top floor had a tiled floor, hanging glass lamps, a flat-screen television, and full air-conditioning. Mr. Zhu was reluctant initially to come out to greet the ODP, led by Ms. Chen. He insisted, on the one hand, that they could not possibly buy a decent home with the compensation offered. On the other hand, they were very happy with their existing apartment, which was conveniently located, and the family did not see any need to move elsewhere or buy another home. Throughout the conversation, Zhu rarely caught Ms. Chen's eye, instead watching a cartoon on television and occasionally making a disrespectful gesture. As Ms. Chen grew weary at this impasse, another ODP took over the discussion, remarking, "Mr. Zhu, I think you have an attitude problem, with a dissenting sentiment against society and the public interest."

"I Also Understand the Leadership's Policy Very Well."

Ms. Hung's 65m^2 home was fairly run-down. Her son was also present but showed great displeasure at the repeated visits to suppress them. When asked about her decision, Hung reiterated her demand: either two apartment units plus RMB100,000 cash or one three-bedroom unit plus RMB180,000, saying that their home was in a good location and that some of the family members were elderly. The ODP replied that the request was in breach of government policy. Hung became emotional and claimed that such a compensation ratio had been enacted in other districts of Chongqing:

> Explain to me, how come the same arrangement became invalid here only? Are the government policies interpreted differently in different places? I tell you, I also understand the policy of Bo Xilai and Wen Jiabao very well!

BARGAINING: POWER AND RISK

As far as I could ascertain, more than two-thirds of the evictees in the demolition field were requesting a 2:1 compensation ratio without paying the presumed difference in valuation. From the demolition office's perspective, this demand failed to acknowledge the higher market price of new units compared with their current accommodation, which was in a poor condition. Some ODP explained that there had been cases where two apartments were allotted, but that was mainly because the original unit was so big that a compensating apartment of corresponding size was unavailable on the market. In addition, there were exceptional cases in which a small 30m^2 unit was compensated for with two units because of the household's extremely crowded living conditions. Moreover, when the demolition work entered its latter phase, the authorities would offer better terms to expedite its completion, but these exceptions had become an ongoing problem for the present task.

Most of the evictees believed that, the later a deal is struck, the better the terms would be. The impression that early birds might have been disadvantaged was based on the chaotic situation prevailing between 2007 and 2009, when a mode of contract responsibility arrangement was endorsed whereby the demolition companies were given a lump sum within their budget to embark on their own projects and allowed to keep any benefits arising from the squeezing of evictees. Typically, the demolition companies would be more willing to sweeten the deals to settle with the last batch of households before proceeding to forced evictions. Although such contract responsibility practices had been abolished, their legacy continued to affect new evictees' conceptions and expectations. Another issue concerned the municipal leadership's public policy statement. It was claimed that the Mayor had promised a 2:1 ratio of floor area compensation for the occupants, but an ODP insisted that this only referred to extreme cases where households were living under very crowded conditions. Whatever the perceived truth, the actual truth was that the evictees had taken this hearsay as fact, something substantive, and proof of their argument's validity and their demand's righteousness.

Even if more favorable terms could be agreed upon, there may not be an available supply of prime replacement stock to allow a high ratio of compensation. It so happened that the early birds were able to select apartments in better locations. Indeed, most of the replacement apartments were under construction or even still at the planning stage, since the demolition work to build these had also encountered similar difficulties. After selling plots of land to developers, the local officials became very eager to lock in demolition costs by forcing evictees to move out as quickly as possible, but the shortage of built apartments meant that most evictees in transition could wait two years or more before settling into their promised new home. This is a serious systemic bottleneck, which was partly to blame for the ongoing chaos and apparently justifies the households' refusal to consent to move out within the government's notified schedule. At the same time, the evictees were resistant to the cash option even if they could push it up to the market valuation, as they believed that only compensation in kind allowed them to demand an over 1:1 compensation. Such was the formidable dilemma confronting all evictees who must decide whether or not to sign early. It appeared obvious to me that every household had its own individual logic and insights developed through harsh learning from the turbulent history and brutal reality of the housing reforms and forced demolition. Perhaps no other case exemplifies the contradiction between the principles and pragmatics of protecting one's self-interest better than that of Secretary Hai, a Party committee cadre from a village that was affected by demolition a few years ago.

Many of the affected villagers, along with Hai herself, had subsequently been compensated with apartments located at Site A. I was told that Hai was relatively secure financially: she owned a taxi business worth several million RENMINBI and another residence in addition to the apartment at Site A, which she rented out. The ODP considered it a strategic breakthrough if they could persuade Hai to take the lead in accepting the compensation terms. The following is a record of the ODP team's visit to her, led by Ms. Chen and Secretary Yang from the community office:

> Secretary Yang: We've come to discuss with you . . . hope that you will support us.
>
> Secretary Hai [smiling]: Support entails mutual cooperation. I heard that previously two-for-one compensation was allowed. Why is it impossible to do it this time?
>
> Ms. Chen: Back then, it was because of the special situation related to the unavailability of large units; but the total floor area was not doubled.
>
> Secretary Hai: I was involved in the rural area's demolition work myself. I know that flexibility always exists. Previously, we Party cadres took the lead in moving out, but ended up getting less than those who initially resisted moving out. In our village, back then, one household was evicted by force, but when the negotiations were almost over, he was released and compensated with even better terms. Hence, people are now undeterred by the possibility of forced evictions. As human beings, everybody is selfish. I've learned my lesson; this time, I'll wait.

After the meeting, on the way out, I saw Secretary Hai murmuring a few words to Ms. Chen and Secretary Yang, with her hand on the shoulder of Ms. Chen:

> For my case, please work harder to improve the terms. If my demand is satisfied, I won't utter a word to anybody—I'll just say that I've paid for the shortfall for two large units. I'll also mobilize other *chaiqianhu* to move out early.

Secretary Hai was on the inside when it came to understanding the Party's organizing logic. Demolition was an economic priority, political insiders enjoyed privileged knowledge about when and how to strike a tacit balance to extract the maximum benefit without breaking the rules. Her hint to the ODP to take care of her private interests in return for her public support revealed the logic and practice of the Party cadres in the *realpolitik*. Idealism and sacrifice were no longer the norms of everyday life. A few months later, her case was settled, with half of her extra demands being satisfied. Secretary Hai's attitude and practice hardly constituted an isolated case. Secretary Yang from the community office was ironically himself soon to be an evictee, as he confided to me he had an apartment nearby but with the title disguised under his wife's name. He had formulated a "perfect strategy" for himself, having been engaged in hundreds of demolition cases and having considered his own options and risk-taking capacity. To begin with, he reckoned, one must display a cooperative attitude but try to be vague about the preferred compensation, and only later reveal it at the high end (never the extreme) of a continuum of everybody else's demands, then resist the pressure for as long as possible, but remember never to infuriate the ODP in order to avoid being selected for forced eviction. Finally, keep an ear to the ground, and settle quickly before the authorities decide to handle evictees ruthlessly.

If Yang's strategy represented a well-formulated approach, the actual practice of Mei Mei's family, one of the ODP at my field site, confirmed it as the utmost practical sense. Mei Mei's mother had worked for the government in the 1980s as one of the first generation of demolition personnel. Back then, she was acting in her official capacity, unlike the present-day Dafa, operating as a development company. She later became a private entrepreneur and built a three-story residence, now poised for demolition. I was invited to visit her mansion, where she told me about her "colorful" career. There were a total of six units in the building that she owned, but she had signed the release of only three titles, which were of lesser value. Her consent was designed to demonstrate her cooperation with the authorities while at the same time preserving her most valuable assets. Moreover, by releasing a batch first, she was entitled to choose replacement apartments in her preferred location for her family. She stated that the three vacated units were all on the ground floor so that Dafa could not kick-start the demolition immediately without endangering the structure of the upper floors. Summarizing her family's tactics, Mei Mei stated:

> All of our demands are within the flexibility and limit discreetly sanctioned by the policy. We won't touch the authorities' bottom line, unlike some ignorant *chaiqianhu*, who are making all kinds of reckless demands, as if forced eviction never happens again.

Indeed, during a public hearing, a householder complained bitterly, asking why only their case out of almost three hundred unsettled households had been singled out. He demanded that the formula for calculating the compensation for each case be published and that all households in dispute be called upon at the hearing. However, it was exactly this kind of transparency that the demolition office sought to avoid to optimize its bargaining power and expediency. The discretionary power to select individual cases for a public hearing constituted a warning to feisty evictees, without unduly expanding the warfront.

A PRACTICE OF DISTRUST

Mrs. Shi was a member of the first of the three hundred households to vacate her premises, early in the demolition work. One morning, she visited the site office and complained she had been unfairly taken advantage of, as she had heard that a new compensation scheme had recently been applied to unsettled cases. Shi told me she could not sleep and was under severe "mental pressure," as she felt that she had mistakenly complied too early. On another occasion, I asked Secretary Yang how the majority of early birds felt. *Regret*, he reckoned, was a common feeling for most of them, as they knew that most evictees had not signed. There were three categories of evictee who struck an early deal with the government: households in financial difficulty who thus opted for cash compensation; well-off households who rented out their demolition apartments and so considered the compensation in kind as another kind of investment; and some who placed genuine trust in the government's fairness. Shi belonged to the second category, and her bitterness was attributed to greed and desire, according to the ODP's reckoning.

The case of Mr. Feng, in contrast, was clearly a regrettable one from the third category. During the several visits I paid to Feng's home, I saw his suffering and that of his wife. Both in their seventies, they lived in a 76 m^2 apartment with their elder son's family and their disabled younger son. Mr. Feng's whole extended family was in financial difficulty because of the heavy medical expenses required by Mrs. Feng and their younger son. They were compensated with two apartments under construction, but had to pay RMB80,000 themselves. Feng was persuaded by the ODP during a home visit to sign the agreement without consulting his family. They felt deceived, having been offered no hardship allowance and wanted to renegotiate better terms. One day, the Feng family came to see me to request help. Unfortunately, I was told by the ODP that their case would not be re-opened. Being a retired factory worker and veteran Party member, Mr. Feng had thought that the state needed his place, so he must pledge his support, implying that his family's needs should come second to those of the state, but now he rued his own premature decision and only sought fair treatment. He was ridiculed by his wife and daughter-in-law, who could not understand his "naivety," as they called it. When I asked him whether, in hindsight, he should have teamed up with his neighbors to make a collective demand, he explained: "No, Party members coming together for discussion is a violation of Party discipline." Feng's pure-minded Party loyalty stood in sharp contrast to that attitude of many other Party member evictees. They displayed a more balanced reading of their duty toward the Party and society through a pragmatic apprehension of self-interest as demolition bargainers themselves. The reality was that unfettered Party *loyalty* had become a moral *liability* to one's family.

Nominally, the official policy was not to be violated by either the demolition team or the evictees, for the sake of the public interest and social harmony, but Director Hu once told me he had never heard of a public hearing of a disputed demolition case that resulted in a different verdict from the original one handed down by the authorities. Notwithstanding their tacit knowledge and the inefficacy of the demolition procedure, the evictees and demolishers alike followed a definite set of rules and procedures. However, the real contestation always centered on the households' interpretation of the substantive meaning of the rules and conventions of the demolition as well as routine encounters and engagement with the ODP. Evictees who displayed unreserved trust and obedience toward the government were in a constant state of distress and regret, while those who were resilient enough to be able to distinguish between nominally imposed rules and genuinely endorsed norms remained more hopeful of obtaining a better result in this game of perpetual contestation and gain-seeking. This is consistent with the three key components, "understandings, rules, and life conditions" of the nexus identified by philosopher Theodore Schatzki as linking doings and sayings in order to constitute a practice (1997, 304). The ODP themselves were mere humble salary earners and privately told me that, if they were the evictees, they too would have demanded equal compensation, for who would not? When the ODP emphatically proclaimed to evictees that the compensation rules and schema were fixed and fair to all, they themselves were well aware of the possibility of flexibility, but did not know the exact degree of this, as it lay under the domain of Dafa, the demolition convener. Interestingly, the head of Dafa repeatedly denied the existence and exercise of such discretionary power; rather, time and again, he placed heavy pressure on the frontline ODP to exert a mighty bearing on evictees.

To complicate the situation further, within the demolition team, some members played the twin role of evictor and evictee, thus displaying an oscillating rhetoric between persuading evictees and defending their own interests. This was ironic, as the agency results depended on a distrust engendered by a presupposed body of knowledge of past and present unfairness. The rich data gathered here provide an empirical vindication of both rule-guided and causally induced practices, conditioned by power and intentionality, respectively. Not only was a local relation of power differentials observable, but also articulated was a strong intentionality with conscious plots and plans, cognitively and emotionally pointed toward a clear purpose. Still, individual agency was formidably conditioned by the objective political reality and contrasting moral considerations. What appeared to be a family deliberation was not exactly the family's unconstrained choice.

DESIRES ON THE MARGIN OF POWER

In the demolition field, the representation of power was not unambiguously defined or located. As one householder stated sarcastically, "Everyone says they're representing the state or explaining policies on behalf of the government, but I've never actually come across a single official." Indeed, the demolition convener, ODP, Director Wu, and Secretary Yang were all performing merely on the margin of a power relation; how the interplay of this presupposed power relation was conceived and enacted was blurred, subject to each individual agent's interpretation and contestation. One thing is certain though: none of the stakeholders had either the intention or the capacity to challenge the state's inherent power structure. No matter how contentious the arguments and counter-arguments might be, and how fierce the encounters between the ODP and the evictees, both sides must say a few kind words to avoid hostility and declare that they all genuinely support the government's endeavors toward achieving social harmony and fairness. For example, one evictee, following a very heated argument at a public hearing, said, in a softer tone outside the room, "I hope that you'll explain our situation to your superiors; just give us some extras and we'll be fine," while his sister pleaded with an ODP for help. Here, the contestation fundamentally centered on the desires and nourishment of individuals. The overarching power relation was not subject to challenge but employed dialectically. The evictees repeatedly made use of the local leadership's statements to counter the policy deliberation of the demolition convener who possessed the residue of power. The agents engaged embedded power mechanics, but evoking blatant dissemination of state power was the last thing they wanted. Rather, the evictees' agency was a form of intention and desire, pursuing specific goals and enacting practices of presumed calculated risk.

Outside the demolition office hung another banner that read, "Trust the government; don't believe in rumors; don't fabricate rumors; don't spread rumors." Ironically, in the field of house demolition, an agency was constructed through a history of unfairness and a practice of distrust. Evictees who had struck a deal to move were not given a copy of the supplementary agreement, which detailed their additional compensation, and were warned not to reveal the details to their neighbors. They might privately tell a number of close relatives, who then leaked the information to third parties. Gradually, all this became the basis for rumor and hearsay, and facts were not casually available but reconstructed and believed. In playing out their tactic of counter-dispossession, not all of the evictees are on a level playing field.

They are playing a dangerous game, one in which not everyone possesses the same vital knowledge or is aware of the critical risks ahead. Most of the evictees believe in the existence of flexibility and discretion, but are sadly self-destructive to forming a scheme of transparency and fairness, an unintended consequence of their reinforcement of the demolition convener's tactical power of discretion in picking targets for forced eviction.

The housing privatization process is engendered by the semi-privatized and contracted acts of house demolition and land resumption executed by local authority agents on behalf of commercial interests. Yet, it also functions to allow state agencies to wriggle out of accepting direct accountability and full responsibility. Hence, everybody plays by a rule and a procedure as specifically and clearly spelt out and imposed by the central and local governments, but few agents are naïve enough genuinely to trust in the existence of procedural justice, a situation which I call *following rules and procedure without followers*. Nobody feels confident that adherence to an utterly consistent scheme will be the outcome. In the eventual results of each agent's strategizing, there can be chaos and unintended consequences, despite the agents' inherent intentionality. As Erik Harms (2013) points out, in his study of the temporality of eviction in Ho Chi Minh City, those who are indifferent to time could transform waiting into an expression of one's own agency and the power of their indifference proves a strategy that is hard to resist. In the end, the constrained agency of the evictees, particularly well-versed and well-connected ones, unwittingly reproduces a structure of unfairness and unfaithfulness, in nominally abiding by but vigorously bending the official rules, on the back of their tacit understanding of the actual norm of practicing demolition and counter-demolition.

By behaving this way, the evictees are arguably reproducing a certain structure of rules and assumptions, and their own subjectivity and *habitus*, as conceptualized by Bourdieu (1977) as a socially constituted system of motivating structures and the universalizing mediation that causes agents' individual and collective practices. This habitus ensures the active presence of past experiences, which "tend to guarantee the 'correctness' of practices and their constancy over time, more reliably than all formal rules and explicit norms" (Bourdieu 1990, 54). Thus actions selected by agents always seem sensible and rational to the agents themselves and to other evictees with a habitus produced in the same situation and under similar conditions—a nominal "homogeneity of habitus" (Bourdieu 1977, 80). For the present case, various agents' habitus are structured and produced by the historic practice of house demolition. In this regard, evictees have produced a habitus through their individual but common, routine encounter with demolition practices and tacit knowledge of the unspoken norms and malpractices in the very recent history of housing demolition. Although the historic practices of demolition are relatively recent, mainly emerging less than two decades ago, the coherence of evictees' habitus is evident and comprehensible, albeit still in a process of formation. Nonetheless, the predictability of the evictees' actions and the habitus' degree of homogeneity is a subject for further study.

Moreover, the habitus being analyzed here is simultaneously more fluid and mutable, constitutive ironically of the local leadership's ideal goal of "common prosperity" and many city dwellers' tacit understanding that seeking maximum benefits from demolition projects represents the opportunity of a lifetime to become rich and so secure a flourishing life. The contrast between the ordinary evictees and those who ended up performing the dual role of demolition personnel and evictee is also striking. Noticeably, the variations in the habitus of individual stakeholders are framed by various agents' own ethical consideration (patriotism and Party loyalty) and moral responsibility (to family), even among Party veterans; for instance, the "naïve," trusting Mr. Feng agreeing to initial terms while the "cunning," distrusting Secretary Hai holding out for a tacit deal constitute a fundamental contrast. James Laidlaw (2013) rightly points out that ethical consideration is indeed a crucial aspect of the relational processes and what lies between social structure and the agents' action is more than a merely causal account. Laidlaw explains that ethical terms, such as blame and responsibility, are complex, and not just subjective or psychological, and we are *not* simply more of an "agent" the less effectively we are incorporated into supposedly larger structures; and he thus critiques that the supposed duality between structure and the "acting subject" in practice theory is not a duality at all. I would not go as far as dismissing the validity of duality as practice theory's fundamental building block, but concur that a simplistic structure-agency analysis may prove inadequate. As such, there is no such thing as a truly singular homogeneity or mechanical functioning of habitus, with ethical considerations adding due complications to the chain of causality, which is suggestive of the limitation of the analytical purchase of habitus. Nonetheless, habitus remains a very useful analytical category and the practice theory perspective sharpens my reading of how the evictees are laying bare the faint possibility of transforming the overarching structure, with either the political insiders' opportunistic insights or the reckless evictees' misconceived belief in a different political reality. However, whether their practices are for good or ill, no one can predict.

THE ECONOMICS OF "RIGHTS INTERPRETATION"

During a routine household visit, I found myself sitting with the three daughters of the female householder and two female ODP, listening to their repetitive exchange for thirty minutes. Then, all of a sudden, the householder, probably in her seventies, put aside her knitting and muttered loudly, "My granddaughter's grown up. She'll get married soon and will need her own apartment; we demand three units in compensation, one for her!" For me, this was a most revealing ethnographic instance that illuminated her underlying motivation; never mind all that strategizing between her daughters and the ODP. It is a kind of genuine needs as conceived by a grandmother's love for her offspring: a simple motive, but legitimate enough in her own reckoning.

Of course, one could easily challenge the justification for endowing all of her offspring with an apartment. This claim of needs is logically untenable in this case, because the housing needs of urban citizens have been relegated to the market economy realm and are no longer the local government's principal concern. In the politics and economics of house demolition bargaining, only property rights' claims are deemed legitimate, which is also a reflection of the newly dominant social ethos. Hence, from the perspective of ODP, this grandmother's claim is but a common example of the misconceived desires expressed in a discourse of needs and justifications. Mr. Gao, the head of Dafa, used to emphasize to me, "Mr. Ho, you know, people's desires are boundless; in this society, everyone is striving to secure their own interests." Thus, what appears to an individual as a genuine, legitimate need translates into a mere desire, untamed by a particularized reasonableness. The deep irony is that most ODP privately would not dismiss such a desire as illegitimate. The cases of "insider evictees," elucidated above, demonstrate all too well that such boundless desire is indeed a routinely observable, commonality in the everyday pursuit of well-being. Practice theory per se vividly informs such everyday pursuits, without necessitating a representational category such as need or desire, but we remain interested in a general explanation of actions, the working of the will, a sense of causality; that is, which kind of mental states or relationships (familial or power) compel and steer the agents into certain risk-taking and strategizing practices? Through the prism of practice theory, we see how evictees and evictors alike maneuver in a nominally rule-abiding but actually norm-directed site of contestation. But why have some gone so far in seeking what they want against all odds, while others are trapped in despair and regret? What causes people's differing perceptions of reality and choices of action?

In demolition bargaining, the real rules and risks are neither totally transparent nor easily intelligible; thus strategy and decisions are not straightforward, utility-maximizing scenarios. The state of desire seems to be a convincing representation for explaining the differences. In the regime of pervasive counter-dispossession, the power of need has been largely swept away; now, it is desire that effectively enables an agent's strong will for resistance. Commonly, many states of need find expression in desires and striving, although the notion of need is deeply embedded. Moreover, contesting agents are constantly evaluating their own and their counterpart's actions by way of ambivalent categorization as justification (need) or explanation (desire), both to establish a rational sense of reality and to rationalize themselves. Hence, analytically, needs and desires are probably more usefully conceived as an axis along which agents oscillate and shift, rather than a rigid either/or polarity. I consider that a juxtaposition of the needs-desires matrix alongside practice theory enriches our understanding, rather than diminishing the vigor of the practice perspective.

At the demolition site, all evictees are legal dwellers with their basic needs satisfied at present. It is not merely a case of outright dispossession that inflicts serious harm; rather, the issue concerns also whether their present and future well-being will be compromised. It is true that evictees shall be compensated with a better quality, possibly even larger apartment, as a norm of demolition compensation, but to what extent such utility is diminished by a change in location is subject to each agent's own subjective evaluation. More importantly, the idea of flourishing is a dynamic concept, which encompasses future possibility and potentiality such that harm should be defined as how much the present constrains the future. Against the backdrop of soaring property prices and the discontinued welfare housing, evictees may consider holding out on their possession of a well-located property as the best one for their family's well-being. Forced relocations and compulsory compensation are infringements of private property rights, depriving evictees of voluntary choice and constituting genuine damage to their needs and interests. However, the evictees' own discourses of demanding equal treatment somehow obscure such logic of needs.

In her critique of the late capitalist welfare state of the late 1980s, social theorist Nancy Fraser (1989) noted that needs talk had been re-institutionalized as a major vocabulary of political discourse, in juxtaposition with the discourses about rights and interests. For Fraser, however, the focus of inquiry is not about needs per se but rather discourses about needs, which is a "politics of need interpretation" pertaining to the shifts in the boundaries of the political, economic and domestic, to bring into view the contextual and contested character of needs claims (1989, 163). Fraser's ideas are all the more relevant to this study, because they are the exact opposite of China's emergent neo-socialist "non-welfare" state, in which needs are a discourse that has been "harmonized" (concealed), and talk about needs has often been relegated to the margins of political life. Still, Fraser's politics of need interpretation finds a certain resonance on the demolition site, where conflicts over the interpretation of the needs/desires demarcation and the interpretation of rights come to the forefront of the discussion. There remain elements of need in the compensation scheme, in the forms of minimum floor area per household, and allowances for disability, illness, and so forth; but need interpretation is reduced to a residual concern. At present, as needs talk is buried in desires talk, the rights discourse has become the real site of struggle. Using

Fraser's terminology, housing needs are being de-politicized and re-privatized as impersonal market imperatives and family ownership prerogatives; hence only a game of economics is visible and legitimate. In a nutshell, rights talk had been institutionalized as a major vocabulary of economic discourse, in juxtaposition, and sometimes conflated or even confused, with discourses about (debased) needs, (rhetorical) desires, and (objectified) interests. However, the interpretation of what is a right and which rights are legitimate, as ethnographically expressed, is both ambiguously and ambivalently contested by evictees and evictors at the micro level, thus illustrating the predicament of an "economics of rights interpretation."

NOTES

1. Economist Abhinay Muthoo (1999) considers *bargaining* as any process through which players try to reach an agreement, whereas a *bargaining situation* is a situation in which two players share a common interest to co-operate but experience conflicting interests over exactly how to do so. In the everyday use, negotiation is a broader idea encompassing communication between two parties, entailing open-ended questions about what both sides want and why; thus bargaining could be considered a subset of negotiation, concerned mainly with price and economic benefits. My use of bargaining over negotiating presumes that demolition outcomes need not result from an explicit negotiation process. Indeed, they could result from implicit differences in bargaining power due to asymmetric power relations and unequal access to vital information (cf. Agarwal 1997); for instance, political scientist Erin Jenne (2006) uses "ethnic bargaining" to refer to the process by which minorities negotiate with the majority over the group's claimant status. Bargaining also implies a relational dimension and a dynamics of everyday interaction besides formal exchanges, what management consultants Deborah Kolb and Judith Williams call "shadow negotiation" (2003, 13). Thus anthropologist Lawrence Rosen uses "bargaining reality" to illustrate that "reality is achieved through a process of negotiating the meaning of the terms and relationships of which it is composed" (1984, 4). This relational perspective is particularly relevant to my case of urban demolition practice, which involves evictees as bargaining actors in a close neighborhood setting.

2. Owing to the inherent sensitivity of demolition work, all names of places, people, and companies are kept anonymous, with pseudonyms used where necessary.

3. GFA includes public areas such as corridors, staircases, and the courtyard. The net usable area is roughly 80 percent plus the GFA calculation in the present case.

4. In comparison, rural land belongs to the "collective" and demolition compensation in rural areas is based very differently on a combined per capita/per household basis. For example, Helen, who lived in the Chongqing downtown after her marriage, had retained her household registration in her rural hometown, where her parents still resided. As the Chongqing metropolitan area had expanded rapidly into the outskirts, Helen's family had been offered a replacement apartment measuring $20m^2$ per person, plus a base compensation of $20m^2$ of floor area per household. Helen's grandmother also lived with Helen's parents and thus should be counted a separate household and entitled to compensation in her own right. However, this dual-household status was declined, so Helen's family had refused to move out. Helen said collective land ownership is complicated and confusing; it was always the local cadres who benefited the most from rural land compensation. Economist Peter Ho (2001) reckons that a "legal twilight" still surrounds the transfer of rural land rights, in comparison to the gradual policy move to "valued use" of urban land, and that such ambiguity can become a potentially explosive source for social conflict.

5. From January 21, 2011 onward, all demolitions must comply with the "Regulation on the Expropriation of and Compensation for Houses on State-owned Land," a new law promul-

gated by the State Council. "The Chongqing Municipal Regulations on the Administration of Demolition and Removal of Urban Houses" was repealed subsequently.

6. The statutory minimum wage level in Chongqing's urban districts and taxable income in 2011 were RMB870 and RMB3,500 per month. City sanitation workers earned RMB1,100 per month and taxi drivers RMB3,500–4500, Those earning RMB10,000 or above accounted for 20 percent of all income tax payers.

7. The sub-district is the third level of the three-tier urban administration; the community residents' committee in turn is set up by the sub-district. Benjamin Read (2012) considers that residents' committees form a cellular component of immense systems of urban governance and as an example of "administrative grassroots engagement," wherein its leaders serve as the state's designated liaisons in the neighborhood.

Chapter Four

Investing Citizens

Embracing Desires and Risks

> "There is no longer a sense of neighborhood; but people own their *fangzi* with a strong sense of pride and belonging. Is it progress or regress? At the least, people are free to manage their wealth and control their lives." —Auntie Zhou, property investor

Since 2003, retired medical practitioner Auntie Zhou, in her mid-sixties, had pursued an unusual hobby: she joins house purchase tours in both Chongqing and other cities organized by property agents. The first *fangzi* (housing property) that she owned was a welfare housing apartment purchased in the 1990s for RMB30,000 that had appreciated to RMB200,000 a decade later. Zhou considered real estate tangible and durable, one imbued by its owners with affection and expectations. As a child, she lived in her father's work unit compound. Her neighbors interacted extensively, but Zhou would not consider such relations to be of an intimate nature. Rather, people treated each other as a "source of entertainment" by gossiping behind people's backs and reporting others' suspicious behaviors to the authorities.[1] Now, Zhou lived in a residential compound and rarely mingled with her neighbors. Through transacting property, she felt satisfaction at owning something, a new social identity based on property and possessing. This echoes Lisa Rofel's depiction of new Chinese citizens as developing a "self-conscious enthusiasm for coherence in their search for a new cosmopolitan humanity" (2007, 197). Individual urbanites play the dual role of consumers and investors in the housing market, albeit sometimes proactively, sometimes unknowingly, wherein, as geographer You-tien Hsing reckons, "the dialectical nature of housing embodies elements of risk-taking speculation and long-term financial and personal security" (2010, 45).

Zhou had been involved in more than half a dozen transactions and still owned four apartments when I first interviewed her in mid-2011, but had abandoned her "hobby," after the government introduced severe measures to cool down property prices. Zhou's narrative is hardly atypical. Instead, at the turn of the new millennium, many urbanites across the strata have become investors-cum-speculators in their leisure time. Homeownership in China is probably among the highest in the world. The Chongqing Municipal Government in 2011 estimated that up to 70 percent of households in the city proper owned their premises, with 20 percent owning two or more units of property.[2] Real estate scholars (Wang et al. 2012) point out that the level of household housing assets accumulated over the generations in Western market economies were reached in just a few years by some Chinese families. Indeed, during my field work, I frequently encountered Chongqingers including taxi drivers who told me that they owned two or three apartment units, most of whom had made their first purchase via the 1990s welfare housing program. Likewise, Party cadres, civil servants, and state enterprise employees in the cities were given the option to purchase their living quarters at a drastic discount; then, after several rounds of rampant property price spirals, their dwellings could have appreciated five-fold or more, and a new group of wealthy people emerged. For the younger generation of property owners, who no longer enjoyed such benefit, they probably inherited their property or received financial backing from their parents or even grandparents, who had enjoyed the privileges of welfare housing allocation and thus could use their life savings to support their offspring.[3]

On the back of the seemingly perpetual property price appreciation, many owners traded in their apartments for bigger, better quality premises or for more units as investment, via mortgages. During the real estate bull market of 2009 to 2010, investors queued for a couple of days outside the developers' sales offices. All too often, buyers were allowed only a few minutes to make decisions concerning the few available units. Quarrels and even fights were common. Some property salesmen recalled that, on many occasions, potential buyers at the tail end of the queue, thwarted in their quest to buy, refused to leave, with some even falling to the ground, sobbing uncontrollably. Such was the investment mania of ordinary people who seemingly knew only of one side to the peculiar asymmetry of market risk, that is, an upside without a downside. This recent period reflects a particular historical moment: property possession has gained hitherto unseen prominence and primacy in China as both a social phenomenon and a personal obsession, with people witnessing the re-emergence and dominance of private property ownership over the course of only two decades, after urban welfare housing began to be phased out in 1988.

CITIZENSHIP OF RIGHTS, DESIRES, AND RISKS

In chapters 2 and 3, I explore how demolition bargainers in urban neighborhoods are caught up in housing demolition, as a result of the conjoint government maneuver of massive urban redevelopment and soaring prices of residential properties propelled by momentous property purchases across China. In this chapter, I deliberate on the broader meaning of investment for Chongqingers from three dimensions: first, the pursuit of the rights to possession as a *desire* for material gain and personal security; second, the duality of real estate possession as *investment* and consumption; and, third, a new paradigm of *risk* emerging from the new economic ethos of investment and property rights—informed, constructed, and constrained by an all-embracing statist participation in a market economy.

My ethnographic cases in conjunction with a housing market analysis clearly point to the emergence of a new form of urban citizenship from the practice of investment in housing properties and the endorsement of private property rights as an imperative principle for achieving well-being. I have coined the term "investing citizens" to refer to a propertied class, animated by a common drive and embrace of desires and risks but devoid of the definitive, defining characteristics of a coherent class identity and consciousness. Crudely conceived as status, investing citizens are actually neither defined nor conferred by the state but made and self-declared by the "citizens" through the mere act of investing. Unlike the commonly understood Chinese urban citizens, as defined by the household registration system, investing citizens are less a rigid category of privileges than a fluid but subdued status or identity of becoming. Investing citizens are the product of their subjectivity and the outcome of complex historical configurations, as the definition of people's well-being has changed unequivocally from sacrifice to choice (Pieke 1996, 2009; Jankowiak 2009). Thus, to be more precise, investing citizens are probably better understood less as a clearly delineated category of status or identity and more as a *process* and *practice* of subject formation. This analysis echoes sociologist Engin Isin's (2008) suggestion that citizenship is increasingly mobile and defined by academics as practices of becoming claim-making subjects.[4] However, investing citizens must also be understood in the neo-socialist context of the inescapable, formidable role of the party-state in the realm of the market economy, and be differentiated from an "outright" possessive individual. This chapter's ethnographic data suggest a new moral economy animated by value(s) in transformation, intertwining the state, the family, and the market—a tripartite relationship that is examined in chapter 6 in conjunction with the subject of contesting housing demolitions.

China's real estate development and property prices are critically inseparable from government policy and statist involvement in both the supply and demand sides. The market is also heavily affected by the global liquidity flows in relation to the pervasive, enduring influence of the 2008 global financial crisis. The distant yet immediate force of financial globalization is a crucial factor of which few Chinese property investors apparently are fully aware. Strikingly, those aged fifty to seventy years old constitute an important group of property owners/buyers; many of them do not purchase property principally for their own consumption but as gifts for their children when they graduate from college or get married. Property transactions have become a pervasive social concern and activity. Even for the masses who cannot easily afford to buy property, it is a common topic of everyday social exchange, as they lament how prices have been driven up by speculation beyond what they can afford. Customarily, they blame it on the cohort of property speculators and property developers, as well as the government's pro-business attitude of governance. Moreover, property transactions are not pure products of personal and commercial decisions and activities. On the one hand, they are entwined with the re-emerging centrality of family values, wherein members of families deliberate a distinct logic of why, when, and how to buy. On the other hand, the market is wedded to a statist political agenda and the manifestation of an intricate web of relationships among individuals, families, and the party-state. Simply put, every transactional decision is intertwined with reflexivity over how the well-being of families is affected and structured by a historically engendered relation between the family, the market, and the state power.

PROPERTY MARKET WITH CHONGQING CHARACTERISTICS

If active government participation is a defining characteristic of the Chinese real estate industry in general, then the differentiation of Chongqing from other places is arguably one of degree only. I hesitate to use the word "intervention" to describe the role of the state; because its use implies that the market "ought" to be independent. The government has never proclaimed its substantive withdrawal from the market, meaning that statist control is simply and has always been this way, but how Chongqing sets out to control the market is exceedingly proactive and meticulous, and is said to have left a lasting mark on policy initiatives and the property pricing structure.

As a jokey but vivid example, real estate professionals revealed that Secretary Bo Xilai so disliked the proliferation of Spanish-style villas that he approved only traditional, gray houses for new villa projects. The notion of "Bo's gray" (*bohui*, means a thin layer of ash) has become symbolic of the heavy-handed will of officials in dictating every detail of an otherwise mundane business decision. Another example of micromanagement concerns the question of what unit of measure is used to calculate property price. Until very recently, Chongqing was the only city in which new property sales were priced in terms of their usable floor area (UFA). The difference between unit prices per UFA versus gross floor area (GFA) can be as high as 20 to 30 percent. Two possible reasons for this exist. First, according to one informant, back in 2003, the municipal leadership considered Chongqing's property prices too embarrassingly low compared with those in other second-tier cities. The use of unit price per UFA creates a massaged number for the sake of image building. Second, the local officials explained that disputes were common over the measurement of GFA, as buyers from rural areas were unfamiliar with such a measurement concept which includes public spaces such as corridors, lobbies, and courtyards. However, GFA pricing remained the norm for all secondary transactions and the basis for calculating house demolition and real estate taxes. Chongqing's peculiar and somewhat incoherent arrangement has become a source of constant confusion.

According to several real estate professionals, prior to the mid-2000s, Chongqing had no clear, coherent strategy regarding real estate development. In consideration of the abundant land supply due to its vast suburban terrain and numerous run-down urban areas, the municipal government could assemble any size of land that developers demanded, resulting in a squeeze on development margins. Hence, most of the leading national real estate companies were reluctant to enter the Chongqing market, given the unpromising profitability and shadow of bureaucratic legacy existing in that locale. As the national real estate market entered its bull run in 2006, Chongqing finally started to attract major domestic and international players. With the 2007 arrival of Bo Xilai, Chongqing has embarked on many grand development plans that called for aggressive old town redevelopment and urban expansion but, unlike the first-tier cities or popular holiday destinations, Chongqing's housing demand derives primarily from local users and the intensity of speculation is relatively modest. In addition, the municipality's policy of transferring millions of rural households to the urban area has a bearing on end-user demand. This combination of a supply-demand matrix is frequently invoked by property professionals and investors as the principal reason for the subdued property prices and their confidence that low-end housing demand will remain robust in the long run.

In China, all urban land use rights transactions are controlled by the local government, who can be called the land master because private or state enterprises cannot accumulate directly from or dispose of land reserves to third parties.[5] The central government also stipulated that, after August 2004, all land transactions had to be conducted through one of the three channels: tender, auction or invitation for bidding.[6] This policy is credited with enhancing orderly land sales and developmental compliance, thereby eradicating bribery and bringing in more fiscal revenue, theoretically but, as You-tien Hsing (2010) points out, many localities continue to allow exceptions to the new rules permitting privately negotiated land-use rights transfers. Based on two case studies of corruption in Chongqing, economist Zhou Tao (2010) discovered that planning officials continued to command substantial discretionary power in their dealings with developers regarding concession fees and the total amount of developable floor area. Real estate professionals in Chongqing, from the local and foreign corporations alike, were also fond of telling me and ridiculing how land sales remain subject to backdoor lobbying between developers and local officials.

First, if an "outsider" offers the highest bid price to win at a public land auction without prior government endorsement, for example, officials could conduct prolonged public works projects adjacent to the building site or delay the completion of crucial road access and public utilities in order to disrupt the progress of the property construction. Second, conversely, a preferred developer could boost the land purchase price to support the government, only to be compensated later by means of postponed payments, or preferential tax and financial arrangements, a situation not uncommon even for mega-sized projects involving foreign conglomerates. Third, for the more complicated tender or invitation for bidding, officials could list several bespoke conditions fitting only a certain predetermined partner. One financial journalist reckons that these practices/malpractices are not specific to Chongqing but, as its municipal leadership is very strong, personal interference is particularly forceful. Nonetheless, Chongqing's approach does subscribe to the general statist model of proactive government policies and dominant state enterprise participation, albeit of broader scope and larger magnitude.[7] This hands-on approach is in stark contrast to the rural land administration, on which economist Peter Ho speaks of "deliberate institutional ambiguity" as upheld by the state to create leeway for reacting to societal developments without a clearly delineated structure of land ownership (2001, 400).

For well-connected companies, their property business in China requires relatively low capital input, because bank financing and presales provide the bulk of the cash flow for meeting the land and construction costs. Government relations are key to securing financing, because, in many localities, the local authorities have a prevalent influence over the local financial institutions' business decisions and even credit assessments. Developers also assist the local government in unusual circumstances. For example, they postpone the reporting of the sales of high-end projects until after the end of the fiscal year in order to prove that prices are "under control," thereby allowing the local government to cast its fiscal report in the most positive light possible. This situation is consistent with Li Zhang's (2010) observation that precarious conditions have been created, allowing for the interdependency and mutual protection of political and corporate interests in the property sector. Real estate scholars Ren Hong and Wang Lin (2008) hence attribute property bubbles partially to government interventions and collusion between developers and officials. Actually, such patron-client relationships had begun to emerge when the Chongqing real estate market was in its embryonic stage a decade ago. One local businessman stated that the municipal government first lent money via its investment arm to a few well-connected companies to enable them to purchase land. If they made a profit, the government benefitted financially and politically, resulting in a burgeoning property industry dominated by a few inner-circle players. If the companies went bust, the land was returned to the government, with the loans and land sales revenue balanced out. As such, the government is said to have created and enormously benefited from the real estate industry. Many of the aforementioned accounts represent conjectural statements that could hardly be verified, albeit all are related by experienced industry insiders. Accounts such as these circulate widely and are accepted as anecdotal evidence by ordinary investors in their conception of the state-market relationship. Sometimes, they are also taken as the basis for formulating investment strategies amid routine policy alternations.

Enormous financial incentives are behind the local governments' direct involvement in real estate management, as they receive the lion's share of development profit via a host of taxes and charges such as the 8.5 percent transaction tax, a 30 to 40 percent value added tax, a 5.5 percent business tax, as well as the corporate profit tax. These are in addition to the direct land sales revenue, which, in the case of Chongqing, amounted to RMB131 billion in 2012, equivalent to 42 percent of its total public financial (recurrent) and government fund (non-recurrent) revenues. This revenue source is important for the funding of Chongqing's mammoth infrastructural program upon its elevation as a municipality. In early 2011, Chongqing took the initiative by imposing a real estate tax, notwithstanding its substantially overall lower property price level. The scheme is targeted mainly at standalone villas and other residential apartments that sell at more than twice the city's average sales price, with a progressive rate of 0.5 to 1.2 percent. As a result, the sale of properties costing RMB12,000 or more (twice the average) slowed, while low-end housing prices continued to rise, with the unintended consequence of penalizing first-time buyers who were buying low-end properties. In contrast, Shanghai has imposed a real estate tax across the board on all families' second-home purchases. One foreign property professional lamented that, "This is absurd; ordinary people's affordability actually worsens. If well-off people want expensive properties, so be it; why should the government bother to intervene in the high-end market?!"

The government's reluctance to impose a heavy tax on mass residential properties might also be related to its mass public rental housing program, which, heavily debt-financed, will provide 40 million m^2 to accommodate two million residents by 2020 for new graduates, rural migrant workers, and households living in overcrowded conditions. This scheme contains an add-on purchase option for tenants to acquire their apartment after five years at

70 percent of the then-market price; but with the restriction that householders must sell them back to the government at the original price. Such sales also represent a crucial funding stream for the municipal government to continue with the program, which clause should be attractive for prospective applicants if market prices continue to edge upward. If the market environment deteriorates, tenants are likely to opt to buy in the private market in pursuit of capital appreciation. In short, the long-term success of the rental housing scheme is largely predicated on a lively commodity housing market, with the scheme allied with an explicit developmental mentality that is contingent upon the pervasive adoption of private property rights practice.

As far as the developers are concerned, the total return could be significant, as the actual equity input constitutes only a fraction of the total development cost, particularly for land reserves that were secured a few years ago. Since government relations and support are critical, developers are willing to consent to the local officials' often high-handed approach along with the attendant backdoor maneuverings. Developers play the role of strategic coordinators, subcontracting out almost all of the design and construction activities, while property development at large plays a contentious yet strategic role in creating monetary wealth as well as engendering rapid economic development by pooling society's collective financial resources. Arguably, a closed circuit of government, finance, and production is forged, a model that serves well to deliver the local government's economic and social goals but, as one informant puts it, "Everybody follows the government's 'noncompliance of rules' in order to maximize their benefits," so this is a kind of optimization, a paradoxical exploitation of the local state's concurrent rule-setting and ignoring of rules.

I OWN, THEREFORE I AM

This is not an alternative philosophical statement of existence but rather a pragmatic evaluation of everyday life in contemporary urban China. It is based on the reflection that someone capable of owning property assets necessarily "exists" with a citizenship identity because, with property ownership, one qualifies for urban household status in most cities and so becomes a nominal urban citizen. This evaluation also indicates that, as most social welfare provision and job security have been abolished, the significance of an urban household status has become largely obsolete. Rather, the foundation of urban citizenship occurs via a sense of financial and ontological security derived from the private ownership of tangible assets for self-occupation, for rental, capital appreciation or future bequests to one's offspring in the face of the recurring spiral of property prices. Hence, citizenship is transforming from a specifying category defined by power into a kind of condi-

Figure 4.1. Certificates of Housing Property Rights and Land Use Rights. This photo was taken by the author.

tioning and becoming animated by reflexivity. This is a far cry from the membership-based, tiered urban citizenship of entitlement and segregation in Beijing, as described by Dorothy Solinger (1999), with the right to receive public goods, but resembling more the younger generation's process-based, "contested cultural citizenship of desiring and longing" (Rofel 2007, 94).

It is in this context that I have coined the term "investing citizens" to refer to those who have lived in the cities for a long time and *owe their property possession to a historical urban citizenship* and those who *owe their citizenship to their historic investment act*. In either case, the meaning of citizenship has become more symbolic than substantive, more a becoming than a category, a subjectivity that reflects a story of the past and a past story of longing for the future. Friederike Fleischer (2005) speaks of a citizenship of consumption in housing, whose people's social and economic position is increasingly intertwined with their power to consume; whereas political scientist Luigi Tomba (2005) states that homeowners have become members of communities of consumers, with a new status formed in local socialization in the neighborhood. In contrast, investing citizens, having "constructed" a status for themselves, are actually less concerned with privileges and spatiality than with longing and temporality, while at the same time failing to share a coherent class identity. My study is more about investing citizens' imaginary future in their capacity as investors than their concrete present as consumers or producers. Today, unless they own even a tiny apartment, it is not considered legitimate for young people to get married, as dictated by what are considered the social norms. Unless one owns more than one property, one's disposable wealth will not grow in tandem with the monetary economy at large and one's socioeconomic status will decline as a result of the inflating asset prices. In short, it is the mere act of investing and owning property that guarantees the existence of the self, a self that many believe could live a life without fear of insecurity and uncertainty, a self that fulfils the utmost responsibility to one's family. In the following section, I will chart the life stories of several Chongqingers who possess *more than one* property asset, so that we can apprehend the context and process in which they have become, first, incidental investors and, ultimately, consciously investing citizens.

From Rural to Urban; From Socialism to Capitalism

Ms. Chen, a thirty-five-year-old mother of a five-year-old boy, when we first met, ran a small clothing store. She had been raised by a single parent in a rural area. Unemployed at twenty, she decided to try her luck in Chongqing, where she had no relatives or friends. She recalls vividly that ferry journey fifteen years ago, the first time she had left her home:

> During that six, seven hour journey, I told myself again and again that I must not look back. I come from an unhappy family and have not received much education, so I thought, I've nothing to lose. If I could make it, I could help to improve the lives of my sisters. I didn't shed a tear, despite the uncertainty ahead of me. I slept well that night.

In the mid-1990s, China embarked on state enterprise reform on a massive scale whereby people were "encouraged" to abandon their iron bowl employment and find a new life, without assistance, schooling, or other training. Thus, Chen jumped onto the bandwagon by accepting voluntary redundancy from her factory job, for which she received a one-off lump sum of RMB150 (US$24). On arriving in Chongqing, Chen first worked in a small clothing store. Her boss let her sleep there on a wooden plank for her bed. "I also bought a hard pillow, which was my first item of private property." A few months later, she transferred to a larger store and rented a room for RMB100 a month. A year later, Chen borrowed some money to purchase her female boss's business. She went to the pier each morning to purchase supplies, and did not pay porters, but carried the heavy loads herself. In 2001, after saving up for the down payment from her earnings, she bought her first house:

> Because of the property, I was granted urban household status and officially became a Chongqinger. I could have used the money to expand my business, but I just wanted to have a place that belonged to me, a place that could shelter me in good times and in bad.

In a nutshell, because of her poverty, Chen was exiled from her home and, because of property, she was able to acquire a new and real home. Since that time, Chen's retail business has grown ever further, and she has purchased two other apartments as an investment, hedges against inflation. Married now, with a son, they now live in a 120 m^2 apartment in the urban district. Chen alone made all the property investment decisions, saying that her husband concentrates on his own work. She devotes considerable time to her son, about whom she worries constantly—his personality, his study, his future. Chen said she will sell one of her apartments to finance his overseas education. She initially insisted that she had never considered giving her property to her son, "I want to let him fight for his own future. But maybe ten years from now, I'll change my mind, who knows? [laughs]" By August 2013, Chen had quit her business to become a full-time housewife, as her store had been failing to thrive. She was reluctant to invest more in property, explaining that, previously, she lacked a sense of security but, in her current financial position, she no longer felt the need to speculate. Chen's story reflects the birth of a new generation of private entrepreneurs at the dawn of an economic reform that swept through the whole nation within two short decades. Despite her humble educational and rural origins, Chen has managed to metamorphose into an urban citizen and petty bourgeoisie. While the income derived from her clothing business endows her with resources and hope, she lives a frugal life, taking few holidays. It is her property assets that give her a genuine feeling of security and satisfaction. During the many conversations we shared, Chen expressed concern about the viability of her business, the course of societal change, her son's well-being, and her marriage, but her sense of satisfaction about her property never wavered, though she was no longer keen to buy more. In her mind, ownership offers security, no matter what personal fortune might lie ahead; however, family is the ultimate source of happiness and contentment.

This rural-urban pathway was echoed by forty-year-old Mr. Deng, a retired naval serviceman, originally from a rural county in Sichuan. His original rural home was demolished by the government to make way for the construction of the Three Gorges Dam. The original compensation was RMB30,000, but his family received only RMB6,500 initially; not until the villagers petitioned repeatedly to the provincial government was their payment raised, little by little, to RMB20,000. "Like squeezing a toothpaste tube; each level of governments claimed some of the money; if no one ever protested, then that would be the end of it," Deng recalled.

In 2003, when he first bought his present 1,100 m^2 apartment, it was surrounded by farmland but, on the day I first visited him in October 2011, the vicinity had already morphed into a huge residential district. Deng had received only a secondary school education. He did not want to be a farmer but instead aspired to acquire urban household status, which at that time (the 1980s) meant that one was still entitled to employment, retirement, and other privileges. In 1989, he joined the navy, thinking that becoming a member of the People's Liberation Army was the only option for achieving this. In 2005, on retiring from his naval post, he was assigned to work in a prison in a mountain area, but soon resigned and went to work on the night shift in a factory. While others were sleeping, Deng continued to work hard. His superior was impressed, but his colleagues were unhappy about him setting such a high benchmark. Deng decided that the state enterprises were too rigid, and soon joined his present company to run its office in Chongqing. After getting married in 2001, Deng purchased his present apartment for RMB1,500 per m^2. From 2002 to 2011, his house's market price soared by 350 percent, to over RMB7,000 per m^2. However, unlike some property speculators, he did not sell or mortgage it to fund further purchases, as he had neither the urge nor desire to do so. Only in 2009 did he put down 20 percent to buy another apartment for RMB8,000 per m^2, having watched the real estate market's frenetic activity. Deng and his wife together earn about RMB7,000 a month, a level that he reckons places them in the lower-middle strata. He has a company car, and spends only a few hundred RENMINBI on himself each month, as he does not smoke, drinks little, and does not take holidays. However, he spared RMB100 to buy me lunch after our first interview. Deng stated that he may keep his new property until his teenage son grows up, adding that, "I didn't have much education, so I want my son to have a better opportunity by selling the apartment to fund his studies. I just hope to lay down a foundation for my son's future." Deng agreed that the property price rally has created considerable wealth for many households but, at the same time, property speculation is most unfair for young people and rural migrants, who cannot afford anything. "It's certainly an achievement, but not solid. I worry that it'll become like the United States."

Like Ms. Chen and Mr. Deng, fifty-year-old Mr. Cha came from a rural area, but had become an amateur speculator, because he was able to use the economic and societal changes to his advantage with the maximum level of bank mortgaging. (Both Mr. Deng and Mr. Cha were involved in the homeowners' protest at Hillside Garden; see chapter 5.) Starting with a house that he received as demolition compensation in his home village, he bought another in a nearby township, then upgraded to Chongqing's outskirts, and now lives in the city proper. Altogether, he had been involved in over one dozen transactions, and retains three properties as investments. He stated that he was an excellent example of *nongchuanfei*; that is, the change in household status from rural to urban. When asked what he would do with his property, Cha replied, "Maybe pass it on to my son." However, as the housing market quieted down, he also ceased property trading. In August 2013, almost two years after we first met, Cha informed me that he was financing his mortgage payments out of profit from his previous trades. Nonetheless, he was pondering whether to let his son, who was by then in his late twenties, take occupation of one of his property holdings or help him to purchase a bigger apartment in case he got married. Although Cha was no longer preoccupied with making a quick profit, he remained a typical parental investor whose main concern is the well-being of his offspring. "He didn't do very well at school, so I couldn't spend much on his education; buying him a house is the best support I can provide," Cha added.

From Generation to Generation; From Love to Tangible

The rural-urban pathway may not be the most representative orbit for the majority of Chongqing urbanites who have been long-term residents there. However, it serves to exemplify how the dominant economic thought and urban social relations have evolved within such a short time span. It aptly demonstrates that merely working hard is insufficient to prevent oneself from being engulfed by waves of societal change. One must be willing to embrace critical attitudinal change and ferret out what may be but flickering opportunities to share the momentous tide of wealth created during a period of epochal asset price inflation. Those who are too unfortunate or unprepared must endure a lifetime characterized by misery and hardship. Most urban property owners at present owe their first purchases to the welfare-housing sales of the 1990s. Many of the younger generation, who may not earn enough to buy their own property, have the good fortune to receive assistance or inherit property from their parents.

Mr. Bai was in his mid-thirties; after graduating from university, he purchased his first apartment in Shenzhen for RMB4,000 per m^2, with his parents financing the down payment. He sold it for RMB19,000 per m^2 three years later, leaving him with enough cash to repay his parents and purchase two apartments in Chongqing, financed by 50 percent bank mortgages. Bai related that, in 2008, people had expected Chongqing prices to fall; but instead "the central government policy always got discounted at the local levels; local governments and developers are tied by their common interests into sustaining a robust real estate market." Bai had a friend who, at the market bottom of 2008, snapped up ten apartments by mortgaging them to the hilt, and the rest is history. "2009 was a crazy year; anybody could make money just by getting hold of an apartment. Now [2012], most people are hesitant, waiting on the side-lines." Bai's situation was similar to that of thirty-year-old Mr. Liang, who came from an affluent family and ran a small property agency. Liang stated that, in the city proper, many young people such as himself owned at least one or two apartments. He also described the mundane trajectory of urban wealth creation:

> Ho: How can young people like you afford to own two apartments?
>
> Liang: When I graduated, my mother helped me out with the down payment for my first purchase when they were cheap; now, I couldn't afford one. There's this tradition that parents strive to pass on a house to their children—they are tired, but they don't want their children to be tired. Not only that but, when a young man wants to marry, he needs to own a house; otherwise, his future mother-in-law won't consent to it.
>
> Ho: Then, what about your parents? Do they own property?
>
> Liang: My parents have welfare-housing. Chinese people also have a tradition of and obsession with saving money; wealthy people ramp up property prices because of idle liquidity. Now, being rich doesn't mean you have only one property; and the poor—those without any property at all—must tighten their belt to afford even one.

No doubt, many people would consider Bai and Liang lucky, enviable young men who possess the property that everybody desires, some of which was acquired through the material and affective support of their parents. Another young informant stated that parents fear that their children will be unable to afford a home of their own, and that the later they buy one, the more expensive it will be. Thus, for parental investors, the risk of the housing market is asymmetrical: one finds only an upside but no downside risk. My next example, in contrast, is a fifty-five-year-old taxi driver, Ah Fu. When asked why many drivers own two or three apartments, he responded hotly:

> I can't even afford one! You see, I pay RMB200 to the taxi owner each day, plus another RMB150 for the fuel. I bring home only 4,000 in a twenty-day working month. I can't work more days, because I'm not a robot!

Ah Fu originally came from the suburban area. When his parents' home was demolished, they received RMB130,000 in compensation. Using their savings and a bank loan, they bought a small apartment. Both his parents passed away, and Fu inherited their property and effects. His wife's parents similarly received welfare housing, which also was passed to her on their death and is now occupied by their twenty-eight-year-old son. Fu regretted that his son makes only RMB2,000 a month. "How could my son afford his own property; so how can you say all Chongqingers are wealthy?" Both Fu and his son are *propertied men*, though he always insisted, "I can't afford it," and, regardless of whether people pay for their property or inherit it from their family, they share the aspiration that owning their own accommodation provides a shield against uncertainty in a reform era, and that ownership per se has become a defining feature of urban citizenship. A significant difference exists between those who are content with passive ownership and those who conceive of risk as an inherent opportunity for active investment; but, in either case, both are consciously investing citizens, with a desire for ownership, either by default or choice.

PROPERTY INVESTMENT: A NEW PARADIGM OF RISKS

The purchase of residential property contains the two inherent components of consumption and investment. In terms of motivation and utilization, owner occupation is a basic, common act of consumption, but one that does not exclude the element of investment because its asset price can both appreciate and depreciate, regardless of intention and usage. Bear in mind that the land asset per se does not suffer from depreciation, unlike the improvements atop the land itself; and it is typically the land-use right that accounts for much of the surge in property value. Hence, for owner-occupiers, intuitively they are simultaneously "consuming" the premises while investing in the land. Theoretically, owners could sell their home and rent one if they anticipate that prices will decline, but may fear that their prediction will prove incorrect or that the transaction costs (financial and psychological) are prohibitively high. Moreover, stable homeownership entails a sense of belonging and facilitates the formation of a neighborhood. Thus, the fact that most of them do not sell in the face of government intervention to combat prices actually entails an element of risk evaluation and investment decision. When, for example, Chongqingers embark on the purchase of a second property, it is an explicit investment decision to counter the risk or exploit the chance of future price increases. In terms of temporality, investment involves the postponement of consumption for oneself or one's offspring, which is also a mode of a consumption of love in knowing that one's offspring will be secure when they reach adulthood.

It follows that investment and consumption are not two strictly incompatible or ambivalent categories but, rather, dialectic concepts and concrete practices that constitute the duality of property buying, owning, and selling. If the social actors as described in this chapter are portrayed as investors, then those defying demolitions could legitimately be called consumers of housing in the course of protecting their housing and property rights. Together, consuming and investing constitute the demand side of property transactions; the difference is that the act of owning property for consumption embodies long-term financial and personal security, while property investment/speculation entails risk-taking. If the notion of *taste* is a key parameter in the realm of analyzing consumers and conspicuous consumption patterns to understand social meaning and value (Bourdieu 1984; 2005), then *risk* is the cardinal concept for cognizing investment practices, because the element of risk must be implicit in the investors' scenario analysis and option evaluation in the run-up to the decision-making.[8] Both consumption and investment preferences are construed and structured by the complex conception of *value*, which is not a constant but is itself a product of cultural dynamics and social transformation. The concept of risk addresses situations in which people become aware that something of value to them faces a possible threat (Boholm 2003). Assessments regarding the impact of such a threat are also heavily value-laden. In this regard, evictees are also confronting and incorporating formidable risk in their own endeavors, bearing a similar commonality of value reference, as do their property investor counterparts. In chapter 6, I address the profound question of value(s)—family and property, in conjunction with my thesis on the formation of a new property regime. In the following, I focus on risk as an inherent feature of a new social order characterized by the primacy of private property rights and investment.

In quantitative terms, risk is conventionally construed as the probability of occurrence multiplied by the severity or magnitude of the outcome. In the language of finance, risk is the standard deviation (volatility, dispersion) on either side of the historical average returns of a specific investment, that is, a post facto measure. As an analytical category, risk stands for calculated uncertainty, which can be managed, taken or avoided, depending on one's own and others' actions and motives. An anthropological study on risk should ask how people in certain social settings identify, understand, contextualize, and manage uncertainty in terms of having knowledge of the probabilities and consequences of events. Be mindful, however, that risk implies *uncertainty* for, without uncertainty, there is no risk and hence no chance or need for risk avoidance.[9] For instance, if people believe in a non-negotiable fate or a god's will, absolute certainty is implied, and there is no case for risk perception and management. In a similar vein, during the radical socialist transformation from the late 1950s to the 1970s, the Chinese people's routine thoughts and practices were directed and dictated by the Party; there was no other road for the future but grand socialism and absolute faith in Chairman Mao, with no expressed doubts and uncertainty whatsoever. On the contrary, at the beginning of the 1980s reform, having been thrown, virtually overnight, from a communist world into a capitalist one, underpinned by a commoditized economy, the people, long accustomed to the party-state's absolute power, felt unmoored, set adrift in imagining their futures, with their unreserved faith and holistic social relations cast out onto unknown seas. This was a temporary situation of absolute uncertainty, when any effort to mitigate risk was futile. A coping strategy for risk in the economic arena became more necessary since the 1990s, when millions of people were relieved of their job due to the state enterprise reform and when urban households were no longer entitled to free social assistance, but were given the possibility of making a real change to their life in the realm of epochal market and property rights reform. It follows that risk assessment is only meaningful after the reform reveals clearer evidence and patterns of its impact on society. Such is the new regime of risks confronting investing citizens in the 2010s.

In the realm of property rights reform, the pertinent risk is unfamiliar for the majority of Chinese urbanites, who have been accustomed to the allocation of living quarters with neither the right of possession nor the fear of being dispossessed. Even when people were encouraged to purchase the welfare-housing apartment in which they lived, most took this as a mere change of formality but, when they saw the nominal price/value of their quarters rising multifold, they knew that this was important to their whole family's well-being. Property prices soon became an experience-near, formidable category of knowledge and risk in the 2000s and, within even the short span of one decade, time and again, the central government's warnings and measures about preventing property bubbles turned out to be token gestures, or "got discounted at the local level," as many informants lamented. Such everyday experience informs a kind of tacit knowledge and belief that crystallizes into the basis of a perceived risk. In addition, the ubiquitous collective narratives communicated via micro blogs and gossip concerning the corruption of government officials and malpractices of developers fuse together to create the interface that, along with everyday experience, informs everyone's own assessment of risk. In Åsa Boholm's (2003) schema of understanding of the cultural variation with regard to risks, the science-driven scenario is an important mode of risk knowledge but, in our context, I find little evidence that the expert opinion of the officials, property practitioners, and academics matters much in people's vernacular assessment of risk.

Regarding the impact of risk, the magnitude is often non-commensurate for different people, even under similar circumstances. A consensus has formed, nonetheless, that property prices are now adhering to a "secular" uptrend that extends well beyond the normal wage increases of working people. There is an inherent bias and worry about the consequence of failing to buy real property, but such an impact assessment could well be distorted by ordinary people's past experiences and the belief that property prices could, at worst, decline modestly, notwithstanding the stringent government measures. In the face of the rampant price increases, many people grew frantic, adding to their property portfolio or becoming first-time buyers financed by bank mortgages, which has resulted in a new period of risk regarding household affordability. For example, between 2009 and 2010, mortgagers were typically offered a preferential 20 to 30 percent discount on the official base lending rate, as the government was keen to divert private savings into the economy but, after stringent property controls were imposed, the interest rate was rebased at a 10 to 30 percent premium to the base rate, and the weighted average mortgage lending rate in August, 2011, was 7.5 percent, whereas a year earlier it had been a mere 4.7 percent. For ordinary people, interest-rate risk is masked by the way such rates are linked to inflation trends. For example, when the consumer price index (CPI) rises from 4 to 7 percent, consumers are supposed to pay 7 percent more for consumer goods than in the previous year. In the event that the lending rate is also adjusted upward, from 4 to 7 percent, to neutralize the impact of inflation (on floating rate mortgages), borrowers' perceived interest-cost increase could be three percentage points higher, but their monthly repayment actually would increase by as much as 25 percent. Hence, a borrower's intuitive projection of his financial cost could be misunderstood until he receives his new bank statement.[10] For a household with a family income of, say, RMB8,000 and a mortgage of RMB500,000, this is an additional expense amounting to 10 percent of income, probably unbudgeted for when the purchase decision was made. For investors who entered the housing market before 2009, the interest-cost differential could be as little as RMB50 per month. For those who danced to the tune of the property boom, though, the financial risk could be substantial.

During the Asian financial crisis of 1997–1998, mortgaged owners around the region experienced the saga of having "negative equity"—wherein more is owed than the property securing the loan is worth. For instance, property prices in Hong Kong dropped by 60 percent and in Singapore by 40 percent to below the average mortgage amounts. Borrowers who lost their job in the recession were unable to pay the interest; neither could they sell their property to repay the banks as they could not afford to cover the balance. Thus, investors were trapped and the banking sector was confronted with the prospect of loan defaults on a massive scale. This situation is best described by Marilyn Strathern when she says, "Possession gives the possessor market opportunities and opens up a world of choice. The other side (debt) becomes choice which has been preempted" (2004, 96). However, none of my informants mentioned a fear of such a fiasco befalling them, as they trust that the Party could fine-tune the economy to avoid a recession. As such, investors willingly turn into voluntary risk-takers, by buying more or at the least being reluctant to sell. Noticeably, every time the market entered a consolidation phase, with softened sales prices, demand slackened, thus echoing Marshall Sahlins's insight that, "Scarcity is a function of value rather than value of scarcity" (2013, 38). Anyhow, it seems most paradoxical that investing citizens place high trust in the Party's ability to manage the economy but simultaneously distrust its determination or efficacy in damping down property prices. These voluntary risk-takers are striving to hedge the risk arising out of the immense (but not absolute) uncertainty in the post-reform era. The irony is that, the greater the need to counter such risk, the greater the demand for property and reliance on price increases, hence exacerbating the inherent systemic risk.

In the course of creating enormous wealth for millions of households, a real estate bubble and a new investing ethos have been systematically accompanied by the latent risks hidden from many social agents, although the latter unwittingly believe that they are actually tackling the perceived risk of perpetual price spirals by embracing it. Chinese people are genuinely conservative financially, with the bulk of their money kept in cash rather than invested in the stock market. Hence, this new investment ethos contains a highly particularized understanding of risk as *not* risk. Recall a reflection by one of my investor informants that was indeed shared by many: "I have this investment consciousness; I just feel that I should go and make this money. I can't imagine that property speculation could be a losing proposition; impossible." Although this may sound slightly naive to a cool-headed observer, in all fairness, it constitutes an astute judgment and reflexivity about a social reality induced from abundant anecdotal evidence. A new practice of property rights thus emerges as a counter-risk endeavor.

This salient risk evaluation echoes the central premise of sociologist Ulrich Beck's (1992) thesis of a highly individualized "reflexive modernity," in which the main social issue is the distribution of the risks and hazards produced by society between the social classes. It is true that China remains far from leaping past the social positions and conflicts of a wealth-distributing society, hence the party-state agenda of "common prosperity," but the issue of "risk-distributing" has become genuine, as far as ordinary people are concerned, with the ruling Communist Party also on full alert for possible social disorder in the event of a property meltdown. This also resonates with Jane Guyer's (2009) observation that risk now figures pervasively in price composition and capital accumulation, as both an addition and a subtraction. For the younger generation of urbanites who are not endowed with welfare housing or parental inheritance, they may relinquish a significant share of their wages and commit to almost a lifelong liability to buy housing. Elsewhere, in the United States and Europe, this has been a standard way of buying real estate but, in China, this is a new mind-set and foretells an emergent risk culture.

The new Chinese economic agents may assume that they have achieved a kind of bourgeois freedom by virtue of their property possession, wealth, and satisfaction returned from the shrewd employment of capital, but investing per se is essentially classless, for there is no additional criterion, such as family status, education level, political affiliation, ethnicity, and so forth, for qualifying and legitimizing investing citizenship. Capital endowment is the sole prerequisite of investors' endeavors; hence, the idea and appearance that investment, risk, and responsibility are all individualized choices, mimicking a rudimentary form of Beck's *risk society*, although the source of the risk is completely different from that in the field of manufacturing and technology. Hai Ren (2010) also reckons that China has become a risk society, with the state redirecting responsibility and redistributing risks to the middle-class individuals, who are defined as a successful neoliberal subject through consumption practice. In the light of the global financial crisis, neither Ren's notion of consuming class nor my own conception of investing citizens offer the option of *not* taking any risk; but the crucial difference is that investing citizens are classless or cross-class, as they do not share common class attributes and civility, as middle-class individuals do.

Expanding on his original idea, Beck (2002) considers that global financial crises signify different dimensions and dynamics of the *world risk society*, whereby entire regions on the periphery can be plunged into depression via an exogenous shock that is propelled by decisions made in other countries.[11] This precarious situation, as revealed by the global shock waves engineered by the Western programs of quantitative easing, further obscures the Chinese risk-takers' reflection and reflexivity; for they may misread the housing market as merely a domestic contest between the central and local governments, and a venue for their individual investment decision. Economist Michael Hudson (2012) indeed talks of a global "Bubble Economy," based on debt leveraging in search of capital gains; that everywhere in the world new homebuyers are obliged to take on a lifetime of debt to obtain housing. As Barbara Adam and Joost van Loon argue, "Even the most restrained and moderate-objectivist account of risk implications involves a hidden politics, ethics, and morality" (2000, 1). I believe that the use of risk as an analytical parameter could reveal an emerging relational order, through which connections between people, ownerships, and rights-liabilities are constituted. In revealing their desire for property, investors are not merely rational agents, but themselves subjects of economic action who are deeply rooted in their collective past and integrated into a complex modernization project of the party-state and an intricate global financial system. Until they become fully aware of the latent risk and potential social repercussions of their actions, that is, *rights* and *risks* go together, however, Chinese investing citizens will not be fully reflexive, and "modern," yet (the notion of Chinese modernity is explored more fully in chapter 8). With this caveat in mind, I will discuss a case study of property owners' collective rights defense in the next chapter, which illustrates that aspiration to rights claims that are predicated on a desire for investment gains can be ephemeral and fragile.

NOTES

1. Martin Whyte and William Parish (1984) discover that work unit compounds in which workmates are synonymous with neighbors with the minimal separation of work, residence, and other spheres of life can often be stressful. Work unit compounds are also places with considerable political pressure and the threat of political criticism that offset the potential closeness of neighborhood ties, with less mutual involvement and harmony in larger cities because of the greater number of bureaucratic services and control.

2. See *Chongqing Morning Post* (2011: A02). This is higher than, for instance, both the U.K. and United States, where 65 percent of housing is owner-occupied (sources: U.K. Statistics Authority and U.S. Census Bureau). Chongqing's high property ownership also deviates radically from sociologist Louis Wirth's premise that "overwhelmingly the city-dweller is not a home-owner" (1938, 17).

3. At the same time, many drivers who were originally from other localities lamented that they could not afford their own living place. The key factor is the urban household status, which provides holders who have a permanent job with state enterprises or the government with the opportunity of acquiring welfare housing apartments at nominal prices.

4. It has now become customary in the anthropological literature to add an adjective before citizenship such as "cultural citizenship," "consumer citizenship," "intimate citizenship," "cosmopolitan citizenship," "ecological citizenship," "insurgent citizenship," "graduated citizenship," "proxy citizenship," and "biological citizenship," which illustrates that new identities could be investigated as the "formation of new subjects, sites, and scales of claim making" (Isin 2008, 17) and recognized as the "contingencies of political membership" (Lazar 2010, 121).

5. See You-tien Hsing's work (2010), which contains an elucidation of the local state's role and strategy in the politics of land and property. She first uses the term "socialist land masters" to refer to central-level government agencies and state enterprises that have exclusive use and management rights over the land they occupy. Here, by *land master*, I refer generally to the municipal government's jurisdiction over primary land use rights transfer.

6. Tender (*zhaobiao*) requires interested parties to submit a detailed proposal and bidding price to compete. A public auction (*paimai*) offers to sell to the highest bidder openly. An invitation for bidding (*guapai*) refers to the solicitation of prospective buyers who could satisfy prerequisite conditions and bid for the highest price.

7. Ivan Szelényi (2011) indeed questions the sustainability of Chongqing's heavy reliance on surpluses from land and property for financing its public projects. He worries that the possible collapse of its real estate bubble could lead to the dismantling of Chongqing's so-called "Third Hand" or "Third Finance."

8. In Pierre Bourdieu's (1984) reckoning, taste is an acquired disposition to establish and mark differences by a process of distinction, and implies a practical anticipation of what the social meaning and value of the chosen practice or object will probably be; housing as a principal form of property certainly situates the owners within the social space of taste (Bourdieu 2005).

9. In the finance field, the distinction between risk and uncertainty hinges on the probabilities of occurrence. Uncertainty is a necessary but not sufficient condition for risk, and reducing uncertainty does not necessarily reduce risk (see Gough 1988). Frank Knight ([1921] 2009) formalizes a distinction between the two, with risk applying to situations where the parameters of the risk are known to the decision maker and measurement of the odds is possible, while true uncertainty exists when subjects have little information about the form of the uncertainty and is not susceptible to measurement. Michael Chibnik criticizes that the social science literature is dominated by economists' models and psychologists' experiments, which largely ignore "Knightean uncertainty," thus failing to consider the vast majority of decision-making situations (2011, 88). Chibnik argues that anthropologists could make an invaluable contribution to our understanding of the complexities of decision making in particular risky and uncertain situations.

10. This paradox can be illustrated with a simple calculation. Assume an apartment worth RMB700,000, with a 70 percent mortgage for twenty years and lending rates rising from 4 percent to 7 percent, the mortgage payments would be RMB3,212 and RMB4,028, respective-

ly, or a surge of 25 percent. The change in actual repayment is less than the increase of 75 percent in the nominal interest rate, because part of the repayment goes to paying off the principal.

11. Ulrich Beck (2012) differentiates between three different axes of conflict in the world's risk society today: Ecological conflicts, global financial crises, and the threat of global terror networks. The intertwining theme is *global* but only financial crises can be individualized and nationalized.

Chapter Five

Affective Ownership

Situating Rights in Desires

"At first I thought there's nothing I could do if the *kaifashang* (developer) was dishonest. In the end, we had achieved something substantive through our spontaneous efforts." —Mr. Deng, activist homeowner

After purchasing an apartment under construction at Hillside Garden in 2008, Mr. Deng could not resist occasionally visiting the site to monitor progress. He observed that the main entrance to his apartment block appeared less impressive than depicted in the original plans but, after all, felt that he had been very lucky to have snapped up even one unit during that frenetic period of property presale. Buying the property represented an investment of his life savings, but he had only had a few minutes in the sales office to make his decision.[1] One morning, in August 2011, Deng visited Hillside Garden to take occupation of his apartment but instead was urged by other owners to participate in their protest against the developer's cheating. Since then, he had become one of the principal leaders of an eight-day protest. I was present from the beginning of the eruption of discontent until the moment the activist owners settled with the developer, and personally witnessed the spontaneously organized action; therefore I can provide invaluable information into the practices of local investment and protest in this chapter.[2]

Unlike rights defense actions taken by owner-occupiers, the buyers of Hillside Garden are predominantly investors who have no intention of taking up residence in the property in question.[3] The investors' temporary presence at the property development was driven primarily by their desire to realize investment gains. These buyers come from a diverse set of backgrounds—active investors, civil servants, senior staff members of the developer itself, entrepreneurs, and retired schoolteachers. Community solidarity or class identity is thus conspicuously lacking among this set of property owners. Their decision to purchase at Hillside Garden was incidental and transient, both spatially and temporally, with little bearing on their day-to-day life. The subjects from my field site were quite different from those end-user buyers, whose purchase of residential space is said to have "become one of the prime arenas of the dynamic processes of social and spatial reconfiguration in contemporary urban Chinese society" (Fleischer 2010, 146). Hillside Garden's investors are also markedly different from Li Zhang's (2010) description of an urban geography of the middle class that emerges through homeownership status, consumer practices, and property-based activism. My subjects are more appropriately labeled "investing citizens" (see chapter 4). I discovered that, beneath their veneer of public emotions and apparent solidarity, amid the vast majority of the several dozen owners were found individuals behaving more like opportunistic free riders than genuine supporters of the protest leaders' cause. Some owners even suspected betrayal by leaders who made concessions to the developer for a back-hander. Meanwhile, the core members also were far from being either unanimous in their rationales or united in their actions. What appeared to be a mighty display of anger, solidarity, and well-reasoned strategy was actually a hectic, contingently crafted platform, lacking meticulous behind-the-scenes planning.

This chapter explores the homeowners' restricted protest and limited resistance vis-à-vis the developer. One might be surprised by the efficacy of these homeowners' spontaneous actions for, in the end, they did prompt both the local officials to intervene and the developer to grant a concession. I shall also pinpoint the intricate relationship between the developer and the local officials in resolving what should have been a purely commercial dispute. As it turned out, both the homeowners and the developer scrambled to define the situation, respectively, as "rights defense" and "rectification at the owners' request," in order to set the record straight about dictating the "nature" of the situation. In the everyday politics of China, "determining the nature" (*dingxing*) of an event is of major moral significance in defining its political seriousness and assigning political responsibility for it.[4] In the days of radical socialism, an event defined as contradictions "among the people" or "between the people and the enemy" was a matter of life and death. Even today, the nature of a social incident or a criminal case matters substantially in terms of its legal and political ramifications. Yet, *dingxing* is more a matter of politics than legality, and how it is actually carried out remains obscure. For instance, Secretary Bo Xilai had been expelled from the Party and dismissed from his public post for alleged disciplinary violations and criminal offences as a political decision before his case was passed to the court for criminal trial but, typically, once a Party cadre is no longer referred to as a "comrade," the issue involved becomes no longer a matter of contradiction among the people and the cadre's fate is already sealed prior to judicial proceedings. For homeowners, the "nature" of their protests determines whether or not they are troublemakers with ulterior motives and subject to repressive dealing by the authorities. For the developer, it determines whether it is deemed by officials to be fulfilling its social responsibility of supporting government work. As far as local officials are concerned, how the situation is defined has a serious bearing on whether they would be held responsible for failing to meet the cardinal objective of constructing a "socialist harmonious society" as set out by President Hu Jintao as the guiding principle of governance. Such a definition of the situation is always determined politically by the Party; and, once determined, further resistance, protest and struggles would probably prove to be in vain.

THE AFFECT OF PROTEST

Notwithstanding the confrontational situation as witnessed in the field, it is intriguing to discover that the majority of dissenting owners were generally in a relaxed mood. I recall a lady laughing as she was about to march to block the road one particular afternoon. The owner-protesters were concerned about the potential loss of property value due to the controversy, but their sense of agitation was apparent only when they were among other owners and involved in such actions. Many of them came to the property site expecting to take possession of their property, an asset that was expected to appreciate handsomely in value. Few had actually noticed the alteration of their apartment building's main entrance until the leaders of the protest raised the issue. Emotions heated up when the protesters arrived in the reception office, reaching a climax in subsequent meetings with the developer's senior management but, when the parties involved sat down to chat with each other, they were mostly calm and relaxed. Still, one minute, they were gathering comfortably in an air-conditioned lobby, out of the suffocating heat, and the next minute, they were assembled, holding a long protest banner and blocking a main road to exert pressure on their opponent. The property had not yet been inhabited; therefore, there was no intimate connection between the owners and the property. Rather, the owners' emotions appeared to have been manipulated from the "outside," via intense encounters with other unknown owners, and their mood was animated by a commonality of desire and rights pertinent to an incidental site and space to which they held little or no emotional attachment.

Indeed, the specificity of this site and space is of secondary importance, as it merely functions as a metaphor for investment desires and a mediator for materializing financial gains. Given their diverse social backgrounds, the homeowners seemed to relate to each other purely through the property object or specifically through the disputed building entrance. The majority of my interlocutors stated that they had never before participated in such a protest. Their unusual action in organizing and participating were not primarily prompted by their own prior personal experience but instigated by this mood and relational capacity, which was essentially "pre-individual." At the same time, many of the protesters had heard about similar incidents and claimed to know how the government officials backing the developer were compromising property buyers' interests. Thus, this mood is not "pre-social" either, as it is partially constituted and provoked by the owners' presumed knowledge of social inequality and power asymmetry. In this regard, the notion of *affect* is inspirational in cognizing this particular mode of "mood" and I would like to employ affect to shed light on the analysis of protesting owners' actions in this chapter.[5]

Unlike emotions, affect is conceived by anthropologists as not residing within the interiority of a subject, but is synonymous with the forces of encounter and affect's characteristic spontaneity suggests a high degree of non-intentionality (see Clough 2010; Seigworth and Gregg 2010). This approach offers a contrasting perspective on the intentionality of agency as analyzed in my study of demolition households in chapter 3. In the production of subjects through practices, agency's behaviors inadvertently express internalized social norms, leading to the reproduction of a predominant social reality. In contrast, as Kathleen Stewart explains, what the question of affects begs is "where they might go and what potential modes of knowing, relating, and attending to things are already somehow present in them in a state of potentiality and resonance" (2007, 3). Hence, affectual theorizing in the main is more concerned about relational capacities than meaning and representation; and, unlike the theme and approach of chapter 4, narrative, identity, and subjectivity in this chapter become more the backdrop to watching as events unfold, and in wondering how one happening leads to the next.

THE OCTAMERON

My narrative opened one hot, sunny Saturday in the summer of 2011. I had originally arranged with a developer's management to visit the site of a recently completed residential project. My aim was to conduct interviews with owners who were arriving to take possession of their newly built apartments.

Day One: All Is Not Well

This was the first day of registration for owners to take possession of their apartment but, when I arrived, I saw two dozen people engaged in a loud dispute with the developer's staff. In front of the entrance hall of Block C hung a few large, colorful balloons and the sidewalk was covered with a bright red carpet decorated with flower baskets on both sides. A huge banner on the wall read "Welcome Homeowners." However, the otherwise celebratory mood was spoiled by anger. One man was using a tape measure to calculate the width of the elevator lobby, while others were photographing the main entrance, and still others were complaining of construction flaws. I overheard people saying that Block C and D apartments were not what the developer had promised and that their quality was inferior to that of Blocks A and B. They mainly complained that the main entrance door was supposed to be 4.7 meters high rather than its present 3.5 meters (see Figure 5.1). Furthermore, the door was supposed to be fitted with glass panels instead of a tiled wall. Suddenly, a disgruntled man came forward, demanding:

> Why would we look at the design details when buying? Everyone took reference from the sample flats of Block A. We're given only two to three minutes to make up our mind. Now look, the main lobby's entrance door, the sunlight passage, and the height are all different, and the lift lobby's corridor is so narrow!

The crowd grumbled that they had bought the property not to occupy but to rent out; thus, the layout and finishing must be as grand as in Blocks A and B. As the owners walked past Block B on their way back to the developer's reception lobby nearby and saw its grand entrance, one lady murmured, "The more I look at it, the more annoyed I feel." "Exactly. We arrived here feeling happy—now how can we be happy?" asked another. A female retiree, who had used her pension plus some money given to her by her children to buy a seventy-meter unit, uttered, "I intended to rent it out; now . . . there is so much trouble, I really want to return it. I have high blood pressure, high blood lipids, and high blood sugar. My heart is also not in particularly good shape. I can't bear all these disputes." Mr. Dai, in his mid-sixties, wearing a worn-out college T-shirt, stated that he could wrangle with the developer and make things difficult, while his wife revealed that they used to live in welfare housing provided by the school where she had taught:

> We've worked hard all our lives. For a long time, I haven't eaten any meat or taken a taxi, so we could save money to fund our son's doctoral studies in the United States. Now that he's married, we want to make our first investment and pass it on to him.

As the crowd waited, their patience waned. A robust, outspoken man, nicknamed Big Brother Tian, who was one of the eight volunteer representatives, directed people to block the entrance and reception desk. Indeed, throughout the week-long protest, Tian, who was a businessman and property investor in his mid-forties, played the role of field marshal, often inciting the crowd to act. Likewise, Mr. Du (early thirties) and Ms. Bao (around fifty) were Tian's most loyal, dedicated lieutenants, leading from the front at all times. On that day, within a few minutes, some thirty owners, mostly women and elderly people, split into three groups and sat near the entrance, inconveniencing passersby. The security guards and company receptionists looked on passively. Then, the activist owners started to intercept each new owner as they arrived to complete the paperwork, demanding, "Are you owners of Blocks C and D? There're serious problems—don't take possession." After a while, they also worked on a correspondence list and a draft of the main issues in dispute. As more owners arrived, they gathered more than one hundred names and contact details.

I introduced myself to several activists and asked about their grievances. Tian was enthusiastic upon learning my intention to conduct social research and wanted me to give them some good ideas. One woman asked whether anyone had called *630 Everyday* (a popular television chat show). "Yes, but they only took our phone number, they didn't promise to come; the *Morning Post* also said no, this *kaifashang* is its biggest advertiser," someone replied. By late afternoon, the owners had decided to return the following morning to cause further disruption and mobilize more owners to join them. As we were leaving, Mr. Dai waved his hands and said, "Today you saw what happens. This is the price of development, which is the hardship of the working people."

That night, the protestors decided to launch an online forum on the popular Internet portal QQ.com to enable all owners to share information and express their opinions about how to continue the fight. I was allowed to join the forum as an anonymous participant.

Day Two: Confrontation

The next morning, the crowd returned with two white banners that stated in black characters, "Serious cheating by the *kaifashang*; resolutely defend the owners' legal interests." There were still many owners who were unaware of the situation before they signed the papers, being led in through the office's side doors by security guards. The staff had been very restrained and even allowed the owners to sit in the air-conditioned lobby but, by afternoon, the situation took a sharp turn. A few security guards had rolled up banners that the activist-owners had not been watching. Upon learning of the situation, Big Brother Tian rounded everybody up to rush outside. The crowd shouted at the security guards, "What right do you have to take our things?" and "Solidarity is strength." Some kicked over the plastic flower pots. At that moment, a security guard took some photos of the crowd, prompting Mr. Deng, the chief representative of the owner-activists, to demand that the photos be deleted. A retired naval serviceman, forty-year-old Deng came

Figure 5.1. The Entrance in Dispute—The "Bad" versus the "Good". This photo was taken by the author.

from a rural area. Always soft spoken and calm, Deng had been instrumental in the movement, playing a central coordinating role. Deng and Tian performed complementary roles, corresponding to their polarized personalities. The guard became agitated and kicked Deng on the leg. Tension heated up within seconds. When some owners threatened to sleep in the road, the police warned that they would be arrested. In response, the crowd taunted that many more police vehicles would be needed to arrest them all. Without hesitation, Tian led a dozen people on a march to the nearby four-lane main road to block the traffic, taking a banner with them (see Figure 5.2). It was 2 p.m. and, as the heavy traffic was held up, some drivers became angry, saying, "Go fight the *kaifashang*; why hold us up here!?" When the police arrived twenty minutes later, in a matter of moments, half of the protesters disappeared, and those remaining soon decided to back down.

The developer agreed to hold a meeting later that afternoon with the owners, with district government officials participating as arbitrators. I later learned that the Municipal Party Secretary, Bo Xilai, was going to visit the district government and his convoy was likely to pass through that area. The district officials were in a panic and notified the developer to contain the situation by any means. The owners' representatives then prepared a document called "Ten Clauses of Rights Defense." All of the owners were urged to sign and fingerprint it. At 5 p.m., the meeting between the developer and the owners began. The developer's general manager, nicknamed Boss Zheng, and representatives from the district housing management bureau and public security bureau were present. Mrs. Ma, in her late twenties, who handled the logistic support for the owners, handed out the "Ten Clauses of Rights Defense." Tian opened his eyes wide and shouted, "You changed the height and width without informing us. Now, the property is worth less. That's why everybody thinks you are cheating us." At this point, Mr. Du pulled out a pile of the company's flyers and asked Zheng, "Look at these graphic layouts. It is not merely that one or two of us got confused, but several hundred of us were misled!" Boss Zheng responded hesitantly, "We can consult a solicitor about whether we are in breach of contract; there's no point in wrangling here." When Mr. Cha suddenly stood up to speak, everybody listened. He concluded, "Your procedure may be legal, but it's unreasonable. The contract law says it clearly: integrity and equality come first." The crowd clapped loudly. Fifty-year-old Cha is an experienced investor, who works in publishing. I would describe his role in the protests as a political commissar, making strategic speeches to boost morale at critical times. The official from the housing management bureau then urged everybody to have confidence that the developer would come back with a firm reply. He was followed by the head of the district public security bureau,

> Earlier today, some owners' attitudes were not commendable. You should convey your opinion to the government instead of blocking the road. This is a law-abiding society—in case of any extreme behavior, the police will take action accordingly.

Upon hearing that, several representatives said that they staged the protest only reluctantly as they are weak compared with the developer. The crowd was becoming restless again, with people shouting and swearing. Boss Zheng reaffirmed his position, "I truly can't give a guarantee here, but I promise that, whatever we tell you today, the company will honor it." The meeting reached deadlock after almost two hours. In the end, Zheng only promised a reply within six days.

Days Three through Seven: Preparing for the Fight

Over the next few days, key representatives took it in turns to patrol the site to solicit further support. Tian informed me that, although the developer had promised a reply by Saturday, it was continuing to process registrations for new owners. He was concerned that, if many more owners took possession of the apartments, the protesting owners would become a minority of troublemakers rather than legitimate representatives of the majority. Tian joked that they were like the Communists using guerrilla warfare against the Japanese,

Figure 5.2. Protesters Blockading the Road. This photo was taken by the author.

a struggle involving the use of mental and physical strength. One elderly woman stood outside the "good-looking Block B," muttering, "The *kaifa-shang* has no heart." A manager passed by and scolded her, "You made your purchase blindly; now you come here to fart ignorantly!" In order to obtain as many owners' contact information as possible, someone spent a few hundred RENMINBI to buy the full list from a renovation company, which had bought it earlier from the developer's sales personnel. This was certainly a breach of privacy, but no one seemed surprised.

In the evenings, the owners' online QQ forum became very busy. Mrs. Ma reported that she had received a call from the police, reminding them not to blockade the main road again. She also appealed for help from the forum participants and asked if any owners were from the legal profession, but to no avail. Overall, people were most concerned about the overall design defects of the main entrance and the elevator lobby. Some mentioned the loss of potential rental income due to the delayed occupancy. Debate ensued over whether the owners should inform the domestic and international news media, but some were concerned about the repercussions of this for their property's reputation. One anonymous participant said, "The impact of our restraint protest is too mild; we should go to the other development projects of the *kaifashan* to create trouble and sabotage their sales activities!" Others agreed, even suggesting reporting the case to the Hong Kong media. Nonetheless, suggestions concerning more radical action were not endorsed by the majority. There were also inconclusive discussions on legal issues and the possibility of hiring lawyers to advise the group. The issue of compensation was raised also, with some owners insisting on 10 to 20 percent of the purchase price as their bottom-line demand. Noticeably, those who owned multiple units all refrained from participating. Some participants gossiped that several floors in Block C had been allotted to local officials and employees of the developer at a significant discount and that this was why they did not support the protest. Many were also worried that spies might join the forum, posing as owners, and requested more stringent screening of the forum membership.

Day Eight: The Final Showdown

On the morning of the eighth day, almost one hundred owners gathered again, expecting to hear the developer's definite reply. Before the meeting, Mr. Cha stood on a rock to address the crowd, appealing for solidarity and determination. The meeting venue, which was the reception lobby of Block B, had been well-prepared, with four large, square tables covered with a decorated cloth. Fresh fruit and bottled water, plus a big projector, were provided. The meeting was chaired by the vice director of the sub-district office's public enquiry department, who sat in front of the podium.[6] Flanking the vice director were Boss Zheng and an official from the district bureau of industry and commerce. Also present were officials from the district building commission, planning bureau, housing management bureau, fire services, and police. The sub-district official opened by stating that the government took the incident seriously and that the bureau of industry and commerce would investigate whether rules had been breached. He hoped that both sides could resolve the issue harmoniously. Mr. Deng expressed thanks for the government's efforts in settling the dispute and appealed to the participating owners to refrain from talking while others were speaking. A company employee video recorded the activities.

Manager Wang from the developer reiterated that all construction work and design had complied with the relevant building and fire safety regulations, and had been carried out in accordance with the master design plan. However, for the sake of community harmony, the company would be willing to undertake improvement work at its own cost. The crowd grew disgruntled, and some shouted from the back of the room. Deng rejected the company's reply as an evasion of responsibility and demanded a definite answer on the improvement work and compensation. About an hour into the proceedings, the meeting had reached a total impasse, with accusations, screaming, and cursing from those in attendance. Zheng and the officials looked grim. A fierce-looking woman suddenly shouted, "Why waste time on the details? I just want results!" At this point, Mr. Cha stood up and delivered a fifteen-minute speech. He stressed that the interests of small investors are actually in line with those of the developer, which are to enhance the prestige of the project and increase the value of the properties. The sub-district official then summarized the discussion, concluding that if, any wrongdoing by the company was to be found, there would be a criminal proceeding. Until then, the incident would be considered a civil and commercial dispute, which the owners could take to the courts. He appealed to both sides to avoid confrontation, and then all the officials left their seats. The crowd exploded with anger. Several owners tried to stop them from leaving but were prevented by police escorts. I learned that the officials had actually waited in an adjacent office to monitor the situation.

The anarchic, vociferous situation lasted for half an hour, as three-quarters of the people gradually departed. Events then took an unanticipated turn. Several owners approached Boss Zheng and urged him to make substantive changes. Before long, Zheng was seen sitting side-by-side with the owners, chatting casually and laughing. As they talked, Zheng and several owners sometimes put their hand to their chest as if they were speaking with sincerity. Zheng asked his staff to produce some graphics to illustrate the renovation schemes. I asked Mr. Cha what had happened, and he replied, "The *kaifashang* senses that our protesting could stir up concern among the government, so they backed down. What is important now is to provide a ladder for the *kaifashang* to step down from its position while saving face." This marked a sharp contrast between the owners' earlier rhetoric and their real-life pragmatic approach post-confrontation but, still, it was surprising that, after elevating their moral appeals to such a high level as accusing the company of dishonesty, the activist owners could suddenly retreat from such a position and accept a watered-down solution to their complaints, thereby clearing the developer of all legal liability. By midday, the majority of the owners had left and Big Brother Tian was conspicuously absent—later, this became a controversial issue regarding his "loyalty." In the interim, the company ordered boxed lunches for those who stayed behind. Who would expect Goliath to feed David to prepare David to fight him? While everybody waited, Boss Zheng stepped outside to have a cigarette. I took the opportunity to chat with him; this was all he had to say to me: "We just do what we ought to do."

Later, the company prepared a questionnaire, asking whether the owners agreed with the proposal. The proposal would have to be endorsed by a two-thirds majority of all the owners in accordance with the 2007 "Property Law." Mrs. Ma was unimpressed with the outcome. Nothing was agreed upon regarding compensation. The questionnaire only addressed five of the ten points originally raised by the owners, who were only allowed to choose between agree or disagree or their forms would be invalidated but, as Mrs. Ma said, the trickiest part was the wording of the questionnaire:

> The questionnaire about altering certain sections of the public space of Hillside Garden blocks C/D: In the course of the lawful handover of the project's completed properties, some of the owners of Blocks C and D have proposed that certain improvement work should be carried out. This survey is intended to solicit the opinion of all owners with regard to the alterations as proposed by certain owners.

It seems clear that, once the questionnaire has been endorsed by the majority of owners, any delay and inconvenience would not be the developer's responsibility, because it would be a collective request on the part of the owners. This concern was echoed later by many owners who had not attended the meeting. On the owners' online forum, heated debate erupted that evening. Several participants noted that this drastically watered-down scheme intimated that the developer was generously doing them a favor. Some even queried whether the developer had bribed their representatives. One participant predicted, "Whichever representative no longer speaks out over the next few days is the traitor." Noticeably, the most vocal criticism came from those who had not participated in the past week's activism. Others countered that these hardliners could have been infiltrators sent by the developer. In reply, Mr. Cha said that the proposal represented some progress, as the developer would bear substantial renovation costs. He appealed to those who wanted to continue the fight to shoulder the responsibility for doing so.

The Aftermath

Over the following week, the owners' representatives were preoccupied with collecting endorsements from all of the apartment owners. In the end, adequate endorsements were obtained, and the developer proceeded with the alteration work, which was completed four months later. Before long, the owners' concerns had shifted to the business related to renting out their apartment. Some said that perhaps they ought not to emphasize the difference in quality between their units and those of Blocks A and B or they would have to accept lower rental payments. Gradually, the owners were realizing a hard fact: that an open fight might be detrimental to their economic interests as investors. This was the dilemma confronting every owner—that their interests are neither diametrically opposed to those of the developer, nor a singular proposition but a matrix of trade-offs.

On the owners' online forum, many participants persisted with the idea of taking legal action, but those who suggested this did not dare reveal their identity, much less commit to bearing the burden of legal costs. Anonymity has revealed itself as counter-productive and reactionary, which is in sharp contravention with many other instances of social mobilization worldwide wherein young people are the core participants, driven and coordinated by the new media platform. During the Egyptian Revolution in January 2011, Facebook facilitated a qualitative leap in the human rights movement (Saad 2012) while, in the #Occupy Boston movement in October 2011, the use of Twitter (plus smartphones and Facebook) served to produce a sense of connectedness and co-presence, potentially eliciting powerful feelings of solidarity (Juris 2012). However, the assumption that the Internet naturally brings dissidents together in an alliance of shared sentiment is challenged by Sarah Kendzior, who demonstrates how, within an "Uzbek political culture of cynicism and distrust," the Internet allows existing doubts and antagonism to be more easily perceived and exacerbated (2011, 560). In the similar context of China, Zhou Yongming (2006) contends that the decisive factor regarding the effectiveness of a technology platform is not the technology per se but the receiving context in which its potential is exploited. This context includes the state's firm control of societal forces, and the lack of collective and organizational participation that severely limits public online text's authority and credibility in times of political mobilization.

AFTER THE CURTAIN CLOSED

In hindsight, the rapid deterioration of solidarity within the owners' group was unsurprising. First, the representatives were not elected but volunteered on the very first day of the dispute, before the majority of the owners were even aware of the situation. The idea of asking all owners to re-endorse the representatives was never pursued. Nobody dared to challenge their legitimacy, probably because the vast majority of owners only wanted to free ride on the benefits of others' efforts rather than wholeheartedly participate in the fight. Notwithstanding the repeated calls for more people to take the initiative, throughout the eight-day drama, the core team never expanded in number. Second, the composition of the owners of the 680 units was very complicated. Among the four blocks of property, Block C was the first offered for presale, at a low price of RMB8,000–9,000 per m^2, with the developer's own staff members guaranteed a slot through "internal allocations." This was considered special treatment at a time when all properties were being snapped up frenetically by long queues of buyers. Hence, many of Block C's owners were understandably reluctant to support the defense of rights. In contrast, Block D was the last to be offered for sale, with an inflated offering price of RMB12,000 per m^2, and had been marketed as an "elite and boutique style" commercial building. Most of the buyers intended to rent out their unit, believing that the property's premier location was an attractive spot for small-to-medium-sized companies to set up a modest office. Such huge differentials in the various owners' cost-risk profiles thus led to a substantial division of perceived interests. Most representatives took a conciliatory position as they soon became disillusioned by the lack of support from the majority of owners. As such, once the scheme of alteration was endorsed, the owners' moral high ground crumbled completely.

A few months after these events, I spoke to some of the core players, including the owners' representatives and the developer's senior management, to explore this intense but short-lived rights defense. "A complete failure," is how Mr. Tian gloomily labeled it, adding that, initially, everybody was passionate so much was achieved spontaneously but, as more people became involved, the group became divided, and the final showdown with the developer was a wash-out:

> Nobody wants to make the decision. If you put things right, people may thank you; but if you mess up, everybody blames you. The chaos seen at the meeting was due to the absence of a nucleus of thought. Boss Zheng cleverly saw that the situation was turning favorable and guided several representatives toward his way of thinking in order to strike a deal. You see, the representatives didn't know each other well, so I can't say or criticize much. And, of course, some people did warn me not to go too far.

Tian's disappointment was not only due to most owners' behaving as free riders, contributing nothing to their efforts, but he also felt sickened by the way some owners attacked the representatives, despite the latter's selfless efforts and contribution. Mrs. Ma was similarly disappointed by the result. She had been engaged in photocopying, data input, and contacting the owners. "Many people cheered me on verbally, but never did I come across anyone actually helping," she recounted. In addition, it was puzzling why the owners of Block C also participated in the protest. Block C was presold first, at the lowest price, and the buyers were not promised anything when making their purchase. Thus, it is fair to say that they were less motivated by a principle of rights than by opportunistic self-interest, though many of the protesters appeared to embody both causes in their discourse. Mr. Cha, also an owner of a unit in Block C, confirmed this observation. When he purchased his apartment, there had been no information available at all about Block A's exterior design. He did not see the difference between Blocks C and A until the day he took possession, and only then did he feel uncomfortable. Thus, a new mode of rationale emerged spontaneously: *there were differences between the buildings, which constituted a breach of contract by the developer*. Evidently, not only the body but also the mind is affected by this "affect of ownership." Cha confirmed that about one dozen owner-activists had come together several times for brainstorming, but they hardly had a meticulously crafted action plan or strategy, and much of the observed action indeed happened spontaneously. Nonetheless, to render these "spontaneous" actions effective, a lot of groundwork remains necessary. Mr. Deng was instrumental throughout the events by organizing and executing every aspect and detail. With no initial intention of staging a protest, he had been affected by Tian's passionate call to action and, within a split second, Deng found himself thrown onto a path of no return. Nevertheless, his stance was much more conciliatory than that of Tian:

> We must come up with a simple collective request, for the *kaifashang* will never admit its mistakes. Many owners insisted on forcing the *kaifashang* to agree on the true nature of the incident, which is to confess its breach of sales contract. Is that achievable? Maybe we could indeed have achieved more, but our hearts are not united. . . . What a shame.

In his final analysis, Deng believed that the district and sub-district governments had been behind the developer's sudden concession. He said that he later learned that there would be a nationwide social survey about "becoming a civilized city" and Secretary Bo had passed a "must be done" instruction to all district governments. Hence, the officials were under pressure to force the developer to settle the dispute and avoid any fallout. "But, publicly, the officials and *kaifashang* sat together in the same boat and maintained the same tone, refusing to bow to public pressure." Deng's information and analysis were unknowingly echoed by Manager Wang, who told me that the owners' twenty-minute road blockade had led the district officials to intervene, because they feared that Secretary Bo Xilai might learn of the incident that afternoon as he was on his way to a meeting with district officials. The company had been instructed to restrict the activist owners to the sales office and its top management was forced to come out to handle the situation. Wang himself was an owner of Hillside Garden and said that, personally, he had no issue with the property's quality. He reckoned that the whole "rights defense" was an opportunistic act rather than a matter of rights protection. Wang recalled that Boss Zheng, throughout the negotiation, insisted on only tackling technical issues related to the rectification work, while refusing to budge an inch regarding the nature of the incident, that is, on whether there had been a breach of sales contract. Zheng had reached a consensus with the district officials prior to convening the meeting with all of the owners. Wang had high praise for Cheng's negotiation skills as he recalled Zheng saying, "This morning, I've had a big bowl of noodles—if necessary I'll sit here all day long." Three months after the incident, Wang still felt excited about the company's efficiency in handling the issue: "That night, we went out to celebrate. Our boss exclaimed, 'See how rapidly we resolved it; isn't it a miracle?' I replied, 'Yes, it's a miracle!'"

But was it a miracle? Did Boss Zheng actually lack confidence that the dispute would be resolved quickly? Or does this reflect a deeper unease regarding what kind of endgame an opportunistic combination of rights and desires could create among the contesting parties? Unlike resistance anchored by a principled cause that is collectively shared, revolt prompted by the sporadic private interests of a mass of individuals can mutate, disrupt, or discontinue unpredictably due to a lack of concerted efforts and unified objectives. As evident from the spontaneity of disparate events during the eight-day saga, affect as desire, which circulates among individual bodies, is fluid and amendable to change. This contrasts with the individualized private interests that reside permanently within each individual subject. Zheng would be right in believing that only a miracle could have led to such a clear solution against the power of desires, which had been evoked and manipulated to force the local officials' intervention, but this case actually illustrates the kind of open-endedness and messiness inherent in the unfolding of events, characterizing both an immense potentiality and profound fleetingness of the notion of desire in activating the owners' protest. This resonates with Lisa Rofel's thesis that desire is unpredictable, that "full control over where desire might end up is impossible" (2007, 140). In the end, desire at once creates and handicaps the condition of possibility.

AFFECT IN PROPERTY OWNERSHIP

From passion to emotion and action, the set of protest activities started with an appeal by a charismatic individual, and then a few dozen owners were drawn into an intense but short-lived protest against a property developer's alleged cheating. Many investors had visited the construction site many times to watch the work in progress, with great dreams for their future. Even so, as they watched the rising of their building, story by story, week by week, they either failed to take note of the problem or gave greater weight to their luck at having been able to buy a unit over a matter of principle regarding any suspected wrongdoing on the developer's part. Soon-to-be owners, particularly small investors, feel excited at the prospect of making money. They put the property assets into discourse and symbolize them as a sign of lifelong achievement or success, financial profit or security but, once they feel that their dream is threatened, they reinterpret the whole situation as an oppression of the weak by the mighty, and as a conflict between honesty and greed through their performative construction of the good (themselves) against the bad (developer). The owners' vociferous and random accusations concerning the developer's alleged cheating apparently served to consolidate the protesters themselves, demonstrating that speaking as an everyday embodied practice is generative of affect (Moore 2011). Emotions can certainly flare up;

but, while emotions are observed to bind owners together from time to time, such sentiments come and go circumstantially. As Sara Ahmed (2004) argues, it is the "non-residence" of emotions that binds together subjects and creates the very effect of a collective. Hence, emotions in this context are "pre-individual," and would be better understood as not simply *personal emotion* but as *affect*, circulating in the exteriority of and between subjects. The accumulation and mobilization of this affect becomes the driver for the subjects' mental and bodily action of collective order.

My analysis in this chapter takes reference from Christina Schwenkel's (2013) studies of affect in relation to Vietnam's postsocialist urban reconstruction, which bears a close resemblance to the situation in China. Schwenkel depicts how bricks came to signify unfulfilled promises of care, renewal, and inclusion of a socialist past, while generating anxiety and despair, as well as new sentiments of disenchantment and desires for state care and belonging as part of people's everyday experience of capitalism. For the present case, the property investors at Hillside Garden also take the material form of real estate investment as an "entry point" to express their desire and aspiration for monetary gain and family well-being, implicitly denoting a reflexivity of the socialist rationality and a long-lost ideal. My attempt to approach property ownership from an affective perspective also relates to recent multidisciplinary efforts to attend to affect's centrality in inducing economic effects and for theorizing post-industrial capitalism and neoliberal economic transformations (Anderson 2012; Clough 2007; Massumi 1995; Negri 1999; Richard and Rudnyckyj 2009). A common attribute is that the market realm is no longer separable from the noneconomic fields and domains in an economy based on desire, affectivity, and pleasure, with life itself becoming increasingly articulated to capital. At my field site, the vast majority of owners come from different walks of life and are endowed with vastly different economic resources. Investment capital is the owners' least common denominator, which intertwines their affective feeling and desire, engendering their thinking and action. Owners may have accumulated their capital for investment through saving, entrepreneurial activities, stock market speculation, or even bribery and corruption but, once the money becomes capital spent on property purchases, its source, root, and history are no longer identifiable or relevant. What matters most is an appreciation of property prices and, hence, their investment value. Owners may sell their property for a profit or remortgage it to expand their investment portfolio. Property and capital continue to circulate in the market, premised on the assumption of and hope for a perpetually booming market. Hence, many owners are readily animated by an affect that connotes the image and joy of making investment gains, suggestive of a future characterized by financial security and familial happiness. In a sense, the desire and affect of property ownership constitute a platform of agency. The root of such affective ownership is a temporal attachment to the future, not the past, rather than a spatial attachment to the materiality and vicinity of the property itself. Sociologist and philosopher Antonio Negri states that affect constructs a commonality of a desire among subjects and I suggest that capital forms the cornerstone of an affective ownership of property that manifests itself as a common desire for possession, ubiquitous in China.

However, while the analytical scheme of affect is illuminating and promising, it is unclear how the limit of affect's potentiality can be discerned and verified in relation to explaining actions. My ethnographic account reveals that both the developer and activist owners are constantly reviewing their strategic positions vis-à-vis the incident's critical nature. Once the owner-activists discovered that the local officials were unlikely to side with them in condemning the developer's wrongdoing, they became anxious that the nature of their own protests could instead be defined as troublemaking and a threat to the social stability, rather than a due defense of their legitimate rights. The affective intensity is accentuated in tandem with the activist owners' interactions but without cementing any lasting solidarity. The circulating affect animates and energizes people's propensity and capacity to think and act in unison. These individuals *affect* and *are affected* by each other but only to dissipate and disintegrate precipitously after the final showdown with the developer. The owners are overwhelmingly unprepared to make sacrifices wholeheartedly for their discursively just cause. Beyond their noisy bluffing and apparent solidarity, the activist owners know only too well that they are in no position to fight for principles and their rightful claims through costly litigation or radical street resistance. Thus, the property owners' "collective subjectivity" is shaped predominantly by the social reality of the asymmetrical power relations with the developer vis-à-vis the government. The owners share a dream—the appreciation of their investment—but their divergent socioeconomic backgrounds and interests do not lead to the cultivation of an intimate comradeship. Individual subjectivity evidently remains at work, in the interface with pre-individual affect and, interestingly, once the actors cannot see each other (for example, on the owners' online forum), affect as a capacity to act and to be acted upon falters, and individual interests and subjectivity prevail, causing internal strife. What appears from this case of the owners' rights defense is that affect both coexists with and shapes subjectivity but is simultaneously conditioned by and amendable to individual and collective subjectivities. This reading resonates with Analiese Richard and Daromir Rudnyckyj's (2009) discovery that affect actually sheds light on contemporary subject-making and self-making.

Moreover, unlike the endeavors and solidarity of owner-occupiers, which may involve hundreds of participants in extended protest organization (Zhu Jiangang 2011), the aspiration of rights and action of rights claim that are *not* predicated on spatial attachment and neighborhood belonging appears to be ephemeral and fragile. This is in sharp contrast with the perspective on homeowner activism as provided by several political scientists. For instance, Benjamin Read (2008) and Guan Bing (2010) sound upbeat, variously arguing that private ownership has the potential to effect a substantial reallocation of power at the neighborhood level and that, through homeowners' exposure to grassroots democracy training, pressure is building to alter the traditional mode of governance at the local level. Likewise, Luigi Tomba (2005) notes that some owner-occupiers were willing to act even confrontationally, which he attributes to the drive to protect both property rights and community interests, which creates a relatively autonomous space for socialization and limited action. He notes that protesters are concerned about both the "interest of exchange" (investment value) and the "interest of use" (security and lifestyle) of their ownership. Zhengxu Wang et al. (2013) even suggest that a remarkable shift has occurred, in which vigorous efforts are being made to move out of gated communities and establish cross-community, city-wide and even nationwide alliances, having realized that property-related disputes have their roots in the existing legal and regulatory institutions. Along this line, geographer Yihong Jiang (2013) also shows that organized homeowner activists have moved "upstream" in the policy process in terms of agenda setting and rule-making, while acknowledging that their impact is hard to discern. On the contrary, my Chongqing case reveals a sharply localized and contingent mobilization, lacking a "struggle for recognition" (Tomba 2005, 950) or "cross-community alliances" (Wang et al. 2013, 413). Although dozens of homeowners at Hillside Garden did participate in collective action, their enthusiasm and activism proved transient; and, even among the leading activists, the solidarity was hardly genuine. My reading echoes that of anthropologist Zhu Jiangang (2011), who rejects a simplistic view of democracy propagation, albeit acknowledging a new trend of rights-based community governance prompted by such collective action. This comparison and contrast indeed demonstrate the importance of contextual factors and cautions us against deducing a broad-stroke causality between property rights and the formation of rights consciousness. In the emergent moment of conceiving and practicing property rights, affect as desire reveals itself as both a prima facie limitless potentiality and a limiting condition.

NOTES

1. The developer would start advertising a few weeks prior to the opening of property sales but, in reality, when the market is hot, a large portion of the offers would have been allocated internally to related parties, thus allowing only a small quantity of supply available for open sales. Moreover, many projects on offer are still under construction, so prospective buyers can base their decisions only on the layout design plan.

2. Owing to the inherent sensitivity of rights defense protest, all names of places, people, and companies are kept anonymous, with pseudonyms used where necessary. My effort and

approach in this chapter resembles Max Gluckman's (1940) classic social situation analysis of circumscribed events taking place in a relatively restricted time span, from which and their inter-relationships in a particular society he abstracts the social structure, relationships, and institutions, etc. of that society. The purpose of using such a method is not to draw generalizations from a particular case or social situation but to acquire illuminating insights. As Clyde Mitchell ([1956] 2006) and Don Handelman (2006) variously explicate, the analysis of a restricted, limited set of events could reveal how the general principles of social organization manifest themselves in a particular specified context, so that the ordering of the social life of institutions could be theorized through the analysis of particular events.

3. Since 70 percent of households in Chongqing city proper own their premises, the majority of buyers of the relatively high-end Hillside Garden are likely to be either investors or owner-occupiers with the intention of upgrading from their present residence but, given the limited availability of complementary facilities in the vicinity, most interviewees considered that Hillside Garden is more suitable for office leasing.

4. As Erving Goffman (1958) notes, when an individual enters the presence of others, the initial definition of the situation projected by an individual has a distinctive moral character, in the sense that s/he also makes an implicit or explicit claim to be a person of a particular kind, which automatically exerts a moral demand upon the others, obliging them to value and treat her/him in the manner that persons of her/his kind have a right to expect.

5. The conceptualization of affect as the power to act and as potential builds upon the line of philosophical thought from Benedict de Spinoza through Gilles Deleuze and Félix Guattari. According to Michael Hardt (2007), Spinoza explains the power of affect in terms of the mind's power to think in parallel with the body's power to act, as well as a correspondence between the power to act and the power to be affected. Hence, affect straddles between the mind and body, and between actions and passions. The Deleuzian interpretation further refers affect to sensual intensities that may move through human bodies and considers affect to be diametrically opposed to subjectivity theory (Navaro-Yashin 2009).

6. The sub-district is the third level of the three-tier urban administration, and its officers-in-charge are appointed by the district government. For details, see footnote 1, chapter 2.

Chapter Six

The Property Question

Meanings and Values

> "I am a beneficiary of the superiority of socialism; but mister, what I really mean is, you must put the word 'superiority' in quote marks." —Mr. Lei, a retired teacher

Mr. Lei, in his late fifties, used to teach at the municipal Communist Party School. Notwithstanding his humble salary, his work unit's special status endowed him with the privilege of purchasing welfare housing as early as 1987, before the housing reform even started. Lei paid RMB4,000 for his apartment which, by his own reckoning, was worth RMB30,000. His wife was also allotted another unit, because her household registration had not yet been transferred to the city proper, together with Lei. They later sold their two apartments to buy commodity housing for investment, financed by mortgages. When I last saw him, in mid-2012, Lei still had five apartments, mostly under his son's name; wearing his usual faded T-shirt and sandals, he had just returned from the prosperous city of Shenzhen and was aiming to buy another apartment for his son there. Lei once sarcastically stated, "It's a privilege due to the superiority of socialism, but only a small proportion of people share the benefits." In the town where he was born, he said that perhaps 30 percent of the households received welfare housing. The Lei family's double property allocation was as rare as a double jackpot, but only two decades later could he fully comprehend the significance of such a fortune bestowed by the state and its impact on the well-being of his family. A veteran Party member himself, would Lei consider socialism an equitable system? He smiled. Perhaps the question is simultaneously all too trivial and too complex to answer.

The Lei family's story of incidental wealth creation vividly recounts an unusual historic regime change that affected the well-being of millions of urban households. Lei recalled that, up to 2001, all of his purchases were deemed to be merely following the state's policy and only thereafter did he form the intention to "act out" an investment. The redirection of his mind-set toward the act of risk-conscious property investment reflects the experience of millions of others. All of this happened under the orchestration and gaze of the state. It is surprising, however, that, first, within barely twenty years, property ownership has changed from a pejorative concept into a dominant economic ethos and practice and, second, the family has regained its centrality in constituting personal value in spite of the decades of ideological preaching about absolute loyalty to the Party and sacrifice for the collective good. As evidenced in the previous chapters, there is a mentality of property first that animates the prevalent transfer of property to one's offspring, even among the middle and working classes, and this also preoccupies many house evictees during their stern compensation bargaining. As Ms. Chen, who is featured in chapter 4, commented: *ownership offers security* and *family is the ultimate source of happiness and contentment*. This mentality is at once an unmistakable manifestation of normal human desire and love and the engendering of a new (or indeed "renewed") value, but filled with particular historic and social significances.

This chapter represents an attempt to synthesize my ethnographic observations on active possession (chapters 4 and 5) and counter-dispossession (chapters 2 and 3), which demonstrate that a new tripartite relationality has emerged among the state, property, and family. It illustrates housing property's historical transformation as assets redistributed by the party-state to urban citizens, transacted in the market between developers and investors, and gifted by parents to their children. Housing property also acts as a formidable mediator of social relationships in the broader context of Chinese privatization and global financialization. My aim in this chapter is to detect whether a new regime of meanings and values is emerging out of the neo-socialist engendering of private property rights and peculiar parental gift phenomena. In so doing, we require a dynamic theory of value, which, David Graeber reckons, is "to bring together society and human purposes, to move from meaning to desire" (2001, 21), while heeding Marshall Sahlins's (2013) caution against the "disabling effect" of subsuming the cultural and historical forces that constitute the values of persons and the objects of their existence as individual preferences in the understanding of economic change. In a nutshell, what appears as the individual or familial choice of investing citizens and demolition bargainers may well be essentially a result or manifestation of complex historical changes and cultural configurations, encompassing both macro and micro factors.

At the macro level, my informants as portrayed in this book, be they demolition bargainers or investing citizens, are mostly consequential products of the housing reform, and all bear witness to a historically engendered housing and property question. The policy deliberation of the party-state is at once reinforcing the gulf between the propertied and the propertyless, while also vowing to tackle the rampant social inequalities premised on the socialist promise of "common prosperity." With reference to the acute housing shortage for industrial workers in Germany of the 1870s, Friedrich Engels ([1872] 1979) saw the essence of the bourgeois solutions as, trivially, that "the worker should own his own dwelling." He dismissed such an idea of raising the propertyless classes to the level of the propertied classes en bloc sarcastically as a "utopian social order," in which all wage-workers are turned into capitalists without ceasing to be wage-workers (Engels [1872] 1979, 42). Instead, Engels believed that the exploitative essence of bourgeoisie society dictates that the savings of the workers, invested in property, would, in the end, become capital for the capitalist employing them. Hence, the orthodox Marxist position is that there is no such thing as a "housing question" but *the* social question; and the solution to this "housing question" will be made possible only by solving the *social question* through the abolition of capitalist production and the property relations that it creates. Based on this perspective, if China's unfettered aspiration and discourse of walking the path of socialism is fully acknowledged, the events of recent years must have been a grand detour, with the practice of private property rights being embraced in every facet of public and private life. At stake is whether the seminal change from an era of socialist monopolistic distribution may lead China on a perpetual path of no return away from the communist ideal (though many ordinary people now believe that it is just another utopian social order). How do emancipatory possibilities coexist with the rapidly widening social differentiation? Can the spread of private rights coexist unproblematically with the regulative state action in defense of public assets?

The People's Republic, after all, should be based on the constitutional socioeconomic rights of the people and the public ownership of land and resources. There is thus a broader *property question* as part the social question, rather than a mere housing issue related to how the revival of private property rights is embedded in the continuity of the political system. Recall Karl Marx's declaration that, in all revolutionary movements everywhere, Communists "bring to the front, as the leading question in each, the property question, no matter what its degree of development at the time" (Marx and Engels [1848] 2005, 89). As such, the property question never loses its relevance and significance in any political regime which proclaims itself the orthodox heir of Marxism.

At the micro level, in their respective deliberations regarding bargaining for better demolition compensation and investing in property for gain, many

Chongqing urbanites are dealing with housing not just as a basic necessity and a commodity, but simultaneously as an immensely important parental gift for their offspring. Recall how, for example, Mr. Gu threatened to detonate a bomb unless his demand for an additional apartment unit for his son's family is satisfied (chapter 2); a seventy-year old grandmother muttered to the demolition personnel that her granddaughter is getting married and needs her own apartment (chapter 3); Mr. Liang received financial support from his mother to purchase property upon his marriage; Ms. Chen, a rural-urban migrant entrepreneur, invested in property to finance her son's future overseas education (chapter 4); and a retired couple used their life's savings to buy a property for their son when he returned from the United States with a doctorate (chapter 5). Hence, property purchase and demolition bargaining are not always straightforward, isolated economic transactions, but are often embedded considerations. Housing fulfils a dual function as both a commodity and a gift, entailing both instrumentality and relationality. Through housing, the state's dramatic welfare reform has become intertwined with the property booms and evolving parent/children and marriage/property relationships. I consider this a new regime of value, because it primes the possession and price appreciation of properties as the prerequisites for personal and family well-being, which actually could be considered as a mere revival of traditional value. Moreover, noticeably, the gift-commodity dialectic as discovered in China's contemporary housing arena also has long been a classic anthropological focus of inquiry, as Hirokazu Miyazaki (2013) states that the chief anthropological insight about the gift is exactly the impossibility of defining its contours. My present effort also draws on Marilyn Strathern's perspective that gift exchange "involves a process in which human value *is* made apparent" (1988, 167; original emphasis), with a view to introducing the fresh angle and contextual complexity of a neo-socialist, industrialized market economy.

NEO-SOCIALIST HOUSING AND STRUCTURE OF PROPERTY RIGHTS

Many welfare housing owners like Lei stated that they were initially "unaware" of their new propertied status because, in their everyday life, they have simply experienced the same kind of right to use as before. This situation is similar to some other ex-socialist states. Stephanie Platz describes this as "pseudo ownership," whereby the citizens in Armenia, having received apartments, had little flexibility or security with regard to matters of housing (2000, 119). On the face of it, the old socialist housing provision was alien to the private property right regime. However, if we employ the notion of a bundle of rights for dissecting property relations, we see that the paradigmatic shift toward private property rights is an abrupt but not necessarily complete break from the socialist institutions, as the right to use indeed forms an integral part of the totality of property rights.

Institutional economists' treatment of property rights as an analytical tool offers a useful perspective for ethnographic investigation. In a nutshell, property is said to comprise three basic elements: the right to use a property, the right to earn income from it, and the right to transfer ownership, which entails the open possibility to contract, resulting in a complexity of rights (Alchian 2008). Economist Stephen Cheung (1982) further points out that exclusivity with regard to the use of resources and the transferability of rights is a matter of degree, so an ownership right may *not* be required to determine private property. Thus, there could be many parties participating in each specific domain of property, diluting the sense of exclusivity. Applying this approach to an analysis of Chinese rural enterprises, Xiaolin Guo (1999) discovers that the crucial right of control is ambiguous under joint administration with the local government, with the latter's interference being the norm in the post-privatization era. As such, property as a bundle of substantive rights facilitates a critical examination of the complex relations pertinent to epochal social transformations.

The new propertied persons' consciousness of becoming and being property owners emerges clearly only after they realize that the holding of their property assets is given a whole new meaning by the dominance of a new monetary system of value. The right to use is no longer the primary content of their dwelling; rather, it is the right to earn income and gain from capital appreciation that becomes the paradigm setting in terms of wealth creation and altering the well-being of the family. In chapter 2, I present the cases of Cao and Pu, whose status as long-term tenants did not entitle them to gain from property disposal, which makes a huge difference in terms of financial security. Such deconstructive treatment is crucial not only for understanding the transition of urban dwellers' property rights entitlement, but also for clarifying what housing property rights actually mean. In China, land, the most critical value constituent of an urban property asset, is owned by the state, as represented by the municipal and district governments. In the course of my discussion with demolition personnel, it was commonly stated that, since the land is owned by the state, it should be sufficient to compensate the occupants merely for the building and renovation costs. Ordinary people know, however, that the largest portion of property's capital appreciation comes from the land element, as property prices have soared several times more than the cost of construction. The owners of urban properties in China possess land use rights for a fixed number of years but do not own the land outright. This situation resembles that in Hong Kong, for example, wherein all land is leasehold; however, this has not prevented a phenomenal surge in property prices. The key lies in the realization that the "ownership" of housing built on leasehold land includes the crucial exclusive right to transfer the land use rights and reap the gains arising from this. Hence, whether or not the householder actually "owns" the land is irrelevant when determining his rights and privileges; and when the authorities impose a price based largely on compensating for building structures erected on state-owned land, they are seriously infringing the evictees' property rights.

Until the end of the 1980s, more than 70 percent of China's urban quarters were provided by the state through the workplace (*danwei*) and household registration (*hukou*) systems, as the housing market had been virtually eliminated during the Cultural Revolution (Huang 2004). An individual's welfare provision was rigidly associated with his/her legal classification as an urban citizen and status as a *danwei* employee.[1] The principle of egalitarian distribution was, however, merely a matter of degree, as one's seniority and rank both determined the decision regarding the location and size of one's quarters; as Mayfair Yang (1989) demonstrates, the conception of neediness is intertwined with the normative categories of the "deserving." Social control was made impeccable by the *hukou* system, instituted in 1958, which effectively divided the population into those of agricultural (rural) status and non-agricultural (urban) status, to stem rural-urban migration. Only the lucky urbanites were entitled to benefits such as job allocation, subsidized housing and food, schooling, healthcare, and a pension. Sometimes called a "rural-urban apartheid system" (Zheng 2009, 196), *hukou* created massive birth-based inequalities (Wang 2010), effectively segregating the population into two tiers of citizenship. In recent years, the Central Government has attempted to bridge the urban-rural gap, but the results have been far from satisfactory due to the breakneck speed of urbanization. As Chi-Pui Cheung (2012) notes, by the late 2000s, the urban-rural differences were actually being reinforced in the absence of adequate fiscal resources, paradoxically prompting rural people to cling to rural *hukou* due to the precariousness of the new urban life. It was not until July 2014 that the State Council put out a consultation on abolishing the agricultural and non-agricultural divide, to be replaced fully with a unified resident registration system by 2020.

Housing hence has been intricately tied to the historical legacies of the *hukou* and *danwei* systems. In 1988, a nationwide urban housing reform was launched to transform the welfare system through privatization by gradually selling off work unit-controlled housing at huge discounts (Huang 2004). In 1998, the government finally resolved to phase out welfare housing by subsidizing workers' purchases. In place of public housing provision, a limited amount of low rental housing is provided for extremely low-income households and a special type of affordable housing with government-controlled prices is promoted for purchase by lower income groups. By 2000, 59 percent of urban households were homeowners, increasing to 76 percent by the middle of the decade (Mak et al. 2007; Wang et al. 2013). Geographers Youqin Huang and Chengdong Yi (2011) state that China is becoming a "nation of homeowners" and note the explosive growth in second-home ownership (11 percent of all urban households owned second homes in 2005) as an indication of the significant housing inequality, grounded in the generous welfare housing provision. As a ballpark figure, the urban population accounted for 30 percent of the national total by 2003, which marked the deadline for welfare housing.

Urban dwellers without a permanent job with *danwei* and adequate seniority were omitted from this once-in-a-lifetime property distribution. As for the rural households, they were endowed with allocated plots of farmland and house land, thereby being assured of their basic living needs, but their land is collectively village-owned, and all too often only the local village and Party heads possess power over land disposal (illegal as this may be). Only in the event of urban expansion will the rural land located at the urban periphery become monetized. For remote villagers, their land has no market value and they are lost in this epochal translation of state assets into personal endowments. Until the mid-2010s, only a minority of China's households (say 20 percent) were fortunate enough to enjoy the privilege of purchasing welfare housing and the subsequent multiplication of wealth. Using the framework of property rights, this minority transformed their mere right to use to encompass the right to disposal; this made a huge difference to life chances.

THE "BRACKETED" SUPERIORITY OF SOCIALISM

This epochal property distribution was massive in scale and created huge windfalls for many millions of families. Yet, these nonetheless meant that only a "large minority" of the nation's population was given an opportunity to share in the national wealth; hence Mr Lei's sarcastic reference to the "superiority" of socialism. Lei's leverage strategy of cashing in his welfare housing units to expand his investment portfolio, financed by bank mortgages and rental income, multiplied his wealth further from the property assets' phenomenal capital appreciation. Housing privatization has separated the citizenry into perpetually economically differentiated groupings and induced a general lack of trust. This can be illustrated by comparing two drivers who earn a similar income. Ah Fu inherited two apartment units, from his parents and parents-in-law, respectively, which had originally been acquired via welfare housing. By contrast, Ah Tong, originally from a rural area, had been driving a taxi for ten years. On his and his wife's meager income alone, they would never have been able to buy their own apartment. In Chongqing, I came across several taxi drivers who own two or three apartment units through welfare housing allocation from their previous jobs or their parents. The key lies in the tricky process of welfare housing reallocations, embedded in the larger institutional context, rather than income disparity, individual competence, or personal choice, as welfare housing metamorphosed into the springboard for property investment by the lucky, large minority. When asked how he compares with other Chongqingers, Ah Tong said,

> Of course, this is unfair, but what can you do? I don't know whose responsibility it is; maybe only my own incompetence is to blame. I keep working hard. I believe that, if someone works very hard but still can't earn enough to fill his stomach and have a roof over his head, he can only become a robber, and this society does not have any meaning.

In 2011, the municipal government initiated a large-scale public rental housing project to accommodate two million people. The scheme contained a purchase option for tenants to acquire their apartment after five years at 70 percent of the then market price, but with the restriction that householders can only sell them back to the government at the original price plus the financing costs. The scheme's targets were peasant workers, new college graduates, and residents with a small per capita living space. The initial response was mixed, because most housing estates are situated in the suburbs, with inadequate transport and community services. The rent is RMB11/m^2, including the management fee; for example, an 80m^2 unit for a household of three costs RMB900, not much lower than the private market rents. I visited a couple of these estates; from my own reckoning, the layout looked acceptable but, inside the buildings, the renovations are crude. Interestingly, many of the tenants were young; most of them applied with their parents, but some lived alone. Overall, the majority was quite content with their situation and would not consider buying their rental unit after five years, considering the inferior quality and the stipulation that they cannot benefit from property price increases. One fresh graduate, Mr. Jiang, told me that his application for public rental housing is "a show of support for the government policy." He still had rural household status and did not intend to change it; after all, an urban status no longer endows people with any particular benefit. Another tenant, Ms. Fang, in her early twenties, was a freelance snooker coach, earning around RMB3,000 per month. She applied for the unit with her retired father, who had managed to obtain a fake employment certificate to support their application. She estimated that, in her former secondary school class, only 60 percent were allocated government welfare housing, but she did not think much about inequality, because "that issue has existed for a long time." She probably would not buy her apartment, because she preferred to have her own property rights, though she was unsure whether she could eventually afford this. Jessie, an Internet portal editor, came from a rural area and now lived alone on the estate. She said that the high property prices were attributable to the high land cost, pushed up by the government:

> For a couple earning less than 10,000 RENMINBI, it would take more than five or ten years to afford just the minimum down payment. Then, to pay for the mortgage, it is difficult to raise a child; and they must not lose their job, while their parents had better not fall ill. By squeezing the surplus from land sales, the municipal government is overdrafting the future, and I haven't a clue what will happen to this city in the future.

Another interviewee put it even more vividly: "The first and second generations are prospering at the expense of the third and fourth; like grabbing the money of future generations for your own pocket and then going round giving charity to them." This contrast between the propertied and the propertyless, attributable primarily to the single factor of welfare housing, informs a kind of systemic "original sin" of the neo-socialist state distribution of property, magnified after a decade of skyrocketing property prices. However, whether they are the fortunate ones or not, a deep sense of salience regarding property ownership has become inherent in people's mind-set when considering how to organize their life and their future. The repercussion of this historically engendered inequality will be felt over the generations, with no recourse for rectification. As sociologist Xueguang Zhou (2004) puts it, initial endowments of resources have a lasting effect on social positions because private property rights stabilize and reinforce the relative opportunities of various groups based on their pre-existing social and economic resources. Original sin cannot be cleansed, only ignored and forgotten. This systemic inequality also fosters an endemic "atmosphere of distrust," the antithesis to cementing social solidarity and a new morality that intertwines the tripartite relationship between the party-state, family, and housing.

THE NEO-SOCIALIST PERSON AND THE NEO-SOCIALIST STATE

The new appetite of the Chinese people for risk and reflexivity, in the domains of both housing investment and resistance against demolition, represents a new ethos of rationality, risk-taking, and self-responsibility. Bill Maurer and Gabriele Schwab note that, in the global age of accelerating possession, there is a pervasive expansion and transformation of property, accompanied by concomitant changes in the "self-as-proprietor and the self-as-investor," wherein social and cultural identities, subjectivities, and cosmologies of personhood are deeply affected (2006, 9). With China's momentous privatizations and integration with the world capitalist economy, this observation could not be more appropriate in the contextualizing and reading of Chinese neo-socialist personhood.

Some recent ethnographies on China offer lucid expositions of the new urban subjectivities that manifest themselves as a new scheme of virtue which fosters particular forms of self-conduct and visions of the good life in a "neoliberal world" (Ong 2006, 22). Lisa Hoffman (2010) holds that a focus on subject formation allows us to understand how neoliberalism and socialism may intersect. For instance, Nanlai Cao (2010) delves into the dynamics of the wealthy, moralizing Christians who seek to assert their identity and elite status; Li Zhang (2010) envisages a pathway of consumption practice to new middle-class membership based on distinction and exclusivity; while Carolyn Hsu (2007) discovers a unique ideology of human capital that collectively shapes the moral discourse to support market socialism. However, while a "neoliberal" descriptor is convenient and common in characterizing China (Pieke 2009, 7), such a fashionable academic term is often contradictory in its usage (Kipnis 2007, 388) and does not actually shed much light on the otherwise intriguing elucidation by these anthropologists. On the contrary, I reckon that these new subjectivities are indeed not shaped randomly or freely but are being co-transformed with the party-state, and thus can more appropriately be coined "neo-socialist subjects." The party-state continues to maintain its firm grip on many aspects of politics, the judiciary, media, communications, culture, education, finance, and investment; hence, there is no such thing as an innocent birth of a neo-socialist subject out of thin air. In each and every circumstance of the new subject's adventurous journey, the socio-political landscape of the people-state relationality must be duly located and explored.

From the micro perspective, the situation resembles to a certain extent that of Japan, overwhelmed by the financial and corporate reforms in the 1990s. Although China and Japan differ significantly in terms of their ideological and economic underpinnings, a similar sense of helplessness and anxiety confronted ordinary people with the advent of capitalist rationality and fierce market competition, after decades of job security and stable family routines. As Miyazaki (2013) notes, individuals were urged to calculate their own worth, imagined as a social, personal component of the wider neoliberal economic reforms. Taking pains not to reify neoliberalism as an overarching trope and convenient explanatory tool (Kipnis 2007) or a "coherent project" (Mains 2012, 6), however, I call this new ethos an ethics in transformation at the intersection between "classic" socialism and neoliberalism, to define what a neo-socialist person may look like. In relation to understanding and defining a neo-socialist state, Zhou (2004) reckons that, to understand the social stratification under state socialism, one must place squarely the role of the state and its redistributive institutions at the center of any theoretical explanation. Similarly, Katherine Verdery (1991) pinpoints that the central imperative of Marxist socialism is to maximize the bureaucracy's allocative capacity and power by monopolizing all goods and services. The result was a mass-scale, centralized redistribution regime, but the caveat is that it actually failed to maximize the resources available for allocation—thus the mundane occurrences of long queues on the streets, backdoor lobbying and bribes, hoardings and black market activities. For instance, Caroline Humphrey (2002) describes the "Russian queue" as a social principle, one that regulated social entitlements in time, while Yunxiang Yan (1996) notes that the redistributive nature of the socialist economy has led to the instrumentalization of gift-giving from villagers to cadres in Chinese rural life. One may be intrigued but unsurprised by Patrice Ladwig's (2008) discovery of the Lao socialist state's interest even to appropriate the economy of Buddhist merit as an allocative power to create new socialist subjects.

In socialist China, the state's all-embracing allocative power was not restricted to the material base, but included those who has access to higher education, what cultural goods were allowed to be created, in which academic areas intellectuals were permitted to conduct research, where people were allocated to work and reside, whom to love, hate, and marry, and how many children to have, etc., all of which were dictated by the Party machinery in various ways. The state redistributive economy represented a total relationality, encompassing the economic, social, political, and familial domains, while the centralized state also monopolized the resources for social mobilization, thus denying the legitimacy of organized interests outside its control (Zhou 2004). The redistributed goods and services also represented a total gift. In reciprocating, "the social body must repay by making itself available to be reshaped and put into order by a new mode of power" (Yang: 1989, 35), thus resembling an "atmosphere of the gift" as exposited by Marcel Mauss, where "obligation and liberty intermingle" ([1950] 1990, 65).

In post-reform China, certain crucial elements of the previous redistribution function have not disintegrated, as discussed in reference to the real estate market in chapter 4. Moreover, just as Arthur Kleinman et al. visualized, the new Chinese "enterprising self" continues to be under the restraining power of the state, although it "speaks the language of neoliberalism more often than that of Marxism and Maoism" (2011, 4). Admittedly, in the private sphere, the party-state's totalizing hegemony has diminished substantively but, as political scientist Shaoguang Wang (1995) observes, the state still hopes to shape people's leisure patterns in order to channel their excessive energies into activities that it believes are proper. Moreover, the state's setting of interest rates and executive directives on bank lending limits continue to subject corporate investments crucially to its regulation. Private enterprises' loan requests are constantly shunned by the state banks, giving rise to a burgeoning gray market. Credit, after all, is the most precious resource all over the world in the regime of financial capitalism. In the natural resources, telecom, transport, banking, and insurance sectors, the party-state has retained its formidable status as the largest shareholder of strategic enterprises and upheld the nomenclatural system, wielding personnel control concomitantly over the bureaucratic system and corporate world.

It follows that even the bundle of rights approach may not be able to dissect this complex and multifaceted situation satisfactorily. I echo sociologist Liu Xin's (2009) emphasis on the importance of understanding the relationship between state power and property rights that reveals multi-dimensional bases of stratification. Zhou Xueguang (2005) even argues that, in such contexts, where property rights are often blurred, ambiguous, symbolic, and constantly under renegotiation, property rights as a "bundle of relationships" is more robust in analyzing the stable and sustainable co-participation and co-ownership between the enterprises and local governments. Indeed, unlike other ex-communist states, Deng Xiaoping's reform recapacitated the economic agents and instituted a peculiar symbiotic party-market relationship: the Party claims political legitimacy for championing a high-flying economy, while the impetus of the socialist market economy is predicated on proactive statism. Perhaps no other sector could illustrate this relationship better than real estate. Transactions of land use rights remain state-monopolized, and property sales prices and even sales methods are subject to the local authority's scrutiny; yet the efficacy of the reforms is solidly reflected in the vast housing supply, incentivized by the rigorous pursuit of corporate profits and the high dependency of the local government budget on property-related transactions and taxes. The at times incoherent policy objectives between the central and local states in the real estate sector are a genuine reflection of the divided power of such an allocative monopoly. In summary, the defining socialist redistributive function has undergone massive adjustment but is definitely far from being taken over by the market's integrative role. In housing, specifically, we are witnessing a metamorphosis of the state-market relationship with its pertaining logic at once marking a continuity of the old socialist regime and a radical transformation with far-reaching ramifications regarding what constitute a neo-socialist state and a neo-socialist person.

In describing Ulan-Ude's experience a decade into post-socialism, Humphrey (2007) notes that privatizing housing is not an attractive option in situations of poverty and uncertainty. In China, the housing reform was rushed through so rapidly and thoroughly that many urbanites were not even able to reflect on the implications before it was completed. Then, as property prices soared, the lucky ones suddenly witnessed an explosion in their nominal wealth. Because of their strong vested interests, the propertied urbanites are likely to support the state's efforts to maintain a stable property market. This propertied class may still lament the Party's corruption, or this or that shortcoming, but are unlikely to challenge the legitimacy of neo-socialist governance. These beneficiaries of social inequality know all too well that it was sheer luck that they were born in a city and allocated a job with a state work unit, with an advantage over many others in the present and next generations. Knowing that their own offspring will be unable to afford to buy living quarters, many propertied parents are self-reflexive in preparing to bequeath a property to their children or finance their children's purchase. As such, we are witnessing a paradox of partial distributive equality for the urban minority, but systemic inequality for the populace at large. Market institutions have reduced older forms of social inequality, but the historical and institutional legacies of the socialist era persist and continue to determine the life chances of individuals (Ren 2013). Thus, rooted in the neo-socialist state's allocative injustice, the inequitable ownership structure is being perpetuated across the generations.

PARENTAL GIFT AND FAMILY VALUE

In most cities around the world, parental property gifts among the middle income class are uncommon. Instead, low-income families would count on their children to excel at school, secure a good job, and then support their parents in purchasing their first property. Parental housing gifts cannot be conceived as uniquely Chinese; what is striking is their sheer commonality. I am amazed at the high ratio of urban household double property ownership, and how Chinese parents devote their life savings to finance property purchases for their children or consider property compensation for their children as a crucial factor in hard bargaining against demolition. In a sense, this puzzle inspires an inquiry into the role of gifts in a commodity economy. It is obvious that the one-off urban property allocation was instrumental in making phenomenal differences to the housing arrangements in China, so that even many low-income urban households are now blessed with property ownership. The rural households in the suburbs, affected by the rapid urban expansion, also represent a second-tier beneficiary with cash compensation to buy private housing in the townships. The ensuing, three-decade economic boom, coinciding with hitherto unseen global monetary easing, has further underpinned a material base that heralds a huge sociocultural swing. Chinese parents now see housing as an indispensable part of their care for their children, having themselves endured the hardship of poverty and the insanity of selfless sacrifice in the propertyless, utopian, revolutionary era.

During my field work in 2011, China Central Television reported a story about the youngest ever doctoral student in China. Yang, who started university at ten, had just embarked on a doctorate in Beijing at sixteen. Coming from a low-income family, Yang thought he must become a "man of the men" and could not engage in love affairs unless he had obtained urban household status and owned an apartment, so he pressed his parents to purchase a property in Beijing, threatening them that he would not pursue his doctorate otherwise. He told the reporter:[2]

> It's more proper to say that my parents are forcing themselves to fulfil an unrealistic dream. My own dream is basically an inheritance of theirs. [Reporter: So you feel that you don't need to be responsible for your living?] From the very beginning, it was "you" who wanted me to stay in Beijing, so "you" ought to strive to achieve that goal.

Yang has been a media focus because of his academic excellence, but his situation actually reflects a broader social phenomenon; that is, somewhat abusive parental care for every facet of the daily life of the younger generation, born under the one-child policy imposed on the urban population since 1979.[3] Where parents are not endowed with welfare housing, but channel all of their savings into supporting their children's property purchases, this could translate into a critical latent social problem, given the minimal social security and high dependency ratio. As the first generation of single children are starting to have their own children, an inevitable, violent reversion of state-imposed collective values back to the traditional ones is unfolding, but the future trajectory is hardly comprehensible. In an extreme case, a couple, both second-generation, single children, by 2030, might be caring for twelve parents/grandparents.[4] The following comment was made by a thirty-year-old property agent about the phenomenon of pervasive parental care and property ownership:

> It's related to our traditional culture. People think that only after they get property rights will they feel at ease. They're tired because of the socialist past; but they don't want their children to be tired. If you've a daughter, you'd want your future son-in-law at least to have his own property. There's a joke that mothers-in-law now control China's property prices. You may say that love is a splendid, pure thing, but this is simply impractical. Many Chongqingers buy property with the help of their parents. Like me, when my wife became pregnant, both my parents and parents-in-law gave us a sizable amount of money.

Fifty-year-old active property investor, Mr. Cha (discussed in chapters 4 and 5) originally from a rural area, spoke succinctly about the meaning of property rights. I asked how the concept of property ownership has become so prevalent, bearing in mind the long vacuum from the 1950s through to the 1980s. He replied:

> I've put some thought into this question, too. The key is the concept of the family for five thousand years in Chinese culture. Like a cultural gene, it can't be altered easily. The Cultural Revolution was merely a brief blunder in the

> long river of history. The desire to own a home is an embedded family concept, but to make sacrifices for one's children is not necessarily related to the property rights concept. Rather, it's driven by the one-child policy; parents are obliged to take care of the livelihood and education of their offspring.

Traditional thinking about filial piety entails the obligation of children to take care of their aging parents but, as the social safety net is being dismantled, the burden of providing support for elderly dependents will fall to a generation that consists primarily of single children (Fong 2006). For the low-income parents who use their life savings to support their children's property purchases and the evictees who bargain for additional property for their children, heavy material and emotional reciprocities are likely, though none of my evictee informants ever spelt out this concern or expectation yet. In the case of affluent urban dwellers who possess several property assets, parental gifts are not likely to be reciprocated in material form. This is an example of what Graeber (2001) calls "open" reciprocity, which implies a relation of permanent mutual commitment, with an alienable gift being employed to reaffirm and reinforce an inalienable relationality.

I raised the question of "what parental investors expect from their children" with many parental investors and members of the younger generation; interestingly, the majority of the informants from both generations stated that they rarely thought about it. Most parents would say that they just do their best to alleviate the hardship of their children due to the fierce competition in the real world, considering it their duty as a mother or father, without linking it explicitly with an expectation of reciprocal care in their old age from their children. When asked whether they are caring too much for their adult children, which may prohibit them from maturing into independence, many parents would say, roughly: "This is the reality, if we don't take care of them, they can't handle the hardships of life; I'm merely fulfilling my parental duty." Mr. Cha stated that his wife once questioned whether they should do so much for their adult son, but since his son was not a brilliant student, Cha considered that buying him an apartment was the best he could do to support him, but he has never considered whether his son would thereby take good care of him in the future. Ms. Chen, also discussed in chapter 4, recently closed her shop to spend more time with her son who was turning seven; she said that she would respect her son's will and support him no matter what, but would not expect him to repay her in any way, sentimentally or materially. Another mother in her late forties said that young people these days have no idea what they want to do; she took care of every detail of her postgraduate student daughter's daily life, and said that she would not expect her daughter to take care of her in her old age.

Amy, a fresh graduate working for a real estate company, had just purchased an apartment with her mother's support with the down payment. She said that filial piety was a concept she had learned about at an early age but that has little substantive sense of it, because her parents never discussed or hinted at what they expected from her; she felt that perhaps all would be done "naturally." Ms. Qian (in her early thirties), her husband, and their one-year-old daughter lived with her parents in their duplex apartment. She said that her parents had given her great freedom concerning her studies and career, and she had never thought about what they would want from her, until lately when she became a mother herself and thought she should be more sensitive to her aging parents' wishes. Thus, curiously, we are witnessing apparent lopsided obligations between filial piety and parental duty. Yet, the subjects themselves appear unaware of anything unusual; rather, the givers and the takers alike take the "arrangement" for granted as a natural manifestation of the totality of family relationships and obligations. Strathern (2006) suggests that kin groups could be defined by the interest they have in their members' reproductive capacity, as they "own" persons through the perpetuation of the identity that the person carries for them. In this sense, the parent-offspring relationship carries a most intimate, perpetual relationality of identity, with a highly intricate, inseverable, and even transcendental tie of reciprocity; hence the puzzle and inquiry of who the givers and takers are become irrelevant. Nonetheless, Graeber attributes to parental gifts an "ambiguous" form, as they are simultaneously *not* an act of pure self-interest but responsible for most of society's fundamental inequalities (2001, 211). In contemporary China, most such property transfers take place at an earlier point in the parents' life cycle, which should have far-reaching implications for both social inequalities and the burden of social dependency, an unintended consequence of parental love and gifts.

The relationship between property and marriage has also become contested, in response to the government's intensified curbs on property speculation. By early 2013, a government plan to charge a 20 percent capital gain tax on second-home ownership had led to couples with multiple properties to their names hastening to divorce in order to become singletons with one property each and to remarry after disposing of it. Some other couples divorce for the exact opposite reason: to buy an additional property, with the first property being nominally assigned to one party to get around the purchase restriction.[5] In considering this bizarre divorce mania, a government office in Shanghai displayed the following warning sign: "The property market contains risk; divorcing couples ought to exercise caution." However, while this latest divorce craze may be merely tactical and fictitious, in reality, the Chinese divorce rate is soaring, from a mere 0.85 (number of divorces per 1,000 married population) in 1979 to 2.62 by 2007 (Wang and Zhou 2010, 258). In light of the as many as two and half million couples who divorce each year, the Supreme People's Court of China's August 12, 2011 judiciary interpretation of the "Marriage Law" reflects a genuine concern and has a fundamental bearing on marital property. It directs that a house bought by parents for a newlywed offspring would be the latter's sole property unless otherwise specified, and that the person who made the down payment for the marital home shall own it, meaning that divorced couples no longer have the right to an equal share of their home as part of their pooled assets.

This interpretation has also sparked debates on the fundamental meaning of the Marriage Law, and marriage per se. As the interpretation is commonly perceived as unfair to females, I took the opportunity to obtain feedback on this from a dozen or so female Chongqingers. Unexpectedly, more than half of the interviewees, particularly the better educated ones, considered it fair, as they did not feel that women should take advantage of pre-marital gifts from their parents-in-law. While a few protested that unfaithful husbands would find it easier to divorce their wife, most regarded China as a gender-equal society. Still, on the online forum, there was heated discussion about whether married couples should add the name of their spouse to the property certificate. While most people would not dispute the fairness of equally dividing the marriage property acquired after marriage, it is controversial whether gifted and pre-acquired property should be shared. To benefit from the anticipated tide of registration, the local tax bureaus in the cities of Nanjing and Quanzhou announced a 3 percent surcharge on intra-family property transfer. It was explained that such a rule always existed but now, with the clarification, adding the spouse's name to the property certificate constituted a clear case of post ante gift-giving or transaction. Understandably, this sparked a strong public response. Then, on August 31, 2011, the State Administration of Taxation announced an exemption from deed tax. This U-turn revealed the problematic rationale behind the new interpretation of the law. According to the "Marriage Law," Clause 17, the husband or wife's property, inclusive of inheritance and gifts, unless otherwise specified in the contract, should be deemed to have become pooled after marriage, and hence there does not exist a situation whereby property ownership is transferred or gifted.

Now it has emerged that the different decisions on whether to charge deed tax are based on contradictory executive and judiciary interpretations of the "Marriage Law." The tax authorities were inclined toward the conventional understanding of what marriage means with regard to the concept of pooled assets, whereas the Supreme Court, ironically, pays more regard to the issue of property rights from the perspective of legal clarity and social reality. The controversy over what this law entails arguably reflects a deep sense of social insecurity and moral ambivalence. Stretched to the limit, the controversy recalls the relevance of the dowry system whereby, ideally and conceptually, parental gifts are given for the bride's keeping, benefit, and disposal, continuing to be identified as the property that a woman receives from her kin rather than being merged with that of her husband. A rudimentary, albeit gender-neutral, form of dowry appears to be resurfacing, as housing gifted for newlyweds need not be conceived as a conjugal asset and is suggestive of the emphasis of kinship over affinity. Some Chongqingers informed me that parents now feel less hesitant than previously with regard to giving property to their son or daughter for fear of their eventual divorce. This new mode of parental marital gift arrangement, strangely, seems to be congruent with the ancient practices, in which, according to historian Bettine Birge (2002), property was regarded as being attached to a woman for centuries BCE until until the Yüan Dynasty's (1271–1368) radical transformation of marriage and property law brought about the patriarchal Chinese society with which we are familiar. Thus it may be tempting to connect the latest changes to the image of an emancipated woman in the heyday before Yüan. The caveat is that these modern dowries are gender-neutral and a double-edged sword, as women (particularly the less well-off) may be deprived of their share in the conjugal property. Ruby Watson (1991) remarks that marriage is closely bound up with the world of property relations and economic inequality; for the present case, the possibility regarding gender equality is wide but hardly predicable at this stage.[6]

VALUES: RECONFIGURING THE MEANING OF PROPERTY

The image of a "parent state" has been invoked by Verdery (1996) under an implicit view of society as a family, headed by a wise Party that makes all of the family's allocative decisions under state socialism. She also reckons that socialist property instituted an entirely new set of values, based on an ideological opposition between socialism and capitalism. In neo-socialist China, in contrast, real parents have largely replaced the parent state's historic role, once material resources had been partially repossessed by urban households via the state's epochal property redistribution. In their mundane acts of investing for property possession or counter-demolition against property dispossession, Chinese urbanites are inadvertently embracing (or being forced to embrace) a new economic ethos. The primacy of private property rights has swept the country, inducing a new understanding and definition of personal and family well-being, against the backdrop of the market economy and substantive withdrawal of state welfare provision. Animating the new practices is an implicit value, prioritized through parental care, replacing sacrifices for the common good and collective entitlement to the state's redistributions of resources. During the high socialist period, values were ideologically determined for both commodities and human beings' worth. Now, in a time of mixed market-economy and party-state power, a new frame of value proposition is unfolding.

Paul Eiss and David Pedersen say that the *value* of value as a theoretical concept rests in its capacity to transcend oppositions of "choosing between focusing on social relations or objects, the makeup of persons or of politics, systems of meaning or patterns of action" (2002, 283). Thus, for my topical focus of housing property, the notion of value could be employed to analyze and explain the hitherto unseen euphoria of property purchases and investments, encompassing both the meaning of material possession in the familial relationship and the emergent social relations pertaining to the counter-demolition and investment practices. Marx is conventionally viewed as prioritizing the locus of production over exchange as the principal source of commodity value and domain of critical analysis, although he was certainly aware that the fetishization of commodities is only made possible through a series of market exchanges. Thus, in the context of my research concerning neo-socialist property regime change, it is imperative to note how value is related to the intertwining arenas of production and exchange, without losing sight of how a dominant capitalist value proposition is contextualized and paradoxically engendered by a Communist ideology. In contrast, drawing on the thesis that value arises from exchange and is largely an effect of individual desire, Arjun Appadurai (1986) advocates breaking with the production-dominated Marxian view of the commodity to focus on the total trajectory from production, through exchange/distribution, to consumption. In this perspective, exchange plays a crucial role in the valuation and the determination of subjectivity. Indeed, we are reminded that, since the 1980s, the World Market has become the most gigantic, totalizing, and all-encompassing universal system of evaluation (Graeber 2001) and, today, one cannot imagine a definition of use-value that "could be given even partially independent of exchange-value" (Negri 1999, 81). Conceived at its extreme, this totalizing market system subordinates everything, from property to relationships, to a single standard of value as *price*. In China, the property market and spiraling housing prices have engendered a new value proposition that is incidental to welfare reform and the supremacy of private property rights. Against the odds of surging property prices, the capability of owning a house for marriage and gifting a property to children has become almost a universal yardstick for well-being and the value of hope.

At this juncture, it is legitimate to ask from where exactly does the multiplying value of housing property in the form of market prices arise in the context of socialist regime change, and where and when is work often still perceived as the main source of economic and sociological value. For land property, specifically, in the classical thinking, private ownership is justified in terms of the work invested in land and the improvements thereby accomplished (Hann 1998); while, in the post-socialist setting, in rural Bulgaria, for instance, it is also work that determines an individual's sense of rights over ownership, both of the land and of the products created from it (Kaneff

2002). What then about housing that the owner holds *passively* for self-occupation; what is the specificity of its labor content? Engels ([1872] 1979) once stated that he would not call such an owner-occupier worker a "capitalist," although he is also no longer a "proletarian." He argued that the worker's "rent-free" situation will lead to the reduced cost of production of labor power and ultimately result in a corresponding drop in wages; in this way, the savings and investments of the worker become capital, but for the capitalist employing him. In reality, we know that the wages of Chinese workers never fall in tandem with the surge in property prices, nominally. Chinese workers' average wages have certainly failed to match the rising property prices so, before long, this real asset price inflation may filter through to housing rentals and cause a relative decline in wages to rental costs, and hence a decline in wages in real terms. However, it is definitely not the capitalist employing the worker who has "stolen" the capital as purported; rather, it is the property owner who sees his capital inflated by the worker's contributive savings and investment. Another critical difference is that, when a worker owns more than one apartment, s/he becomes at once a proletarian and a capitalist, such is the change and difference over 150 years, conceptually speaking. Thus, conceivably, none of the "work" rationales explain housing property's price spirals—only the logic of exchange value/price. One must study exchange, not production, to comprehend the particularity of property ownership in a world of financial capitalism and perpetual flows of credit. Just as Jane Guyer indicates, "An anthropology of value that fails to address prices is unsatisfactory" (2009, 219).

Still, such an analysis addresses only the macro level of value production that is incidental to a particular historical and systemic context. My ethnographic materials clearly point to a deeper familial, more holistic notion of the relationality between parental investors and demolition bargainers vis-à-vis the state. My ethnographic investors and bargainers alike take the reality of the absurd runaway property prices as a given in evaluating and reordering their options and preferences, then strategizing their behavior accordingly. In a sense, to "theorize" value is to recapture the moral principles embodied in the practices and preferences of all societies. For the present case, it is particularly important to relate the new economic ethos pertaining to the property regime change to the re-emergent centrality of the family amid the party-state's engendering of individual responsibility yet insistence on the socialist project of "common prosperity." Commonly, the idea of value may encompass notions and criteria as wide-ranging as success, wealth, prestige, purity, respect, love, obedience, and loyalty. In everyday life, intuitively, some of us may believe that happiness and harmony are more important than power and profit. But, in the reality of China, most would acknowledge the harsh fact that happiness is contingent upon making profit and money, while the party-state's everyday propaganda on a "harmonious society" is meaningful only if the Party retains its absolute power. Hence I share Verdery's (1999) cautions on the "fuzziness" of property in the postsocialist context because of the complex overlapping rights, obligations, and claims that emerge from the past socialist property relations; and her call for understanding postsocialist property by focusing on meanings, relations, and powers remains resoundingly valid. *Value*, for ordinary Chinese people, is not a mere matter of individual definition, hope, or choice, but a practice conditioned by certain systemic prerequisites and inequalities, and acted out in accordance with the official rules.

In Chongqing, as in every Chinese city, there is a peculiar "circulation of value" (Graeber 2001, 81). The whole saga started with the massive but discriminatory state redistribution of housing assets to a fortunate minority of urbanites, followed by a decade-long housing boom that turned real estate into a formidably valuable commodity, then culminating in the domestic arena producing the pervasive phenomenon of parental property gifting across the economic strata, animated by the resurrection of the family value that itself is groomed by the state's autocratic one-child policy. The caring *parent state* has given a gift to a certain socialist child, who then becomes a caring *parent* and gives a property gift to his/her biological child via the commodity market or through demolition bargaining. In the course of twenty years, the past socialist value of centralized allocation and redistribution first gives rise to a dominant commodity value, which in turn transforms into a renewed family value that is observable everywhere. In terms of reciprocity and relationality, the people's absolute obligation to the party-state has mutated into an impersonalized commodity economy, with new forms of parental gifts and conjugal property relationships. It is suggestive that there is a conflation of desires at work for property owning and family relationships that animate the production and circulation of new forms of value. Moreover, one may claim that global financial capitalism and the market economy are sweeping away every facet of society, subordinating the old socialist and family values to the margin of pure market logic. However, my ethnographic study points to a multiple dimension of *values*, which is simultaneously shifting and transforming. With regard to the redistributive effects on the changing Chinese welfare system, political scientist Jane Duckett (2011) also sees clear ideological underpinnings of the state that reflect particular political values, preferences, and interests; while, in the contested realm of housing demolition, historian Qin Shao discovers that protesters are utilizing the different regimes of value afforded by the "hybrid nature of Chinese society" (2013, 278). My own reading follows a similar vision of screening and employing multiple values in both the state and private arenas.

In their ordinary seeking of and contest for well-being, meanings, and values, Chongqingers make their decisions regarding housing investment and counter-demolition based on a desire or need for a short-term yet critical transaction. Their pursuits do not end there; instead, their meaning of life is intimately tied to their family and children, as evidenced by their reasoning and practices. In this regard, insights could be drawn from Jonathan Parry and Maurice Bloch's (1989) formulation of the divide between a short-term, impersonal transactional order/cycle and a long-term one that gives rise to the reproduction of the moral values of society. They premise that, if that which is obtained in the short-term individualistic cycle is converted to serve the reproduction of the long-term cycle, then it becomes morally positive; but if the short-term cycle becomes an end in itself, then it would evoke the strongest social censure. For the present case, are we witnessing a triumph of values of the transactional order of individualistic behavior over any long term, collective moral order in present-day Chinese society? Thus far, ethnographic materials point to such a possibility but are hardly conclusive, in consideration of the dual emphasis and reemphasis of transactional and family values in barely two decades of their emergent development. Parental investment is indeed immensely more profound than a mere self-centered, individualistic act. The crucial question is, whether profound parental love would develop and transform into broader concerns and a general system of social value and morality. Noticeably, the notion and practice of private housing property rights have been engendered and imposed by the government, I am thus curious about whether the party-state may intentionally or inadvertently desire to turn a partial and truncated rights discourse and practice into the co-construction of a neo-socialist moral imperative. However, so far, the masses are largely unconvinced that pervasive private property rights would become an enabling factor for the party-state's grand objective of "common prosperity." It is true that many demolition bargainers and investing citizens embrace the idea of property rights, but few would believe that such an endeavor is leading to a fairer, more just society. Hence, more importantly, one should first clarify how the distinction and contrast between the two moral orders represent a meaningful theoretical question for the case of China.

A new doctrine of "core socialist values" was advocated at the Communist Party of China's 18th National Congress in November 2012, which are said to be the soul of the Chinese nation and serve as a guide to building socialism with Chinese characteristics. The list comprises a set of twenty-four moral principles that encompass the three realms of the state (prosperity, democracy, civility, and harmony), society (freedom, equality, justice, and the rule of law), and citizenship (patriotism, dedication, integrity, and friendship). Thereafter, the doctrine evolved into a national campaign, with President Xi Jinping urging the comprehensive implementation of these values and to "make them all pervasive, like the air."[7] However, having witnessed in history how the Party's indoctrination and mobilization of the people to sacrifice themselves unreservedly for the collective good of society had inflicted widespread calamities, a presumption of the *existence of an achievable collective order of goodness* is exceedingly dubious, no matter how exhaustive and impressive the list of values appears to be (indeed, it is just too good to be true for any society, not just China). Empirically speaking, even if such a collective order may not be a complete illusion, it is far from obvious that it must be superior to a so-called short-term, transactional order of morality, given the calamitous disjuncture between historical hard facts and the purported socialist ideal and value. Moreover, it is crucial to understand and distinguish whether such a conceived long-term, collective order of social values is indeed being constituted and represented by the official or vernacular versions of the moral discourse, or both, as the two do not necessarily converge ultimately. At this point, it is only fair to note that the possible courses of evolvement of the emergent state-property-family tripartite relationality remain wide open, and should have formidable implications and bearing for my ultimate question of whether a universal, coherent rights-based ethics may emerge and proliferate, which forms the topic of the next chapter.

NOTES

1. According to Martin Whyte and William Parish (1984), striking structural elements of the Chinese model of urbanism compared to the eastern European countries are: strict rural-urban migration controls; a penetrating residential work unit organizational system; a highly developed bureaucratic allocation system; a relatively egalitarian distribution system; stress on citizen involvement in public health and social control; and rigid taboos on all forms of dress, expression, ritual life, and communication that did not conform to the official ideology. Through the 1970s, most urban residents grew up expecting to rely on the state for housing, income, a pension, education, and medical care. One consequence of socialism has been to increase, rather than reduce, the rural-urban gap.

2. For a transcript of the TV interview, see www.sina.com.cn (2011).

3. In her critical review of the one-child policy, Susan Greenhalgh sees it as a problematic and deeply sanitized one, reflecting "supremacy of scientistic and technicistic values" at the expense of execrable human costs (2008, 343).

4. In recognition of the social repercussions, since 2007 most provincial governments had adopted a relaxed policy of allowing couples to have two children if both parents were only children themselves. Then, in late 2013, the Central Government further degreed that, in future, families will be allowed two children if one parent is an only child (*Xinhua News* 2013b).

5. See *The Economist* (2013), *Yazhou Zhoukan* (2013), and www.news.cn (Zhang Zhanpeng 2013).

6. Bettine Birge (2002) states that the prominence of dowries, land rights, and gradations of status all place ancient Chinese society firmly within Jack Goody's (1973) model of sedentary Eurasian society. In noting the concurrent trends in declining dowries proper and the rising divorce rate in "advanced" countries, Goody (1998) argues for a return to the earlier notions of endowment, with its distinct advantage of treating property acquired before marriage and by inheritance as belonging to the spouse in question. In contrast, Duran Bell (2008a) categorizes dowries elementarily as consumption goods that are not wealth-related; based on this interpretation, our case and Goody's ethical vision about dowries returning to the bride's side in case of separation may be criticized. Bell also notes the crucial difference between a dowry received

by the domestic unit and one that is the possession of the bride, which is exactly the controversy surrounding the present judicial interpretation and spirit of the "Marriage Law."

7. See *Xinhua News* (2014a).

Chapter Seven

The Real Life of Rights

A Detour from Needs and Desires to Interests

> "Evictees seldom mention human rights or property rights in their resistance; they just want more compensation. Property Rights Law means very little in my work. Does it contain a stipulation about the amount of compensation? No. Does it contain a stipulation about whether houses can be demolished? No." —
> Mr. Liu, a lawyer specializing in demolition compensation

Mr. Liu's law firm specialized in representing evictees to defend their interests in government demolitions. His small office was situated in a run-down building downtown. Having been a lawyer for twenty years, Liu has been involved in the urban demolition field for a long time. He noted that, after administrative eviction was abolished in 2011, more evictees became eager to bargain for better compensation terms and there are even professional nail householders who help evictees to cause trouble. Still, his legal practice was not very lucrative, Liu reckoned, as cases can drag on for a long time and sometimes the firm cannot collect the arrears from its clients, even long after the case has been settled. Moreover, siding with evictees against the demolition authorities carries its own risks, and so Liu must walk a tightrope.

Liu said that, in his routine work, he most frequently depended on "Administrative Procedure Law" to contest the authorities' demolition malpractices, instead of construing cases as breaches of property rights as nebulously prescribed in the "Property Rights Law." He explained that this was because the local regulations in Chongqing were meticulous, so he could exploit this by picking up on noncompliance with the stipulated procedures. He stated that house demolition was principally a matter of the government's priority policy, so whenever conflict arises between the laws and policies, the former must yield. Typically, the government and courts ignore the evictees' petitions for intervention and settlement. Evictees seldom unite to protect themselves; some may have agreed to do so, but are easily divided after being offered a small favor by the demolition company. When evictees engage Liu's services, he brings up the case in court, accusing the demolition convener of, for example, improper procedures and documentation in obtaining demolition approval, the improper certification of extra-legal building structures that were constructed a long time ago, the failure to observe the strict requirements of prior notification, or threatening and brutal behavior. If the court accepts the case, then lawyers have the official capacity to become involved and the government officials must come forward to respond to the interrogation. "We just keep looking for loopholes and minor mistakes in order to irritate the officials and press for compensation," said Liu. In the end, he maintained, the most important thing is to secure an effective platform for evictees to enter into a dialogue with the officials:

> The Chinese don't have a concrete concept of rights; just pay me more money and I'll go away. Thus, for evictees, their interests are their rights. Evictees never insist on fighting for resettlement where they originally lived. Forced eviction remains just a matter of procedure, even though now only judiciary demolition is allowed. There's no such thing as an inalienable private property like that in the West.

Thus, Liu expressed an inconvenient truth: a fight against the government as a matter of principle, based on rights, will prove fruitless or, at most, ineffective. Policy prevails over principle, and picking up on the perpetrator's wrong practices prevails over a plaintiff's discourse of rights. For evictees or lawyers, the efficacy of defending property rights arises not from defending these rights per se but from exposing the alleged "un-rights" of the counterparty. When a right is not always legally recognized and enforceable, its meaning becomes fuzzy and its efficacy to defend one's interests becomes subdued. On the contrary, evictees' genuine interests are represented by the bargaining and optimization of compensation rather than the affirmation of an abstract right. This implies that only when one's interests are ascertained are one's rights in place, and explains the statement that "their interests are their rights." This also means that rights are grounded in interests, rather than vice versa. As Liu succinctly puts it, evictees' interests in the end do become a proxy for rights, albeit in a fuzzy sense, but rights as a legal category rather than a normative principle do not perform much of a function in protecting interests effectively. Thus the verdict about who is right or wrong is more important than rights per se and the situation is similar to a modality of rights which James Holston says depends on being right, and is "a moral condition of correctness" (2008, 255). In the case of China, it is always the local cadres who dictate what is right, often in the name of the public interest. After all, right and rights are not the same thing, and conflating "being right" with "having rights embedded in interests" risks undermining the principle of rights.

In any case, Liu's observation was consistent with our previous discussion and provided a reality check on how the discourse of rights is ingrained in an important domain of everyday life. In chapter 3, I discuss a practice of demolition in which the agents maneuvered on the margins of power but never intentionally challenged the representation of that power. Instead, they tacitly followed certain rules of the game to effectuate their claims, variously based on a notion of needs or desires. These situations were categorically less an agency of power organized around the axis of domination-resistance than a kind of "agency of projects," as conceptualized by Sherry Ortner (2006), in which people seek to accomplish valued goals within a framework of their categories of value. Evictees' agency was a form of intention, as the enactment of a one-off though formidable project of property possession. They may narrate a sense of rights that justified their rationale but rarely became a matter of principle that perpetuated their resistance. A similar situation prevailed in the case of desire-based, owners' rights defense (chapter 5), wherein the participants contested with the developers within a frame of rules and procedures but, when they sensed that they might risk touching the government's bottom line of maintaining harmony, they quickly backed off from their once "vocally" determined position. Owners essentially were contesting for their interests in the name of rights, but were engaged more in a project of limited resistance than a challenge of power based on a principle of rights. In summary, rights are variously deployed by demolition bargainers and investing citizens alike more as a tactical weapon than a genuinely endorsed and employed ethical principle.

Hence, we must refrain from presuming that the formation of property rights necessarily translates into the broader concept of social, economic, and political rights. I agree with political scientist Elizabeth Perry's (2008) caution against assuming that the invocation of rights in China bears a close affinity to Anglo-American conceptions of human rights and civil society. Instead, in addressing whether a principle and culture of rights can become ingrained, we need to know how evictees' and owners' value(s) are situated between their own family perimeter and the broader cultural and political context of a neo-socialist property regime. This objective is the focus of the present chapter. To achieve this aim, I need to solve the ambiguity of legality, the puzzle of power and rights, and the ambivalence regarding navigating disparate values in the realms of property transactions and the official discourse. I also discuss certain key aspects of Confucianism for their imputed and latent cultural bearings on the Chinese people's conceiving of moral values, as well as their re-deployment by the party-state for reconstituting and promoting a new social ethos. My invocation of Confucianism, however, is not to reify its content and determinacy, or due to common acknowledgments of its impact that have emerged during field work or by the party-state. Rather, I take it as an exemplary cultural model and latent cultural resource with a presumed or potentially implicit influence on the routine practices of the Chinese, both historically and contemporarily. Nonetheless, when President Xi Jinping stressed that the implementation of the "socialist core values" must be based on traditional Chinese culture, which he labeled "the root of the values," one wonders what he could possibly mean if Confucianism is not a principal constitutive element of traditional Chinese culture.[1] Perhaps a crucial difference is that, while the central government is "redeploying" Confucianism strategically albeit implicitly, the ordinary people are not invoking this ideology consciously in their everyday life, notwithstanding their noticeable re-embracing of the centrality of family value.

THE LEGALITY OF RIGHTS VERSUS THE MORALITY OF BEING RIGHT

At Gaoshan demolition site, there was a photocopied sheet in circulation among the nail householders, purported to have been issued in 2006 by the Municipal Bureau of Land Resources and Housing Administration. Nicknamed "Document No. 91," this paper called for the "resolute rectification of the problem of the infringement of residents' interests in the course of urban housing demolition and relocation" (see Figure 7.1). It stated that all building structures constructed after December 2001 should be deemed private property and be compensated according to their market value. Moreover, to confirm the construction date, property owners should solicit the signatures of at least three long-term residents of the neighborhood. If this document was authentic, then evictees at large should have a substantive base for their claim to extra-legal property, but the stipulations appeared too good to be true, for they contravened every irregularity that I have discussed thus far.

Tracking down its source, I found that the paper had been first given to sixty-year-old Ms. Wu (featured in chapter 3), who was camping on the demolition site to protest against the forced demolition of her home, by a friend's relative, who was said to work at the bureau. Since her own bungalow had been built after 2001, Wu presumed that she did not fit the requirement. The paper was then circulated to other nail householders, of whom Ms. Li, the young woman who had tried to slash her wrists in order to avoid forced eviction, confronted the demolition company with it, but was accused of forgery and told that the "original" "Document No. 91" did not contain the clause about compensation for pre-2001 structures. The caveat is, if that critical clause (of seventy words) is missing, then the "original" document (of four hundred words) becomes truncated and incomprehensible in its content and objective, even if it does indeed exist. Upon further inquiry, Wu admitted she did not know the real identity of her friend's relative. Still, other nail householders, like Mr. Gu and Ms. Lin, were adamant that the paper was authentic but did not follow its guidelines. "I don't need three neighbors to certify me, for everybody can see that my bungalow was built a long time ago," said Mr. Gu. As for Ms. Lin, she seemed slightly perplexed when asked why she had not used it to protect her interests, though she also insisted that it was not fake. I checked the bureau's website and Internet sources but could find nothing about "Document No. 91." I then asked a couple of informed sources, but the paper's "existence" was categorically denied. Indeed, the photocopied sheet was not written in the format of a normal government document. At the beginning, it stated that it is based on the "Decree of the State Council (No. 256)," Clause 22, Item 1.3, issued October 27, 2001, but, on the back was written "December 27, 1998"; a trivial mistake, but one that would not have occurred in an official document. Also, regarding "Degree No. 256," as actually issued by the State Council, the content is unrelated to the demolition of illegal constructions and it does not contain a sub-item 1.3.

Nonetheless, I do not intend to pass judgment on the paper's authenticity or whether "Document No. 91" ever existed; suffice it to say that evictees habitually employed "documental" materials as resources to back their claims. As I see it, however, evictees did not take this paper seriously as a legal weapon, though many of them continued to keep it safe in a carefully guarded little bag hidden at home. Was this because these people did not actually believe in its authenticity or because they knew that these regula-

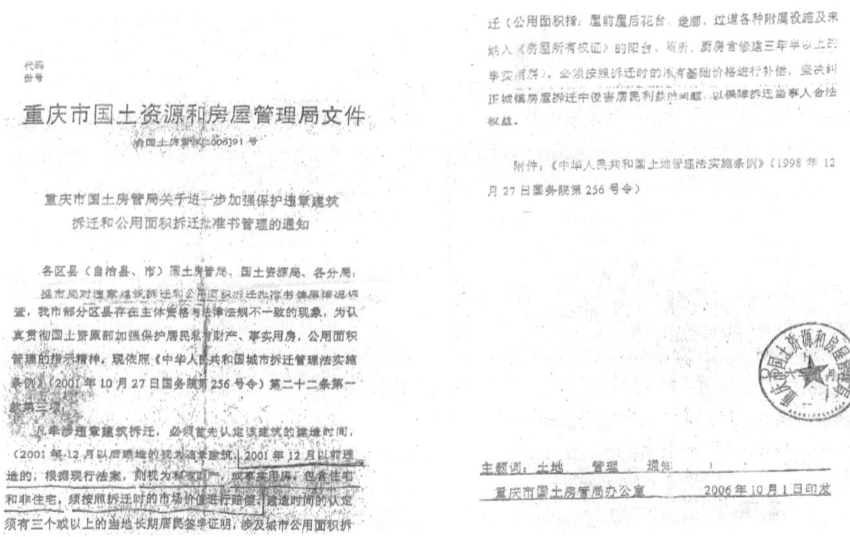

代码
份号

重庆市国土资源和房屋管理局文件

渝国土房管发[2006]91号

重庆市国土房管局关于进一步加强保护违章建筑拆迁和公用面积拆迁批准书管理的通知

各区县（自治县、市）国土房管局、国土资源局、各分局：

据市局对违章建筑拆迁和公用面积拆迁批准书使用情况调查，我市部分区县存在主体资格与法律法规不一致的现象，为认真贯彻国土资源部加强保护居民私有财产、事实用房，公用面积管理的指示精神，现依照《中华人民共和国城市拆迁管理法实施条例》（2001年10月27日国务院第256号令）第二十二条第一款第三项，

凡牵涉违章建筑拆迁，必须首先认定该建筑的建造时间，（2001年12月以后建造的视为违章建筑，2001年12月以前建造的，根据现行法案，则视为私有财产，或事实用房，包含住宅和非住宅，须按照拆迁时的市场价值进行赔偿。建造时间的认定须有三个或以上的当地长期居民签字证明，涉及城市公用面积拆迁（公用面积指：屋前屋后花台、走廊、过道各种附属设施及未纳入《房屋所有权证》的阳台、厕所、厨房合修建三年半以上的事实用房）。必须按照拆迁时的原有基础价格进行补偿，坚决纠正城镇房屋拆迁中侵害居民利益的问题，以保障拆迁当事人合法权益。

附件：《中华人民共和国土地管理法实施条例》（1998年12月27日国务院第256号令）

主题词：土地 管理 通知

重庆市国土房管局办公室 2006年10月1日印发

Figure 7.1. "Document No. 91." This photo was taken by the author.

tions were unenforceable, having witnessed the case of Ms. Li? This apparent ambiguity of legality seems counter-intuitive as, in many other places in the world, which laws and regulations exist is easily verifiable, while in China, the evictees always complained that the demolition personnel withhold the full accounts of the relevant, up-to-date rules and regulations. Even when the evictees agreed to the terms of their resettlement, they were not given a copy of the detailed agreement, nor allowed to share the details of their compensation with their neighbors. The evictees resorted to their own ways of accessing the facts and keeping certain "believed facts," in the form of photocopied regulations, newspaper cuttings, reinterpretations of officials' speeches, or hearsay about compensation cases. These facts then became truths and beliefs. At Gaoshan, what was truly legal or legally true was hardly an easily apparent fact, but rather remained opaque and ambiguous.

In the course of my contact with evictees, many of them said that they keep various kinds of government regulations, notifications, press reports, and tax receipts in a safe place due to a fear of them being seized. Some of them showed me piles of papers to illustrate cases of inequitable treatment. This habit of documentation resonates with historian Qin Shao's (2013) account of housing demolition in Shanghai, as she discovered many protesting evictees had produced an impressive body of materials documenting their own experience of resistance. But these appeared to be of little use as, after her eight years of research, most of the cases remained unsettled. It is perhaps natural for people involved in disputes to collect as many materials as possible as supporting evidence but, in the context of China, the meaning of the legal approach is hardly obvious. On the one hand, people consider that they have to "discover" the policies and regulations themselves, instead of them being straightforwardly accessible to the public; even the authenticity of a "paper" is never incontestable or unambiguous. On the other hand, ironically, the evictees themselves knew all too well that judicial procedures rarely led to fair, not to mention favorable, outcomes. They seldom resorted to legal means, but constantly lamented that the courts, the government, and the developers "breathe through the same nostril." The majority of the Chongqing evictees do not have access to legal advice, not to mention the "luxury" of support from human rights lawyers or transnational NGOs. In such a situation, their embodiment of a particular regime of legality has a unique bearing on their trust in the official discourse and instrument of rights, and hence the indigenization of a purported culture of rights (or indeed, a counter-culture of rights).

Annelise Riles (2006) reckons that "practices of documentation" are ubiquitous features of late modern life and that documents are paradigmatic artifacts of ethnographic research. The meaning of such practices in the demolition field perhaps lies in how truth(s) are discursively produced and how evictees maintain their commitment to the routines of their resistance. Evictees, after all, are like ethnographers in taking documents as artifacts of evidence to prove a point, as a "paradigm of interpretation" (Riles 2006, 6). Hence, I wish to suggest that evictees' documented "papers" should be taken principally, if not only, as discursive and moral resources to substantiate the righteousness of the contestants' cause, though their efficacy is hardly evident. For evictees, proving themselves right is the prelude to substantiating their rights for, in the end, it is not the legal means but their embodied petitioning which are simultaneously the last resort and the more common approach to protect their interests, by begging or forcing officials to change their mind. Katherine Verdery (2004) states that "legality" simply did not have the legitimating function in the socialist property system that it has in market democracies. In China, rights are not a purely legal concept, but always fuzzy and slippery, subject to officials' sanctions in reference to altering political sentiments on whether the tightened or relaxed social control should be enforced or tolerated. It also reflects the Party hierarchy's alternating views regarding how far the people's interests can be encroached on without jeopardizing the Party's power and legitimacy.

ACCOUNTABILITY AS A RITUAL OF DE-POLITICIZATION

In chapter 3, I describe how evictees followed all of the guidelines and procedures in which they did not actually have any confidence, such as the selection of a property appraiser, receiving demolition personnel, and participating in public hearings. I state that there exists "following rules and procedure without followers" to indicate a situation wherein the agents enacted a practice but not genuinely, for even the demolition personnel knew that much of what went on was a mere formality. Many informants, including the demolition personnel, evictees, college professors, and businessmen, instead asked why I was surprised by this at all, for "formality" was a common practice of everyday life. The phrase *zouguochang* (to do something perfunctorily) is often used to describe this commonality of mere formality, whereas *jiaodai* (accountability) is frequently invoked to explain why the government agents must devote such great efforts to conducting acts of formality. Before I discuss the significance of *jiaodai* in relation to the question of rights, let me first describe two cases of *zouguochang* that are drawn from my ethnographic data.

The first case is a demolition public hearing that was held in January 2012 although, as it turned out, I was the only member of the "public" present, apart from representatives from the housing bureau, the demolition convener, the demolition company, and evictees. After the hearing, an administrative verdict was to be passed, followed by an application for a judicial eviction; evictees could then request another public hearing to be convened by the court officials. The meeting was chaired by a middle-aged man from the bureau, with a female assistant sitting beside him. He started by stating the purpose of the hearing was twofold: to ensure that the demolition work was conducted lawfully and to provide a platform for both sides to communicate. A staff member from the demolition company then read aloud the details of the case: the household was a family of three who resided in a 64.8m^2 apartment unit, who were demanding compensation in the form of a one-bedroom unit and a two-bedroom unit without payment out of pocket. He stated that, based on the valuation appraisal and compensation guidelines, it had proved impossible to reach terms that were agreeable to both parties. In response, Mr. and Mrs. Kim stated that they were unaware of the laws and regulations as cited by the demolition company and could not understand why their requests were unacceptable. Rather, because both householders were unemployed, with Mr. Kim disabled by a workplace accident, they should not be required to pay out of pocket. Mr. Kim said, with emotion, "I earned my wages with blood and sweat. Money I've not, life—I have one you can take!" The Kims also asked why, out of three hundred evictees, only they had been summoned to the public hearing, stating that this was unfair, unjust, and non-transparent. The demolition personnel explained that every household is in a unique situation, and family hardship is only one of the factors considered. After fifty minutes, the chair summarized the meeting as follows:

> Both sides' reasons are very normal. The demolition work so far has been conducted legally, because the proposed compensation apartment is larger than your dwelling's unit area. As regards family hardship, both sides should continue to engage with each other in friendly communication and mutual understanding, in order to reach a solution.

The chair's summary confirmed the legality of the procedure. Noticeably, property rights were not mentioned during the hearing. Rather, the key deliberations of the evictees were hardship, need, and fairness, which were not the core considerations of the demolition practices. Throughout the proceedings, the note-taker seldom wrote anything down in her notebook, as if nothing appeared noteworthy. Outside the meeting room, Mrs. Kim spoke to the demolition personnel in an undertone, pleading with them to say a few good words for them. The evictees actually knew where and what was most appropriate to effectuate their demands. Director Hu from the sub-district office, who had been involved in demolition work for a decade, confided in me that he had never heard of a public hearing that resulted in a different verdict from the original one. However, despite the public hearing's inconsequentiality, both sides must follow the procedure. Why? "Because only after this step can we proceed to the next step," explained Hu, philosophically yet somewhat illogically. Why, then, did the evictees participate if it was meaningless? "Because they can't oppose the Party's rules and procedures," Hu added.

Hu's allusion to power, implicit in the formality and proceedings, is also reflected in my second case, the assembly between protesting owners and the developer of Hillside Garden (see chapter 5). After a two-hour, vociferous, emotional exchange, the meeting came to an abrupt end. The presiding officer from the sub-district government concluded that the incident was a civil and commercial dispute, meaning that it had nothing to do with public interest. Half an hour later, Boss Zheng of Hillside Garden's developer and several owners' representatives were seen sitting down for amicable talks. There was a sharp contrast between the owners' earlier rhetoric and their real-life pragmatics, post-confrontation. I chatted with Mr. Cha, an active property investor, who appeared very relaxed.

> Ho: I'm not quite sure I understand what's going on. Just now, you were challenging the company strongly. How is it that, an hour later, you and the management are chatting like a bunch of old buddies, so calmly and happily?
>
> Cha: When the officials were here, the *kaifashang* (developer) had to do everything to rid itself of any charge of wrongdoing. Once they left, Boss Zheng indicated that he was willing to make major alterations, so we are pleased to talk.
>
> Ho: So you mean it's like a stage performance—just a show?
>
> Cha (smile): The hardline negotiation is a necessary procedure for arousing feelings and demonstrating our solidarity. All of these hard words and strong gestures are only a prelude to the real, eventual bargaining.

Manager Wang from Hillside Garden's developer later confided in me that the head of the district government had visited them twice. Before the assembly, officials from various district bureaus and the developers' management had gathered at the district office to agree how to handle the case. The officials' presence at the subsequent assembly with the owners was a display of their authority as the final adjudicators of an otherwise purely commercial dispute. Despite the pre-eminence of the market economy, the public office's power remains critically and ubiquitously present in the realm of commerce. Repeatedly in this book, I suggest that a distinctive mark of China's neo-socialist governance is the non-existence of a disembedded economy, notwithstanding the cultivation and boom of a prima facie autonomous market. On the face of it, even apparently purely economic matters like property selling and disputes between developers and owners could be politicized to involve the interference of officials. Yet, it is politicization that is precisely what the Party is striving to crack down on in the first instance. In China, the party-state's status quo is unchallengeable, with no such thing as residual power being inhabited by a civil society. We talk about market power, and certainly the maturing of the market economy has allowed far greater autonomy for people at large but, in the end, commercial decisions and the market per se are subject to the pre-emption of political power. Nonetheless, in routine, everyday socioeconomic life, conflicts of interest must be seen as being resolved by agreements (not confrontations) by following a set of finely posited procedures (instead of extroverted disseminations of dissent or public protest), which is precisely a process of de-politicization.

In a nutshell, politicization is a privileged, guarded domain, invoked only when the Party deems it absolutely necessary, as in the purge of Secretary Bo Xilai, whose anti-crime campaign and pro-revolutionary rhetoric were discredited as being politically incorrect. The notion of "accountability" (*jiaodai*) in this context means that the officials must abide by certain procedures and formalities in order to "account to" their superiors for their Party discipline and commitment to "smoothing things out." There is another level of meaning in accountability, which is accounting "down" to the masses, which is more like "owing someone an explanation" or making a public statement. As the cadres' power comes from above, not the populace, there is no direct political accountability vis-à-vis the masses, but they need to "exhibit" their adherence to the rules and putative impartiality for the public to see, which is distinctively "moral" in essence, albeit not purely a gestural and meaningless performance. Nonetheless, accountability supposedly means a genuine dedication for the good of the people, but in actual practice it has become pervasively and imperatively a codified rule, a mere formality. In calling it a formality, I do not mean that every procedure is completely inconsequential with regard to the final outcome. Yet, this tendency toward de-politicization constitutes a disguised collective endeavor to exhibit a mode of morality and abiding, to perpetuate a particular social order sanctioned by the Party. It functions more like a ritual, not markedly dissimilar from the extensive forms of symbolic rebellion that Max Gluckman (1954) discovered in African egalitarian tribes. The accusations and screams that I recorded are analogous with the symbolic hatred and attacks in the African rituals, but it is through them that people express their unbridled excess, while remaining bound by the established social order and political discipline. The protesters in my ethnographic cases suddenly became amicable after the "ritual"; their willing participation was to show themselves as good citizens despite all the differences in interest and position. If we argue that African tribal ritual forms do not exist in complex societies because individuals under pressure have more scope for escape, then in China the only alternative to the ritual of formality is to make repeated petitions to the higher authorities to air grievances which, ironically, represents an even higher but more precarious level of formality, as petitions rarely produce a substantive result.

Having said that, the formality of the aforementioned meetings and petitions reflects the protesters' inherent contradiction and ambivalence in their concomitant distrust of the Party apparatus and submissive resistance to the Party power mechanism. Shao (2013) similarly observes that Chinese protesters play by the rules to secure their rights, for the alternatives of operating outside the system are either unavailable or too risky. Be it ritual or formality, accountability is a distinctive form of de-politicization in an exceedingly political regime of governance. In contrast, political scientist Lily Tsai (2007) advocates a model of "informal accountability" in rural China that enhances good governance in the absence of formal institutions for the purpose of holding officials accountable. Tsai posits that in localities with encompassing and embedding solidary groups, citizens and officials are more likely to share a common set of ethical standards and moral obligations. In the urban context of my field site, on the contrary, it is exactly a lack of trust and moral authority that problematizes the "display" of accountability. Be it formal or informal, accountability becomes principally a formality with dubious efficacy.

CULTURAL MODEL AND PRACTICAL MORALITY

In chapter 6, I point out that the emerging tripartite state-property-family relationship has a formidable bearing on whether or not a rights-based ethics can germinate and proliferate. The key question is whether or not the so-called short-term transactional order, based on individual rights, becomes an end in itself or is converted into serving the long-term social reproduction of the moral values of society. Here, the defining characteristics of the short-term order are discussed in relation to the dimension of private property ownership through, variously, one-off state housing distribution, property investments, and counter-dispossession against house demolition. The aspiration to property ownership is incubated by complex socioeconomic factors and evolving value propositions of needs, desires, and rights. The moral imperative of short-term order is *individualized*, instead of collectivized, as evident in the counter-demolition bargaining and resistance, which is based on needs and desires (chapters 2 and 3), and *individualistic*, as understood in the new meaning of rights and risks (chapter 4) and as witnessed in an ephemeral, desire-driven rights defense by property owners (chapter 5). However, I also provide extensive accounts of how property rights are intricately related to the re-emphasis on family relations, as demonstrated by the pervasiveness of parental gift property across the economic strata (chapter 6).

The neo-socialist state's stringent one-child policy since 1979 and dramatic housing reform since 1988 have incidentally engendered an epochal change in this property-family relationship. We may conceive this as a resurrection of family values, but it is uncertain whether it is an outright revitalization or a re-synthesis in the making. But one thing is certain though: that is that the ubiquitous phenomenon of parental investing in China characteristically represents something profoundly more than simply an individualistic act and moral endeavor, which is *not* necessarily a selfish, short-term concern. At the same time, the party-state continues to preach about unceasingly treading the path of socialism. Ordinary people are largely cynical about this propaganda talk, but consider property ownership to be the critical route to material security and family well-being. The Party is not only resorting to the old political discourse for its neo-socialist project, but Confucianism has been "rediscovered" and reengaged as a cultural resource for promoting the state's primary objective of harmony, order, and conformity. In a sense, there is a matrix of moral deliberations simultaneously underlying and transcending the complex relationship between the short- and long-term orders. I argue that there is an immense moral ambivalence given rise by the incidental contestation of monetized value, state ideology, and family morality.

Since the 1990s, there has been a robust intellectual rejuvenation of Confucianism with a strong official endorsement (Bell 2008b; de Bary 1998a; Makeham 2008; *The Economist* 2007).[2] The campaign of building a "harmonious socialist society" for the promotion of values like honesty and unity is generally attributed to echo Confucian themes (Bell 2008b: 9). The government also provided funding to establish four hundred Confucius Institutes around the world to support local Chinese teaching internationally and facilitate cultural exchange.[3] Jennifer Hubbert (2014) describes Confucius Institutes as a constituent part of China's soft power efforts to communicate to the world that its cultural tradition stresses harmony and that its rise to power will be a peaceful and globally responsible process. Historian John Makeham (2008) meanwhile takes the view that the conscious promotion of Confucianism may be regarded as a cultural formation fundamental to the identity consciousness of the Chinese (*Zhonghua*) nation. This is in sharp contrast to the constant denunciation of Confucianism as an obstacle to progress and emancipation since the early twentieth century by left-wing intellectuals and the communists, epitomized in the 1966–1976 Cultural Revolution, wherein the values of idealism, humanism, and conservatism were renounced thoroughly in order to eradicate feudal cultural sins. Makeham remains reserved about the Confucian revival as a potent socio-political force, but I think that it at least reminds people of the once instrumental role of Confucianism in shaping social relationships and moral thoughts historically. Indeed, in my routine discussions with members of the younger generation in Chongqing and elsewhere in China, many of them tell me they have regarded filial piety, family loyalty and obligation, and fraternal duty as "important" since they were very young, though most would not relate them uniquely to Confucian thought. In contrast, concepts like rights, equality, and justice only entered people's awareness (but were not necessarily endorsed) much later.

On the contrary, having endured the deceiving socialist egalitarianism, many parents and grandparents would not even bother to teach their children about anything high-sounding. Sociologists Martin Whyte and William Parish (1984) find it remarkable that the basic elements of Chinese family life have changed so little after radical socialism and they suggest that the bureaucratic nature of Chinese socialist urbanism and its political turbulence may have helped to maintain strong family ties. Similarly, the traditional practice of rural gift exchange in cementing social relationship never ceased between the 1950s and 1980s; it merely underwent complex changes and multiple transformations (Yan 1996). While the notion of culture ought not to be deemed discrete, bounded, and homogenous, equally salient is the realization that social customs and family values, in their tidy or messy forms, cannot be easily and entirely eradicated from the social, familial, and religious arenas. It should be fair and prudent to argue or assume that certain remnants of Confucian thoughts concerning family values must have never ceased to nourish and uphold the fundamental social fabrics. Nonetheless, I admit that my evaluation in this chapter depends on the somewhat "speculative" premise that Confucianism does inform and influence contemporary Chinese society.

On January 12, 2011, people's political imaginations became exhausted when a 9.5-meter bronze statue of Confucius was erected at the entrance to the National Museum in Beijing just off the Tiananmen Square, opposite Chairman Mao's huge portrait that gazes out across the Forbidden City. No less intriguingly, one morning four months later, the statue mysteriously disappeared, having been removed under cover of darkness.[4] The installation and subsequent removal of the iconic statue reflect the ideological debate within the Party, I believe, on how far (*not* whether) Confucianism should be reinstated as the state ideology, along with Marxism. It is immensely ironic that, having once been deemed hideous, private property rights and Confucian values are now revived and redeployed rigorously by the Party to resuscitate the country, both economically and ideologically.

In the philosophy field, Tu Wei-Ming (1985) regards the primary Confucian concern as being to learn to become a good person, which entails a ceaseless process through which humanity is concretely realized, but the cultivation of the self crucially does *not* imply an isolated or isolable entity; rather, the self, in the Confucian sense, refers to a center of relationships, a communal quality. Roger Ames and Henry Rosemont (2011) likewise read early Confucianism as essentially a role ethics, as opposed to the Western virtue ethics, as it embodies a specific vision of human beings as relational persons constituted by the roles they live rather than as individual selves, as well as a specific vision of the moral life that takes family feeling as the entry point for developing a consummate moral competence and a religious sensibility grounded in this world.[5] Thus, Confucianism does not regard the becoming of the self as linear or cyclical, but ceaselessly transformative. Conceivably, Confucius' relational persons are comparable to Marilyn Strathern's (1988) conception of Papua New Guinean persons, who are understood to embody multiple webs of kinship relationships, the very thing that makes them persons. The Confucius persons are also not "outside" relationships, but their personhood is not "inside" or "dissolved" in relationships either. Rather, it is the persons' unceasing self-cultivation and transformation within concentric orders of relationships that make them persons; the self exists as ontologically distinct from the very relationship configuration fostered by the self. It is difficult to locate the Confucian persons on an individual/dividual dichotomy; rather, they resemble more a "dialogical self," a term used by Karl Smith (2012, 57) to denote an orientation to the world around us, an expression of what we believe it is good to do and to be. Mayfair Yang thus makes a legitimate point when she questions, if the persons in the Melanesian and Chinese gift economies are not self-sufficient and autonomous individuals in the first place, then how it can be said that they must be made to lose their rights and serve the demands of society (1994, 298). Hence, I do not mean to reject the meaningfulness of a discussion of rights for the Chinese; rather, it is the "naturalness" of rights which must first be problematized, given that a Chinese "relational self" is in a process of constant and ceaseless transformation.

If I were asked to describe Confucianism in a few words in relation to my research themes, I would say *deeds over needs, rites over rights*, while noting also the doctrine's emphasis on hierarchy, authority, and obedience. Deeds and rites are interrelated. On the one hand, people are expected to strive to behave properly in accordance with a set of codes, even to the point of suppressing their own interests, needs, and desires. Ames and Rosemont (2011) regard the central aim of Confucius' Analects as being to guide his students toward achieving the goal of becoming exemplary persons by way of embodying consummate conduct and behaving with propriety in all of their actions, while Tu (1985) states that human beings are moral because they cannot be circumscribed merely by the instinctual demands for survival or by the necessities and needs for the solidarity of the group. On the other hand, rites are the moral fabric of society that places a premium on the ideal of social and political harmonization. And according to legal scholar Randall Peerenboom (1998), rites are intended to provide the necessary common ground and shared values to make a harmonious society possible; also, rites-based claims are moral claims, contrasting fundamentally with the defining features of rights as legally enforceable. In contrast, the contemporary rights claim, never mind the historical and philosophical root, is a principle-based ethics. Disturbingly, Ames and Rosemont point out that role ethics, such as Confucianism, abjures any appeal to universals, for it "at once respects bottomless particularity and the indeterminacy such particularity entails, and at the same time allows for the development of a more robust sense of regulative ideals that do not require the excesses of first philosophy" (2011, 35). Tu (1998) likewise pinpoints that the Confucian perception of human self-development can be envisioned in terms of a series of outward bounding concentric water circles: self, family, community, society, nation, world, and cosmos; and warns that a creatively transforming selfhood must be predicated on our ability to overcome selfishness and egoism. Following this line of interpretation, it is precisely the malleable particularity and indeterminacy implicit in Confucian influence that may hinder principle-based ethical values and legally enforceable practices such as rights.

Of course, there are indeed many strands and variants of Confucianism and an enormous amount of literature on reinterpretations of it; what is indeed *the* ideal cultural model is constantly contested and debated, not to mention the historical infusions of power and politics into the molding of how such a model should appear.[6] Moreover, while philosophical and theoretical abstractions are illuminative and inspiring, it is quite difficult to prove precise associations and causalities between cultural factors and actual practices.[7] In the real world, only certain elements of cultural traditions and principles are internalized in disparate practices and heterogeneous relationships. Cultural models facilitate our understanding of the ordinary Papua New Guinean or Chinese individuals, *not* vice versa, to demonstrate the cohesiveness of an impeccable intellectual construct of exemplary persons. In this regard, I am concerned with the actual harnessing of ethical principles as endorsed in its concrete social manifestations, possibly informed and influenced by a delineated, idealized cultural model to a (mere) certain degree. Nonetheless, the notion of a contextual and particularistic ethics has been invoked by anthropologists to elucidate and analyze ordinary people's ethical life under state socialism. For instance, Yang (1994) says that at a time when revolutionary idealism seems to have lost its captivating power and when weariness with the universalistic ethics has set in, there will be a retreat to "relational ethics," which start with particular and concrete dyadic relations of family and kin and radiate outward to all types of interpersonal relationships. And in his analysis of the extraordinary extortion cases brought against Good Samaritans in China, Yunxiang Yan (2009a) concludes that the cultivation of social trust between strangers who are still deeply embedded in particularistic and contextual morality poses an immediate challenge in the context of a highly competitive market economy and increasingly risky society. Indeed, Fei Xiaotong ([1947] 1992) has long ago applied the metaphor of concentric ripples to explain the selfish routine behavior of the Chinese:

the self is at the center of the ripples, and each relationship contour entails a different and specific mode of moral order and proper behavior. In his reckoning, sacrificing the lineage for one's household or the society for one's village is "in reality a formula," making it impossible to prove that someone is acting selfishly. The private-public boundary is elastic and ambivalent, and social morality makes sense only in terms of particularized relationship. He states that the Chinese cultivate a moral character by exercising self-restraint, but as I see it, this effort becomes elusive in the outer social space in the absence of an ethical order that transcends differential relationships. In the intersection of fading Maoist and emerging neo-socialist moralities, this self-restraint becomes an even more daunting challenge.

Since Fei Xiaotong's work first appeared, China has been subjected to three decades of Maoist radicalism and three decades of counteracting market economism. A reality check is imperative in order to understand how social morality has actually been transformed. In his ethnography on the private lives of business elites in Chengdu, John Osburg (2013) notes that Fei's characterization of Chinese society still clearly captures the contending and shifting ethical spheres of the networks of entrepreneurs, government officials, and gangsters that underlie real estate development in the mid-2000s. And during the course of my field work, on October 13, 2011, a two-year-old girl, Yue Yue, was run over by two vans consecutively, in the city of Foshan, Guangdong. Neither driver was pulled over; but this horrific scene was captured by a security camera and broadcast on local TV. All told, the media counted eighteen passersby, until a fifty-eight-year-old beggar-woman pulled the child to the roadside. The woman pleaded with the nearby shopkeepers to help but was told it was none of her business.[8] This incident sparked national outrage; within days, Sina Weibo had attracted 4.4 million comments. Yue Yue's father told reporters that he wanted to ask the drivers, "What did your parents and teachers teach you? Is making money all that matters?" The Party Secretary of Guangdong, Wang Yang, appealed to the public to "look at the ugliness in ourselves with a dagger of conscience." I was particularly disturbed by the sight of a young mother who hurried past, gripping the hand of her small daughter. While many parents are utterly dedicated to their own children, selfless parental love does not necessarily translate into a wider empathy for others. The Yue Yue fiasco was obviously a rare case, but not necessarily an isolated one. In recent years, assisting the victims of traffic accidents or other emergencies has become controversial. In attempts to cover costly medical expenses, some senior citizens, who have been injured in accidents that were their own fault, have turned against those who helped them at the scene by suing the Good Samaritans for compensation (see Yan 2009a). In the famous 2006 civil lawsuit case in Nanjing against Peng Yu, the judge intriguingly proclaimed Peng's altruistic acts as having excessively contravened "socially accepted common sense" and fined him RMB45,876.[9] The judge's presumed common sense is disquieting, but perhaps a genuine reflection of the socially accepted moral intuition. Another notable example took place in August 2012, when a young man jumped into a river at Loudi, Hunan Province, to save a family of three who were drowning. After helping the family members reach the riverbank, the man became trapped in the water himself but, when bystanders urged the family to help him in turn, they simply walked away, saying it was none of their business as the man drowned.[10] I certainly do not intend to depict a one-sided moral landscape based on a few high profile cases. There are many instances of heroic self-sacrifice, for instance, the hundreds of volunteers who rushed to offer assistance following the 2008 Sichuan earthquake, most of whom were in the twenties. And based on workplace surveys conducted between 1983 and 2000, William Jankowiak (2004) discovered a transformation in Chinese urbanites' social awareness, with an expansive empathy and increased awareness of human rights. However, I wonder whether the findings may also be attributable to the "talking versus doing paradox," whereby questionnaire respondents would be inclined to say nice things to researchers, without necessarily reflecting on what they actually think and what they routinely behave in the real world. Moreover, people may become more inclined to participate in philanthropic activity but, aside from momentary bursts of empathy, ambivalent morality remains a dilemma in everyday life. Yan (2009a) also observes that the new generation of young people, who work in the market economy with increased interaction with strangers, tend to hold more universalistic moral values; but the market-driven modernization project also brings in ideology of individualism that posts new threats to many forms of sociality and collective morality. My own reading is that the critical question lies on whether an individualized (not necessarily individualistic) rights discourse and practice may contradict or harness a collective order of morality and a universalistic concept of rights. And I think that it is in this context that the Party has advocated the doctrine of "socialist core values" in late 2012 to rebuild faith amid concerns that the world's second-largest economy has lost its moral compass during its three-decade economic miracle.

RECASTING RIGHTS VERSUS DUTIES

The contemporary human rights regime's rootedness originated from the Enlightenment ideal and the natural rights tradition, but whether we can trace its genealogy further back to the classical age is debatable. Historian Peter Garnsey (2007) sees that natural rights theory evolved out of natural law theory, which arose in antiquity and was still going strong in the early Enlightenment; however, while ancient Western societies were locked into a morality of duties and obligations rather than rights, modern rights theory is unequivocally rights-based. Hence, the essential difference lies in the degree of emphasis given to rights as distinct from duties. In comparison, Confucianism also attaches due emphasis to a person's relationality and duties: foremost to one's parents, then to the monarch, one's spouse, siblings, and friends. Many people believe that procreating to continue the family line and propagate the ancestors' honor is a person's utmost duty. Thus, any discussion of rights could not pre-empt axiomatic duties, which is also the point of departure between the Chinese and European cultural models, as there has not been similar, epochal transformation in China along the duties-rights axis to give birth to a rights-based morality. Moreover, to "implant" an element of rights into a duty-bound model demands enduring changes to habitual relations between the rights and duties in everyday practices, far more than a mere "leap of faith" (Hunt 2007, 32).

Ideal cultural models apart, in everyday life, rights of conduct (as opposed to epistemic rights) always pertain to obligations, duties, and responsibilities, constituting a correlative relationship. Positive rights enacted in laws, such as property ownership, marriage, education, and labor relations, typically delineate and define the rights and obligations of the beneficiaries (and their counterparts). A unilateral and rhetorical emphasis on rights could risk concealing the liabilities and uncertainties of property ownership in particular. Thus, when the state distributes welfare housing to urban householders, it is also relinquishing much of its obligation to provide affordable housing to all urban citizens from then on. And when investing citizens rely on bank loans to buy several properties, they have simultaneously secured property rights for hefty capital gains and incurred substantial repayment liabilities. As regards fundamental rights based on basic need claims (say, personal safety, childcare, and clean water), we probably presume that these rights are inalienable and universal, with the right holders not bearing any reciprocal or preconditioned obligation. In reality, this need and right must be first endorsed by society at large for its significance and accepted by the state as an agent to honor and ensure its applicability and provision; otherwise, who will bear the costs of securing such rights and the liabilities for failing to do so? That is to say, even rights which some consider as natural or belonging to persons by virtue of their humanity are not pre-relational or pre-institutional for their applicability and practical enforcement, not merely philosophical theses or normative beliefs. Political scientist Charles Beitz (2009) explains this point neatly when he says that there are indeed both the demand side and supply side of human rights; a right could be (believed and proclaimed to be) universal and yet the obligation to contribute to its satisfaction might not be grounded on considerations of humanity independently of people's social relations. Philosopher David Braybrooke (2005) maintains that an important condition for the efficacy of needs is whether at least a limited altruism exists wherein people are willing to put others' needs ahead of their own preferences and wants; but I would add that, even altruism per se implies mutuality, consent, and relationality, not an outright, primordial, and isolated obligation. Hence the defense of any forms of need-based rights must be predicated on moral consent or authority (if you believe in cosmic moral laws) and/or institutional exercises of power.

As discussed in chapter 3, my notion of "economics of rights interpretation" in neo-socialist China and Nancy Fraser's "politics of need interpretation" in welfare capitalism both pertain to bringing into view the contextual and contested character of need and right claims. Such a contest must be ultimately determined by shifting the consensual social morality or political discourse in a particular historical context. In the realm of property rights to land and housing, these rights cannot exist without a corresponding legal obligation by willing bearers; otherwise, the title holders' interests will be void. It follows that both morality and legality provide the foundation for a regime of rights to be upheld. Talking of absolute rights or duties as a mutually exclusive pair is simply untenable in practice, the critical difference being that rights-based ethics are more legal-bound while duties-based ethics are more moral-and-order-bound. For rights-based ethics grounded foremost in obligations and duties to emerge solidly in China, both realms of *morality* and *legality* are crucial.

Much of this book has been devoted precisely to demonstrating the perils of the enforceability of laws and rules for the substantiation of a rights ethos. On the contrary, in many cases, we see the predicament of the "personalization of rights," the exercise of which depends on the discretion, not the duty, of the officials to recognize the personal merit of the petitioner and grant access to the right (Holston 2008, 257). For instance, evictees either go to Beijing to beg officials for acknowledgment of their inferiority and unfair treatments or resort to *guanxi* with demolition personnel for favors. Be them junior officials or mere frontline personnel working on behalf of government agencies, many people seem to possess discretionary power in converting rights into privileges to obtain what is actually by law a right. Holston says a right creates a duty when it makes someone vulnerable to a claimant's legal powers and hence empowers the claimant; but when theses relations depend on personal interventions, discretion, and mediation, they become legally subverted. In Brazil, Holston says, rights become relations of privilege between some who act with an absence of duty to others, who, in turn, have no power to enforce claims. This disjuncture between right and duty is also prevalent in China, where the ambiguity of legality and dominance of power commonly negate the formation of a claimant's *powers as rights*.

The perils of equating rights to responsibilities in turn is reflected by Harri Englund (2006), who points out that although the two are interdependent, they are often obscured in the relations of power and structural inequalities, and thus not related in reciprocal fashion. This problematic reciprocity is exactly the issue at hand in China. The "Property Rights Law" clearly places private property rights and state property rights, and thus their mutual obligations, on an equal footing, but in reality this is entirely unenforceable, overwhelmed by local officials' discretionary power in the name of the public interest. For the nail householders, property rights are a particularized and elusive legal category imposed on them to deny their housing needs unilaterally. Hence, the issue of rights and duties cannot be resolved in the abstract; it is imperative to unravel the process of disempowerment that underlies the presumption of reciprocity. As long as the political always pre-empts the legal, power precedes rights in the reciprocal relationship between rights-bearers and their counterparties. The ambiguity of accountability compromises the efficacy of the judicial process in ascertaining the value of rights, in favor of political determinations of right and wrong based on whether the dispute may disrupt the state's prioritizing of harmony and stability. Evictees could petition Beijing in accordance with the rules; however, their fate is not determined by whether their proclaimed rights are justifiable, but by political decision regarding the political rightness of their behaviors of resistance. Disgruntled owners may accuse the property developer of damaging their legal interests, but the efficacy of their action was predetermined by officials in liaison with the developer. What is supposed to be a venue for rights dissemination often turns into a ritual for displaying the duty to abide by the rules, and for the attending cadres to exhibit their formality of accountability. In short, the legal domain is not exactly a protectorate of rights, though it sometimes acts in this way incidentally.

In the realm of morality, Confucianism may seem alien to the axiom of rights for its presumable spelling of authority and discipline, limiting of individual freedom, and strengthening of the state. However, the idea of empathy actually pervades all Confucian teachings; as Ames and Rosemont (2011) note, nothing is more defining of humanity for Confucius than the genuine concern of one human being for another.[11] Philosopher William de Bary (1998b) adds that embedded in Confucianism is a view of natural equality that is rooted in shared human sentiments of sympathy, shame, and respect. This view provides a linkage to some contemporary human rights scholars' views. For instance, Richard Rorty (1998) sees human malleability as a guarantee for attaining the Enlightenment utopia, preconditioned on security and sympathy, thereby re-grounding human rights without metaphysics and the rights culture as a "culture of emotions" (Barreto 2011, 94). At the personal level, reciprocity rests on how one's conceived rights and values are projected and propagated toward others outside one's immediate relationship circles. The promotion of social trust, and hence universal values, has become an urgent moral and social issue in China (Yan 2009b). This is a kind of demanding ethical judgment, which involves moral thinking and judgment. I agree with James Laidlaw (2002) that moral thinking is a matter of weighing obligations and deciding where one's duty lies and that moral judgment rests on whether one chooses, whatever one's desires or inclinations, to act in accordance with this duty. Thus understood, it is a taunting challenge to the Chinese society at large on how everyone would behave outside their immediate relationship web, and how they would balance their own interests, rights, needs, and desires with their endorsement of a duty for achieving common goods.

Noticeably there is no lack of expressions of empathy in Chinese society and in the idealized traditional cultural model. Communism per se is exemplary in engaging in discursive moral talk—the promise and virtue of a communist ideal, the Party members' selfless devotion to the people. Katherine Verdery (1991) says language and discourse are crucial vehicles through which the socialist leaders derive their social power from the control of the representations of reality but in China the Party's own encoded ethics have been largely ridiculed at will by the masses, in light of the rampant official corruption and entwined social inequalities. Against the backdrop of the sweeping economic reforms but unaltered socialist power politics, China has seen the nurturing of a convention of rumor, gossip, and selective secrecy, as well as the production of a citizenry who are skilled at reading between the lines. The state ideology is an alienated one, largely unintegrated into the populace's everyday practices. This situation constitutes a moral anti-climax, resulting in a culture of distrust that handicaps collective aspirations and may suffocate common empathy in people's everyday encounters. Agglomerated with the putative revival of concentric moral imaginaries and contextual relations ethics, as backed by ethnographic materials and anecdotal evidence frequently reported by the Chinese media, I argue that the possibility of the genuine acceptance of moral mutuality seems difficult to envisage. On the contrary, both the state-imposed social rules and self-cultivated moral codes are not being taken in their entirety and universality, but invariably formalized (for the cause of social harmony) and particularized (for the well-being of close family members). In short, under the joint enculturation of the (alienated) Communist and (putative) Confucian ideologies, it is unclear whether any universal ethical principles at all can emerge from a cultural system of ambivalent, even contested moral deliberations. Now, Confucianism is being resurrected with the Party's endorsement, ostensibly for the political purpose of locating conservative elements as a complementary ethos to enhance social order and stability. Confucianism, being entrenched in and diffused across the traditional values, provides a buffer by virtue of its emphasis on community and kinship ties, a cultural resource upon which the new social ethos continues to evolve. But despite the official endeavors to resuscitate Confucianism for a particular political project, the vernacular interpretations need not run along the same course. Yet, evocations of cultural resources for an ethical project may lead into uncharted territory, even a moral ambivalence, with the future completely open and uncertain.

In conclusion, China's peculiar and ambivalent situation in the realms of legality and morality is constituting a distinctive socio-political culture in the making, which should have far-reaching implications for the engendering of a rights discourse and practice. Cowan et al.'s (2001) recasting of the various conjunctions between culture and rights presents a useful platform for comparative analysis. I draw on the cases of Hong Kong (Merry 2006) and my present study on Chongqing as illustration. The two municipalities have undergone sharply different historical, political, and ideological processes of governance under the British colonial and Communist rules, respectively, yet in both cases, the traditional Chinese family values were never eradicated. In Hong Kong, the female villagers' grievances against the patrilineal system of inheritance were reframed by activists into the language of rights for more effective public appeal. This scenario fits the category of *rights as culture*, an "understanding of rights as a structuring discourse" (Cowan et al. 2001, 12). In contrast, human rights discourse is conspicuously absent from the Chongqing field sites; rather, my analysis hinges on reassembling the various cultural puzzles of Confucianism, Communism, and the market, and making them intelligible for coherent interpretation. Thus, taking *culture as analytic to rights* (Cowan et al. 2001) facilitates a better grasp of the patterns, contingencies, logics, and contradictions of the social processes. Jane Cowan explains that such an analytical approach is intended to distinguish between object and method without necessarily taking on rights as "total ideological-practical apparatus" (2006, 10). Recognizing the messy status of rights in the shadow of power in China, taking culture as a tool for dissecting and analyzing the formation of rights practice sheds light on the enabling potential of culture that is understood as contestable and open processes. Nonetheless, there is the dilemma that, if meanings are always to be understood contextually, then no fixed, final, or normative understanding of them is possible. Thus Mark Goodale asks, justifiably, who is announcing the transformation of culture "from a noun into a verb," from systems of values, ideas, and behaviors into processes (2009, 88). Most important, I believe, is whether ethnographers actually witness such a transformation, instead of patterning data to fit their preferred intellectual construct. For instance, in chapter 4, when I coin the term "investing citizens," I am making a concrete reference to a specific social phenomenon, entrenched in the wider, changing economic and cultural forces, and when I illustrate the critical transformation of urban housing welfare into property rights that engenders the formation of investing citizens and bargaining evictees, it is a historical, local process that changes conceptualizing and theorizing, not vice versa. Hence, when the elderly woman householder (chapter 3) suddenly put down her knitting and stated that her family demanded an additional apartment as demolition compensation because "My granddaughter's grown up," and another elderly evictee at the demolition site stated, "This society is only concerned with money, not the law; when you don't have the rule of law, you don't have any rights," they, along with other agents of the demolition bargainers and investing citizens, were announcing the transformation and reinterpretation of culture, one that is imbued with a renewed meaning of family value, power, and legality, narrated variously in the claims of need, desire, and right. Notwithstanding, this emergent transformation and reinterpretation of culture and value, pertinent to the ubiquitous practices and primacy of private property rights, could be at once enabling (rights consciousness) and disabling (moral ambivalence) with respect to the germination and propagation of universal rights ethics, which will be explored in the final chapter.

NOTES

1. See *Xinhua News* (2014a).
2. In his study of a private enterprise, Jianhua Zhao (2014) finds that the Party branch established there even promoted Confucian values in the company.
3. Headquartered in Beijing and headed by Liu Yandong, a member of the Party Politburo, the Institute's overseas offshoots usually operate within established universities in the host countries.
4. See Press TV (Ribet 2011) and the *New York Times* (Jacobs 2011).
5. Roger Ames and Henry Rosemont (2011) argue for an alternative, less abstract Confucian conception of family-based "relational virtuosity," to the Aristotelian notion of "virtue" (arête) as acquired character traits; attributing that Confucian normativity is defined by living one's family roles to maximum effect and thus much clearer and more concrete than "putative moral principles." Lee Ming-huei (2013), variously, maintains that Confucius and Mencius ethics belong to deontological ethics and points out that pre-Qin Confucianism may have an ethics of virtue but is far from constituting a virtue ethics. Nonetheless, there has been a growing trend of adopting the concept of virtue ethics to interpret Confucian ethics in recent years. For an extended dialogue among Western and Chinese philosophers concerning the relations between the two traditions, see Stephen Angle and Michael Slote (2013a).
6. Stephen Angle and Michael Slote (2013b) reckon that the tradition of thought and practice stemming from Confucius is rich and complex, and can plausibly be divided into at least five phases of development: classical era, Han Dynasty and thereafter, the "Neo-Confucian" revival, the Qing Dynasty reaction to Neo-Confucianism, and the modern/contemporary period of "New Confucianism."
7. Moreover, one must caution against regarding Chinese culture as directly equivalent to Confucianism. Historian Ch'ien Mu (1979) points out that Confucian and Taoist philosophies are a "dialectically opposed but constitutive duality and two pillars of the Chinese cultural system," asserting that Chinese culture is inclined toward morality and art; while morality is built upon Confucianism's "way" and "virtue," art's most profound form is contemplative manifestations of the transcendent Taoist ethos inherent in nature and humanity. Tu Wei-Ming (1985) also states that in light of their shared concern for self-cultivation, both the Taoist critique of Confucian ritualism and Confucian critique of Taoist escapism are actually dialogical interplays reflecting a much deeper point of convergence, and the two belong to the same "symbolic universe" in which they help each other to grow through mutual influence.
8. See *CNN* (Hong and Jiang 2011).
9. See news.163.com (2007).
10. See *South China Morning Post* (Yan 2012).

11. Andrew Terjesen (2013), in contrast, cautions that there are various forms of empathy (cognitive, affective, conative, and simulative) which may not be all represented in the Confucian tradition, and that it is unlikely that any single form of empathy is the single thread running through Confucian ethics. Nonetheless, the different forms might be "weaved together like a rope that binds all of our moral judgments" (Terjesen 2013, 208).

Chapter Eight

Final Thoughts

The Ambivalence of Rights

The neo-socialist property question in China is essentially one of reflexivity and re-captivating meanings and values, after several decades of disruption to the social order and negation of the traditional culture predicated on the Marxist class struggle and socialist radicalism. Each realm of short-term property transactions and long-term social reproductions of morality by the state and familial efforts respectively contains distinctive logics and value propositions, albeit not entirely unambivalently. In contestation are the monetized value of property, the party-state ideology of social harmony and "common prosperity," and parental morality in pursuing the well-being of the next generation. Intertwining the state-property-family relationship is a ubiquitous practice of individual private property rights, which paradoxically are engendering ambivalent values and moral imperatives. In the course of actively defending or seeking housing property rights, animated by a common embracing of need, desire, and risk, demolition bargainers and investing citizens have emerged as a new form of propertied class. But this new propertied "class" at large fails to exhibit any coherent class characteristics in either its ideological/political aspirations or its consumption patterns; instead, its members share a conspicuous family-based ethical concern. Moreover, private property rights are at once enabling due to the rigorous pursuit of well-being in a market economy, and disabling and agitating for those who resist forced eviction or the infringement of owners' rights. I conclude that a pervasive yet particularized rights discourse and practice, embedded in interests, is proliferating but may risk impeding the propagation of universal rights ethics.

As one of the defining features of neo-socialist regime change, private property rights are reinvented, deployed, and imposed by the state as the overriding principle of welfare housing distribution, the subsequent housing demolition and real estate development in the name of urban renewal and the public interest. Welfare housing represents a most blatant systemic inequality within resource redistribution. There is a circulation of values, first in the form of a gift from the parental state as a privilege for a minority of the population, then appropriated by the millions of fortunate urban households as mediated by the heavily state-interfered property market, and finally passed on as valuable parental gifts. Desperate not to lose their last and only chance of avoiding intergenerational poverty and misery, housing evictees, animated by needs/desires, dance to the tune of rights-as-claim in order to bargain for better compensation. Hence, we see that the neo-socialist China's housing reform and burgeoning private property rights regime is laden with a primordial sinister root. Be it nonmarket-based housing transactions in the form of demolition compensation or market-based transactions in the form of housing investment, the central value determinant is market price, with a bizarre perceived risklessness of investment. The caveats being, first, that the comparative market prices and exact formula for demolition compensation are not determined in a fair, transparent manner; and, second, the alternating and sometimes conflicting policy goals and measures of the central and local governments regarding the real estate market are largely opaque to ordinary property investors' meaningful risk assessment. Individuals' possession of property rights is always partial and partitioned, conditioned upon asymmetric encounters with the discriminatory party-state power at the very grassroots level. Demolition bargainers and investing citizens' conception of rights is always particularized and their practice of rights often situational and even opportunistic, as the legality of rights is routinely regressed to a moral claim of right and wrong, determined by a de-politicized but pervasive power with a fuzzy formality of accountability.

The mundane experiences of property ownership and dispossession are concurrently animated by revitalized family values. They also reflect the salient features of concentric moral values, as embedded in the Confucian cultural model. The notion of property rights is manipulated foremost by the state, resulting in a rights-centered economic ethos and, in turn, an encroachment on the family relationship and conjugal asset arrangement. The private and family realms, however, are no longer a static, passive receiver, for ordinary people embrace and reinterpret certain traditional values in contestation of the state's own deliberation and deployment of the traditional cultural resources. Individuals' rights and duties vis-à-vis the state and the family become oscillating moral principles, subject to reinterpretation and contestation. When confronted with such an obscure social situation, wherein absolute principles and ideologies no long exist, it is easy to proclaim and exclaim a "moral vacuum." However, nothing could be further from the truth. As Yunxiang Yan (2011) notes, even when the personified and mystified moral authority of Confucius and Mao disappeared, in real life, people always make judgments about right or wrong in accordance with some values or beliefs. Now, with the re-emphasis of the statist ideal of "harmony" and the ubiquitous re-embracing of family values, what we are witnessing is clearly not a diminishing of values; rather, multiple modes of values are proliferating, though not necessarily implying a universal ethical principle.

MORAL AMBIVALENCE AND NEO-SOCIALIST MODERNITY

Modernization and development have become catchphrases ever since the economic reform and open-door policy was implemented in 1979, only later being supplemented by an emphasis on constructing a harmonious society and the maintenance of stability. A neo-socialist modernity *prima facie* does not need to replicate Western modernity as a prototype, in consideration of their vastly different historical trajectories and cultural underpinnings. Robert Weller (1999) thus suggests an alternative but uniquely Chinese modernity, with its own adaptation to the markets and new cultural pressures according to the local cultural and social resources. Apparently, this was also the approach adopted by the late paramount leader, Deng Xiaoping. In 1978, Deng advocated the "Four Modernizations" to strengthen the fields of agriculture, industry, national defense, and science-technology, but when the political dissident Wei Jingsheng called for the addition of democracy as the "Fifth Modernization," he was arrested and jailed for eighteen years. Obviously, for the Communist Party, it is only the material sectors, rather than social values or political ideals, which are in desperate need of modernization to construct a rudimentary model of Chinese modernity.

However, the party-state's progressive and linear worldview, complete with the celebrated supremacy of a Chinese nation-state, an obsession with scientific rationality, and the (disguised) adoption of the logic of capitalism, is a defining characteristic of the socialist/neo-socialist ideology of governance, which resonates unmistakably with the European Enlightenment's historical notion of modernity. Beneath the surface, moreover, throughout the history of the People's Republic, the term "modern" has never indicated merely and straightforwardly material advancement. Rather, at heart, lies the formidable political and ideological question of how to handle the binary oppositions between traditional and modern, and between East and West. Between the 1950s and the 1970s, radical collectivization and land reform as transplanted from the Soviet Union together with incessant denunciations of traditional culture were endorsed as a solution to and symbol of a communist variant of the modernist utopia. The tragic failure of radical socialist modernization was followed by a dramatic reversal between the 1980s and 2000s, with the gradual but extensive market and property rights reforms alongside the modernization program being modeled, first on the East Asian experience, then more broadly on Western principles of international trade and the global capital market. This culminated in the reestablishment of rural lineage groups, the tolerance of ancestral worship, and a calculated attempt to rejuvenate certain Confucian elements with a view to complementing the Party's drive to construct and maintain a harmonious society—shorthand for stability and order. The "Wests" are always on the horizon, playing a crucial role most of the time, and only the "traditions" are disposable, to be abandoned and recalled whenever necessary, in a characteristically Communist utilitarian approach to Chinese modernity. As the old saying goes, "thirty years in the river east, then the next thirty years in the river west," and so has the meaning and road to modernity also waxed and waned with the changing political climate and bumpy fortunes of the people. One thing is certain, though: Chinese modernity is inseparable from its Western origins, connections, and burdens.

On entering the 2010s, as China leapt past Europe and Japan to become a prime player in the global economic arena, at once complementing and challenging U.S. supremacy, the drive for modernization finally and inevitably reached a crossroads when it encountered the broader, profound issue of political and ethical values, unless the leadership is content with the liberating force generated by mechanical modernization(s) without a full-fledged modernity. How can China's glorious cultural traditions be reassessed and redeployed to render them valuable to a modern China? How can China engage with the still globally dominant Western discourse of modernity? Is the "universal value" (say, human rights, universal suffrage, rule of law) incidental to European modernity and its legacy also applicable for the good of the Chinese nation and people and, if not, why not? Indeed, China's own quest for and long-held obsession with modernity dates back to the early 1900s, first flagged under "science" and "democracy." As literature scholar Seán Valentine (2006) points out, European modernity was introduced into China's history and culture by force of arms that provoked a lasting, traumatic experience, thus explaining the certain Chinese impetus in recent times for developing an economy and institutions that will serve to create wealth, without imposing values that are advantageous to an already-wealthy "West."[1] Thus understood, Chinese modernity has a specific relationship with the European historical context and hence cannot be un-rooted completely from the legacy, for better or worse, of European modernity. Chinese modernity would be unintelligible in isolation from China's century-long humiliating encounters with the West and Japan prior to this, against the backdrop of a modernized/resurgent Western civilization and a Western-centered discourse of the modern within China, even to date. Any claim or assertion of a unique Chinese modernity is simply factually flawed, and more rhetorical than real. A discussion of Chinese modernity without the referencing of the Western model would nullify its comparative perspective, reducing Chinese modernity to an isolated artifact within a particularized time and space and thereby blocking an understanding of its otherwise nuanced ideological bearings. The theme of modernity, as explicated by Caroline Merrifield et al. (2013), should be understood as something both deeply historical and constantly reinvented through contemporary practices, and as a performance in dialogue with (but never fully determined by) Western ideas of modernity. In this regard, the sociological idea of "ambivalence" in relation to Western modernity provides an interesting platform for dialogue, which may shed light on the discussion of neo-socialist modernity and morality.

Harri Englund and James Leach (2000) suggest that the emergence of sociology at the turn of the twentieth century introduced the notion of "ambivalence" as a key theme in a discourse on modernity, and that ambivalence, understood as the uneasy wavering between hope and despair, is an enduring principle in Western social thought. Within this sociological discourse, Zygmunt Bauman defines ambivalence as a situation with no fool-proof choice, no unreflective knowledge of "how to go on" (1991, 15), adding that, if modernity is about the production of order, then ambivalence is the waste of modernity. Bauman further argues that uniformity and universalism are values that are central to modernity but, for most of its history, modernity has lived in and through self-deception, a conviction that the project of universality remains most definitely on. Putting neo-socialist China into this perspective, the state advocates an uncompromising, unilateral path to modernity, by enforcing economic liberation and promoting personal responsibility, but considering political bourgeoisie thinking to be a dangerous by-product in the pursuit of economic progress that could jeopardize the party-state's political legitimacy and harmonious social order. Thus, we see the probable paradoxes of individual choice without individualism, market economy without freedom of information access, and property rights without political rights. The Chinese party-state considers its project of Communism to be a universal truth, its value of walking the road of socialism as non-negotiable and uniformly applied to every citizen—always incomplete, yet it must remain, definitely and indefinitely. The state is indeed encountering and producing its own ambivalence, in tandem with its unprecedented economic success and unchallengeable political power. Ching Kwang Lee (2009) also takes note of a realm of deep ambivalence among Beijing urbanites, in that they pointed to the unrestrained state power in the form of official corruption as the cause of injustice while seeing the state machinery as the solution, rather than the market or the horizontal solidarity forged out of associations among citizens. This is also my reading of the protest and resistance of defiant property owners and evictees, who nonetheless abide by the official rules and resort to the official authorities to redress their discontent and suffering due to the abuse of power by the grassroots cadres and their cohorts. This is a situation in which the Party machinery's power is taken as the key to redressing people's grievances, while the principles and moral appeal of socialist governance are relegated to a subsidiary role or subjected to constant ridicule by the public as a fossilized motto or a phantom of human fanaticism.

In a society of liberal tradition, tolerance and a politics of differences are the order of the day. In neo-socialist China, political differences and defiance are unwarranted, though moral narrations are being increasingly tolerated, which result in parallel trajectories—official versus vernacular, state versus family—of moral discourses and ethical practices. Sociologist Barry Smart (1999) describes "indeterminate justice" as a condition of ambivalence. In China, the question of justice itself is exceedingly problematic, where the interpretation and practice of legal rules and moral norms are constantly and pervasively doubted within a culture of distrust. Justice and any mode of universal principle becomes slippery, evasive, and even deceptive. The problem and challenge of the ambivalence in the discourse of neo-socialist modernity is not relativism but particularism. In each domain of the market, the state, and the family, the respective value and moral deliberation appear to be concrete; it is the unity of this constellation of disparate deliberations which is lacking, inducing paradoxes and dilemmas. Hence, the sociological insight of ambivalence is fittingly relevant to my discussion of Chinese modernity and its pertaining moral ambivalence, while taking heed of Englund and Leach's warning against the uncritical adoption of a pre-given meta-narrative of modernity, for the potential of engendering "ethnographic ignorance." After all, anthropologists do study modernity, but should pay particular care to analyzing its concrete manifestations. Bjørn Thomassen (2012) speaks of the "pluralizing of modernity" and "multiple modernities paradigm" established from the late 1990s as an escape from the burdening of anthropology by a modern epistemology. A strong motivation behind this is to give modernity back to those who live in it and shape it via their lived realities. In my opinion, however, any attempt to coin alternative or parallel modernities for the case of China to "liberate" modernity from its Eurocentric, modernistic connotations is bound to prove futile and more a reflection of certain anthropologists' own intellectual predisposition to remove the colonial legacy than an unbiased representation of the historical and political reality. I share Thomassen's vision that the "celebratory stance" of the anthropology of multiple modernities toward heterogeneity and hybridity was badly misconceived from the very beginning, for there are no real alternatives and the problem is not Europe or the West, but modernity itself—the tendencies toward limitless growth and excess, that characterize the modern episteme and are exceedingly symptomatic of an emergent Chinese modernity in particular.

Meanwhile, in the realization that a Chinese modernity does not emerge out of thin air and that China is actually embracing much of the capitalist logic in its drive toward modernization, development, and modernity, it is noticeable that the pursuit of personal interests has also become the norm and a hallmark of neo-socialism, although the interests of society and the state are far from fading. Economist Albert Hirschman argues that greed and avarice have been used to tame dangerous human passions and ground in self-interest the moral imperative of capitalism, which is to fashion "a less multifaceted, less unpredictable, and more 'one-dimensional' human personality" (1977, 132). Curiously, for China, it was exactly the lust and craze for power by the Party leadership during the high socialist period that had torn society apart and threatened to decimate traditional values and cultural heritage. Now, the once-excessive political passions are being redirected toward a desire for national development and personal well-being and the promotion of stability and order. As much as the capitalist rationality and its pertaining notion of self-interest is adopted in neo-socialist China, the discourse of interests at large is employed ubiquitously to justify public policy and explain the social contradictions.

Legal scholar Randall Peerenboom (1995) notes that rights as construed by China's moral elites, historically and in the legal institutions of the People's Republic of China, both exhibit a decidedly utilitarian bent, as opposed to the Western deontological rights view. Contrasting rights as moral principles, as ends in themselves, with interests as consequentialist or utilitarian in character, Peerenboom sees that there is a conceptual and fundamental difference between *rights as interests* and *rights as moral principles* that trump interests. He considers that the *rights as interests* view and legal practice actually reinforce the traditional Chinese norms, such as the importance of the welfare of the collective, and hence there is a strong inclination to weigh the good of society and interests of the state above the rights of individuals. Philosopher Stephen Angle (2002), in contrast, holds that it is slightly misleading to say that utilitarians believe that rights are merely one kind of interests that can be weighed against others; instead, he argues that rights could be considered as a particular way of promoting or protecting interests that does not depend on specifically utilitarian reasoning. Angle nonetheless agrees that both the contemporary and historical Chinese rights theorizing maintains a strong tie between rights and people's interests, but disputes Peerenboom's take that Chinese theorists today understand rights *as* interests. Rather, he sees that many Chinese rights advocates are more concerned with grounding normative discourse on concrete, tangible interests than justifying it solely by its contribution to the overall utility of society. In summary, be it *rights in interests* or *rights as interests*, rights and interests are intermingled in the intellectual discourse, which are far more fluid and varied than in the Realpolitik.

In the emergent rights regime, as sanctioned and engendered by the party-state, however, rights exist emphatically as legal-based, formal categories, rather than as normative moral principles or pervasive ethical practices adopted and performed in everyday life. While legislative efforts are always under the supreme leadership and guidance of the Party and the enforcement of laws and regulations are relegated to various government agents, ordinary people's encounters with and conceptions of rights are essentially experience-near and power-laden. As elucidated in previous chapters, China's contemporary private property rights regime has been "created" by the party-state in barely two decades, as housing evictees and investors alike are related to the institutional and legal framework of rights in a most top-down, imposing manner. Thus, foremost in my informants' minds is the question of whether a rights category and claim may benefit them or pose any harm and threat. For instance, when the demolition lawyer as featured in chapter 7 says of evictees that "their interests are their rights," rather than "their rights are their interests," this indicates an understanding of *interest as rights*, resembling the "commonsensical" notion of power as rights. This contrasts markedly with the aforementioned shorthand of *rights in interests* and *rights as interests*, and cannot be labeled even as utilitarian, not to mention deontological. Rather, demolition bargainers and investing citizens alike seem to regard rights more as a discursive weapon and tactical entry into their contestation for interests in the name of "rights defense," but when there is a better alternative or a bigger threat to their interests, rights as claims are all too often retractable and disposable.

All too often, when the image of interests is invoked, it denotes an overarching, objectified representation of what is good for the referent, pertaining to status and identity. Recall from chapter 1's discussion that interests are an objectified attribute and belief-independent; while desires can be instrumental and particular, interests explain intrinsic desire non-instrumentally and are essentially non-particular. Thus, one can straightforwardly define the referent's (collective or self, people's or enemy's) interests without needing to inquire into the particularities and avoid making moral judgments. In many socialist countries, class interest, as defined categorically by the relations of production, has been the most expedient category and instrument of governance. Once a subject has been categorized as proletariat or bourgeois, privileged as urbanite or deprived as peasant, or labeled as the "people" or an enemy of the people, his/her fate is predetermined; social justice and human rights are irrelevant or even reactionary as an idea and cause. As sociologists Martin Whyte and William Parish (1984) point out, once cities have become the producer cities desired in leadership policy, opportunities in education and employment have come to rely heavily on class background and political commitment, thereby disrupting and undermining any sense of predictability, fairness, justice, and stability in society. In this regard, I would like to draw on philosopher Gilles Deleuze's insights regarding interests, desire, and power in Marxism, which is largely relevant to my discussion on neo-socialist China:

> [T]he thrust of Marxism was to define the problem essentially in terms of interests (power is held by a ruling class defined by its interests). The question immediately arises: how is it that people whose interests are not being served can strictly support the existing power structure by demanding a piece of the action? Perhaps this is because in terms of investments, whether economic or unconscious, interest is not the final answer; there are investments of desire that function in a more profound and diffuse manner than our interests dictate. . . . The nature of these investments of desire in a social group explains why political parties or unions, which might have or should have revolutionary investments in the name of class interests, are so often reform oriented or absolutely reactionary on the level of desire. (Foucault and Deleuze 1977, 214)

Deleuze's allusion to desire in explaining the paradox of contradictory interests demystifies the essentialized notion of interests as the cover-up for pretentious Marxist-socialist projects, wherein fluid, changing human needs and desires are negated or suppressed in the name of class interests and a one-dimensional human nature. China's own turbulent history of class struggle and political upheaval has shown how the trivially delineated and opposing interests of the "people" and the "enemy of the people" form the, albeit fragile, roots of misery and injustice. On the contrary, the differing interests of the rulers and the ruled, the privileged Party cadres and commoners are often actually contradicted due to human desires, selfishness, or differing values. What is more, in the real economic life of neo-socialist China, the propertied and propertyless are actually not two clearly delineated classes with distinctively opposed interests. Rather, their well-being and identity are historically and instrumentally determined by politics, policy, and privilege, subject to discriminating endorsement or deprivation by power at the grass-roots level. An abstract or rigid conception of interests merely serves to conceal and undermine the legitimate and viable construction and protection of rights in its own right, and to propagate the enduring moral ambivalence and inequality in society at large.

Angle is correct in complementing the ever-broadening scope of rights as a process of new rights being created when new groups articulate and claim their legitimate self-interest, but I also believe that there is always the real risk of the concrete interests of individuals and groups being overwhelmed in the name of society's greater interests. My concern thus resonates with Peerenboom's caution that, while rights will probably form part of a "post-socialist Confucian China," with the party-state emphasizing the more conservative, authoritarian aspects of Confucianism, rights will probably continue to be understood as a kind of interests rather than as trumping interests

(1998, 253). Whether or not one agrees with Peerenboom's conclusion, his concern is all too real in a regime where rights and interests and their balance are determined almost exclusively by the Party. Hence, with a view to understanding the everyday practices and politics, the particularities of the individual agent's needs and desires in animating and configuring the agent's rights situation must be given due weight, instead of being subsumed or negated under the disguise of decontextualized and generalized interests.

STATE-SOCIETY VERSUS STATE-PROPERTY-FAMILY RELATIONALITY

In the decade after China's early stage of reform, sociologist Deborah Davis (1995) suggests that Chinese urban residents may use their new wealth and autonomy to enlarge the non-state sphere and develop a nascent civil society. Variously, Mayfair Yang (1994) maintains that the prognosis of civil society according to the European model does not suit China, but nonetheless asserts that the search for an autonomous realm of social activity that can counterbalance the state power is extremely important for a Chinese modernity. She further postulated that a new urban sphere of *minjian*, visualized as an autonomous realm of people-to-people relationships and constitutive of Confucian relational ethics, would emerge out of state socialism to deter and challenge the state. In Yang's reckoning, the social fabric of *minjian* is being reweaved on the basis of an "art of *guanxi*" (a discourse of relatedness and obligations), which operates in the space between individuals and society and a transitional space between the state and a fully developed self-organizing social formation, resulting in networks of disparate people that crisscross state-imposed institutions to form a second society.

Yang's prediction twenty years ago of the proliferation of dispersed *guanxi* in every realm of society now seems largely correct. However, her optimism about the development of a separate, disengaged social realm from the state in the aftermath of extreme state penetration of the social order remains a distant possibility. Instead, the neo-socialist state and new *guanxi* relationality, along with the economic ethos of market rationality and private property rights, actually co-constitute each other. The polluted *guanxi*, as envisioned by Yang, had turned out *not* to be totally unregulated. Rather, it is subject to a complex web of official rules and norms in cultivating business connections and obtaining privileges or favors, with the party-state continuing to play an instrumental role in many facets of the political and economic spheres. Moreover, Yang has predicted the formation of a social realm outside the state, probably fueled by a discourse of relatedness and obligations (rather than a discourse of rights), as the cultural emphasis has not been on the abstract universal person but on the person as defined in terms of relationships and roles. Again, I believe that Yang is half-right, as a ubiquitous, though particularized, discourse and practice of individual rights has indeed been re-constituted by the party-state, which ironically has also cultivated a re-emphasis on family obligations and kinship relatedness. In a nutshell, the actual mode of social and moral order that is under formation is neither singular nor coherent, but a condition of ambivalence that is inextricably integral to contemporary party-state governance. In a later article, Yang (2002) suggests that the moral cement of *guanxi* for reconstructing civil society can also counter the new social fragmentation brought about by capitalism. However, when Yang states that what needs to be examined in the commercial society that is now taking root is the encounter between the art of *guanxi* and capitalism, she seemingly perceives and presumes that the socialist redistributive state has largely receded into the background, a point that this book disavows throughout. Instead, I see an even more entrenched tripartite relationality, with *guanxi* cohabiting with state redistribution and capitalism. Instead of constituting an "alternative and even subversive realm of operations" (Yang 1994, 308), *guanxi* practices are inseparable from the state redistributive power and functions. My study demonstrates that state redistribution and statist participation are the norms and imperative elements in China's unique model of market economy or capitalism, whatever one prefers to call it.

In a similar vein of critiquing the rigid state-society dichotomy, Li Zhang (2004) nonetheless sees that, with the rise of real estate development, corporate power and a market rationality are transforming Chinese governmentality itself. Zhang also rejects the overly optimistic view of the concomitant withering of state power and the rise of the free market and civil society; rather, she rightly posits that the "late-socialist state" is reinventing itself as an "entrepreneur state," participating in enterprises to strengthen themselves financially and politically (2006, 475). My own reading also contests a bifurcate state-society relationality while endorsing the view of a new political governance in the making, but I reject a unilateral cause-end perspective. I conceive Chinese neo-socialism as a synthesis in the making of the old socialist and new market moralities and rules, rather than being simply a unilateral or substantive encroaching onto the former by the latter. This view seems to resonate with Frank Pieke's thesis that "under neo-socialism Leninism and neoliberalism have indeed become one" (2009, 192). However, I contend that this neo-socialist synthesis is far from complete for, beneath the unified rationale guiding the running of the economy, the values and moral deliberation pertaining to the market, the party-state, and the family realms, respectively, remain concrete and delineable, thus producing ironies and paradoxes in everyday life.

I also hesitate to share Pieke's judgment that a strengthening of the Communist Party of China's rule *enables* further political reform in the direction of a more pluralistic, consultative form of benign neo-socialist dictatorship. Since Xi Jinping assumed power in November 2012, the party-state has tightened its grip on the Internet, press freedom, and political dissidents. Along with persistent measures for cooling down housing prices and implementing sweeping anti-corruption campaigns (both well-intended, though not uncontroversial), these concerted efforts represent a rigorous pursuit of political and social stability that seeks to strengthen the Party's governance legitimacy without resorting to an election democracy, freedom of speech, and an independent judiciary that commonly characterize market economies.[2] Early signs (up to February 2015) have so far indicated that Xi Jinping has achieved a remarkable consolidation of power, by crushing potential threats to stability at large and imposing a severe top-down discipline on cadres across the local and central government organs, as well as Party and military apparatuses at the very senior levels. In October 2014, the Party passed a resolution to advance the "rule of law" (*yifa zhiguo*) as China's basic road map for socialist governance. While promising sweeping judicial reforms and governance in line with the Constitution, the resolution is categorical regarding the Party's supremacy in leading the legislative works, as Xi Jinping explained that the Party leadership is the "essential feature of socialism with Chinese characteristics and the fundamental guarantee of socialist rule of law."[3] Then, in January 2015, in an written instruction on political and legal work, Xi Jinping stressed that officials in the law enforcement agencies and judicial departments should be loyal to the Party, the state, and the people, in order to ensure that the "knife handle" (*daobazi*) lies tightly in the grip of the Party and the people.[4] The term *daobazi* was first used during the Mao era of fierce class struggle to emphasize the class nature of the judiciary and law enforcement organizations. Xi Jinping's sudden invocation of this ideological metaphor in the present period of relative prosperity and stability is puzzling. His simultaneous calls for *yifa zhiguo* and a firm grip on the *daobazi* also appear ambivalent. At what is the Party aiming this sharp knife? Are there fierce enemies on the horizon constituting an imminent threat to the proletariat revolution and socialist governance?

Notwithstanding, against the backdrop of the Party's absolute power and revival of ideological rhetoric, Xi Jinping's frequent appeals to individual cadres' exercise of self-discipline and cultivation of inner virtue also sound like the Confucius ideal of "being sage inside and being kingly outside" (*neisheng waiwang*); that is, exercising perfect self-cultivation and benevolent governance. Under this scenario, the existence of a sagehood and the accession of this virtuous person to becoming the benevolent leader of an authoritarian regime is a matter of fate and circumstance. Whether this kingly leader will remain benevolent and enlightened is more a matter of self-restraint and an element of chance than a result of rational, democratic choice; and one wonders whether Xi Jinping constitutes such a sagehood himself.[5] Regardless, the curious question arises of whether the Party leadership will ever consider a humble submission to the people's will and rights. Or will it, rather, continue to deem the Party as fully representing the genuine will and interests of the whole people, while the people's rights are proxied and codified primarily as legal rights, the admission, interpretation, and enforcement of which are always and decidedly subject to the Party's full discretion. With absolute power and a "sharp knife" firmly in the Party's grip and the economy and Chinese modernity well on track, China is doubtless heading swiftly toward a new form of governance. The Chongqing model and Bo Xilai legacy may have gone, but a grand-scale, exemplary model of Chinese neo-socialism is actually taking shape under the orchestration of the new leadership. Moreover, just as ordinary people are (perpetually) waiting for more sages to descend from the Party, one's family and a housing property appear to provide the best shelter and protection, after all.

To conclude, in tracking the social phenomena of the pervasive house demolition and parental property investment, I consider these to be a concomitant condensation and vindication of the principles of family values and the emergent neo-socialist governance. This study illustrates that the discourse and practice of rights, as emanating from active possession by investing citizens and counter-dispossession by demolition bargainers, at once cements a platform for securing peoples' interests and nurtures their rights consciousness, yet accentuates an ambivalence of the values inherent in the tripartite realm of the state-property-family. The present ubiquitous housing ownership in neo-socialist China originated largely in the inequitable urban welfare distributions of the 1990s. It follows that the notion and principle of rights cannot be abstracted from the social relationality, since the moral legitimacy of private property rights are compromised by a history of status, privilege, and power. In the neo-socialist context, rights are a slippery concept, the meaning of which is unclear or unfixed and the relation of which with power and duties is inseparable but not unambiguous. There are indeed both manifest and latent contradictions between rights as interests and rights as a moral principle, as well as between rights as interests and interests as rights, which may paradoxically impede the germination of universal rights ethics. Such is the plight and predicament of rights, not as a primordial existence and principle, but as a historically, culturally, and socially constructed concept, which is always contingent, contestable, and even contradictory. In my final analysis, recall one of my research questions as mentioned in the introductory chapter: whether property rights may become and constitute a formative element in China's own emergent human rights regime, or whether and why Europe and China, both premised similarly on the importance of property rights at one point, may be following different historic trajectories? To answer, I believe that the prospects and rootedness of a universalistic human rights idea against the backdrop of moral ambivalence are predicated on whether the legitimacy of needs shall be revitalized in the disputable projects of attaining "common prosperity" and cultivating "socialist core values." It is affirmative that neo-socialist China is walking its own historic path, but it is uncertain whether the practice of individualized rights as embedded in resurrected family values shall anchor, rather than contradict, the proliferation of a moral imperative that also champions the common good of society.

NOTES

1. Seán Valentine (2006) has given an account of the contemporary reexamination of the "Western" model of modernity by Chinese culture studies and political, social and economic thought, with a new postcolonial, postmodern form of modernization with Chinese characteristics proposed. He concludes that the Chinese critique of modernity is both a product of Chinese history and an alternative to the "Western" paradigms.

2. Following the purge of Bo Xilai, the retired vice chair of the Party Central Military Commission, Xu Caihou, was prosecuted for alleged corruption and the retired Standing Committee member of the Party Politburo, Zhou Yongkang, was investigated for suspected serious disciplinary violation, in June and July 2014, respectively. Zhou may become the most senior Party cadre to have been brought down for criminal charges since the Gang of Four in 1976. One interpretation is that these moves signaled Xi Jinping's confidence and determination to neutralize any rival factions inside the Party by asserting his own authority through opening up the Party to closer outside scrutiny. See *BBC* (2014).

3. See *Xinhua News* (2014b).

4. See *Xinhua News* (2015).

5. Historian Chen Joshui (2006) reckons that the links between individuals' self-actualization and a ruler's political behaviors, as prescribed by "*neisheng waiwang*," are logically flawed, because the former is a matter of individual moral choice while the latter is typically a function of complex interests and motivations. Moreover, throughout most of Chinese history, while sages seldom become kings, all kings become sages under the guise of "*neisheng waiwang*," with both power and truth within their grip.

Afterword

Locating and Mislocating Rights in Neo-Socialist China

Throughout the present research, I have been asking myself a simple question: How do I study human rights practice—how do I tell that I am indeed investigating what I am supposed to investigate? This is a fundamental methodological issue when conducting ethnographic research in a context where a tradition and elaborate culture of rights is absent.

The People's Republic of China presents a particularly daunting challenge owing to its complex yet partial transformation from a high-socialist regime to a "socialist market economy with Chinese characteristics," yet with the defining Leninist party-state power structure very much intact. Discursively, the PRC Constitution proclaims many sorts of rights for citizens—the right to own private property, vote, criticize any state organ, work, rest, access material assistance from the state, receive education, and enjoy gender equality. Since 1980, moreover, Beijing has endorsed the Universal Declaration of Human Rights and six of the seven core international human rights treaties.[1] The Chinese government also publishes reports on "China's Human Rights Endeavors" in the form of White Papers, as well as annual reports on the U.S. human rights records. Given that human rights rhetorically has been popularized as almost a universal yardstick for evaluating political and moral rightness in both state and international politics, "a language of progressive hope" (Zigon 2013, 718), it is tempting to perceive China also as a prima facie regime of rights, such that the issue of how the people's theoretical rights are exercised, violated, and contested could be subject to rigorous evaluation and scrutiny accordingly. However, this mode of thinking and methodology carries an inherent risk of taking ideological promiscuity as something real and enforceable, as well as creating an abstract domain of representation which may not necessarily have any bearing on the real-life context. By way of ethnographic observation and analyzing concrete data premised on an imaginary analytical construct, there is every possibility of reaching a conclusion that is no less abstract, misconceived, and fictional.

My caution echoes Richard Wilson's (2006) note that human rights became, in the second half of the twentieth century, a political value with global ambitions, analogous to political metanarratives such as liberal democracy and socialism. In their critique of the uncritical adoption of a pregiven metanarrative of modernity by anthropologists, Harri Englund and James Leach (2000) contend that it risks espousing a new holism, with the metanarrative essentially acting as an explanatory gloss that is imported and placed on ethnographic observations rather than as a theoretical construct grounded in them. In a similar vein, taking for granted and adopting a metanarrative of rights as the basic analytical frame could incur the risk of seeing what we want to see from the very outset, resulting in insufficient reflexivity as to ignore the specificity of its construct and its particularistic applicability to the China setting.

The notion that China is possibly or eventually to become a regime of rights is indeed a far cry from the central imperative of Marxist socialism which is to maximize the bureaucracy's allocative capacity and power, resulting in a mass-scale, centralized redistribution regime for both material and non-material aspects. The state redistributive economy represented a total relationality, encompassing the economic, social, political, and familial domains. Thus, the very principle of inalienable rights is critically incompatible with the legacy of centralized redistribution, which means that a regime of rights against the backdrop of the three-decade-long Marxist socialism must be reconstituted piecemeal, from ground zero. In post-reform China, many crucial elements of the previous redistributive function and state control have not disintegrated, notwithstanding its dramatic market economic reform and tacit tolerance of consumption freedom and personal choice. Moreover, the genuine rights of work, speech, and movement remain very much a function of individual citizens' political correctness, subject to the state's constant surveillance and sanction in the name of *weiwen*. Personal rights continue to reside in the hands of the state authorities and are not a matter of personal endowment or simple personal deliberation. Even in the economic realm, most of the strategic sectors remain under the firm grip of the state enterprises and the rights to commit investment and engage in fair market competition are also closely state supervised and scrutinized. It follows that an inquiry into rights in China must be grounded on the realization that these are not a primordial existence but something that are politically constructed and contested. This point of departure fundamentally problematizes the axiom of rights as a self-evident analytical category in social analysis.

In my routine encounters with people from diverse background in China, I often notice a considerable gap between their habitual usage of vocabulary related to topics of social concern and the rhetorical phrases and categories of representation as quoted in the news story and academic accounts of events related to rights defense. I am puzzled about whether ordinary people and social scientists/journalists are indeed using the same terms, and/or using the same terms but with different or ambivalent meanings. It is not the mere literal meanings which are at issue here; rather, I am concerned with, for example, what exactly evictees are really thinking and conceiving when they talk about rights nominally. I have become increasingly aware of the predicament of adopting and imposing neat, abstract analytical categories as unproblematic social representations in the research field. I believe that if we wish to explore the possible pathways and long-term outlook of human rights development, we must first examine the "rootedness" in society as believed and embodied. This rootedness, arguably, depends on the "indigeneity" and moral appeal of a culture of rights, which demand that we start by interrogating the exact meaning of rights as discoursed and practised. This examination is in turn predicated on specifying the context in which the expression of rights is employed in juxtaposition and in contrast with other (complementary, incompatible, or irrelevant) categories of vocabulary and representation such as need, power, desire, and interest. An anthropological approach ought not to take the idea of rights and its nature for granted as a normative principle, then proceed immediately to the task of empirical inquiry. Instead, we should first ask where exactly they are "located," so as to recognize that we are indeed dealing with an issue of rights prior to rigorous theorizing.

The discussion in this book points to the very need to ground our study of rights in everyday life, understood as an "indigenous culture" in the germination rather than perceived or imagined as an outright implanting and engendering of a principle from afar or from above. This indigenous culture evolves and takes root also from a particularized imagery and terrain of legality. In approaching the study of rights, one option is to take the notion of rights as a political and legal concept. We may then proceed to investigate, for instance, whether and how civil rights as stipulated in the Constitution and laws are honored by the party-state and practiced by the people, whether and how property rights are enforced by the local governments and enjoyed by property owners, and whether and how labor rights are honored by employers and fought for by the workers at large. This relatively straightforward choice is understandable, as not only is the language of rights being used extensively in the PRC Constitution, but the idea of economic contractual rights has been ubiquitously endorsed in routine business practices, following the open-door policy and flood of foreign investment since 1979. Moreover, the dramatic housing reform has led to a proliferation of private property rights in cities across the country. In a sense, the possession (and possible dispossession) of housing property has become a most mundane experience of what the idea of rights actually means for millions of households and how the entitlement (and denial) of rights works out in everyday life. To outside observers (political scientists, sociologists, and human rights lawyers in particular), it is also tempting to imagine that the assertion and guarding of all kinds of putative rights have become a mundane, common practice, regardless of the messiness in people's deliberation and discrepancy in their efficacy. Notwithstanding the fact that the infringement of rights remains a regular occurrence, it is perhaps a convenient proposition for researchers to consider that rights at least have become a normative principle of morality for the evaluation of political governance and grassroots resistance, and it may seem "natural" to conceive a regime of rights being established as officially acknowledged and juridically stipulated.

In a nutshell, it "appears" safe to treat rights as a natural and hence legitimate analytical category for rigorous empirical analysis. However, the "convenient" misconception of this approach should be refuted, as I have shown in this book how an array of economic and property rights claims is sometimes conflated or disguised with the discourses of need, desire, interest, and distrust of power and legality. It is of little help, or even counterproductive, to assume the presence of a self-conscious, rights-bearing individual everywhere for us to discover. Actual aspirations as ethnographically revealed are always fluid and complex, yet often ambiguous, confusing, and even contradictory. Rights in the field, as opposed to a philosophical epistemology, must be understood as neither a singular, pure principle nor a consistent, conspicuous manifestation of the weak and underprivileged (or their counterparts). Rather, rights should be studied in relation to specific social contexts as a plural, fuzzy concept that is being disparately deployed, reinvented, and even manipulated constantly. Wilson describes the fragmented, partial, and slippery nature of the "doctrinal ambiguity of human rights talk," and emphasizes that intellectual abstractions of the general patterns of human rights practices must remain embedded in identifiable empirical findings (2006, 78). Following Wilson, in the ethnographic field, a study of rights means also a study of ambiguity, with no assurance that a definitive classification and awareness would emerge before our eyes. An unsophisticated adoption of an imaginary category as the tool for packing up and ordering data is bound to "mislocate" rights in the broader mapping of how ordinary people actually perform the assertion of rights, thereby compromising intellectual impartiality and the potential ethnographic contribution. However, such a caution comes with a price, which is the possibility and predicament of a perpetual failure in the unambiguous delineation of rights as an empirical fact and its informed theorizing. In return, I am seeking a minute but precious opportunity to witness the germination of an indigenous idea. This could well be a vernacular concept of rights, or a new "compound," being bound up by different old and new, concrete and fictional elements, only to be discovered and identified as such.

NOTE

1. Between 1980 and 1998, the PRC became a signatory to the International Covenant on Civil and Political Rights; International Covenant on Economic, Social and Cultural Rights; Convention on the Elimination of All Forms of Discrimination Against Women; Convention against Torture and Other Cruel, Inhuman or Degrading Treatment or Punishment; Convention on the Rights of Child; and ratified the International Convention on the Elimination of All Forms of Racial Discrimination, but did not endorse the International Convention on Protection of the Rights of All Migrant Workers and Members of Their Families.

Appendix

Research Methods

My research field sites encompassed two demolition areas and one property project. I lived in the vicinity of the demolition projects that I followed. By traveling daily, I gained a personal feel for the area, which facilitated my communication with the demolition personnel and neighborhood evictees. I also conducted casual chats and interviews in restaurants and property sales offices with real estate professionals and investors.

Field Site One: A demolition office where I waited on a daily basis, particularly during the first six months. The head of the demolition office granted me access to monitor demolition personnel's routine work and household visits. I became acquainted with this gentleman through the introduction of one of his relatives, who was referred to me by one of her friends in Shenzhen, who in turn was introduced to me by one of my previous colleagues based in Shanghai. This loop of referrals vividly demonstrates how a relationship, even a loose one, is crucial throughout China.

Field Site Two: A demolition site soon to be cleared for real estate development. I had started to frequent the area after a few months into my field work, for I had gained enough basic knowledge from Field Site One about demolition policy and practices. I walked around to introduce myself and ask for permission for visits and discussions.

Field Site Three: A newly completed private residential estate where buyers came to take possession of their apartment units. A small scale rights-defense by the owners had erupted, providing me a rare opportunity to observe the whole process, which lasted eight days. I had been allowed to frequent the site by a senior manager, whom I had come to know through referral by a real estate professional in Hong Kong.

Participant observation was employed to study the long process of demolition bargaining [Field Site One] and the eventful protest staged by property owners [Field Site Three]. I relied on intensive open-ended interviews and reconstruct the life stories of nail householders [Field Site Two] and housing investors [sporadic contacts, no specific field sites], so as to comprehend their sentiments and values in relation to their perceived pains, gains, needs, and desires. Open-ended interviews were conducted to chart the attitudes and opinions of evictees, demolition personnel, real estate professionals, and other Chongqingers concerning housing demolition and investment, and family relationships. Given the sensitivity of the demolition issue, in particular, many nail householders understandably exhibited caution about my real identity and motive. Nonetheless, as mutual trust grew over time, many informants became willing to reveal their stories and encounters, their ironies and discourses, their resistance and hopes.

I prefer unstructured, open-ended interviews to allow maximum leeway for ethnographic efficacy; but this comes with a risk and trade-offs. The risk is that there may not be a singular truth for me to "discover," and I am tasked with the daunting challenge of ordering and generalizing individualized stories without losing particularities. However, for my study, such an approach is crucial to comprehend the significance of homeownership, and the personal experience of sudden dispossession or affluence for urbanites. Such listening to narratives is an imperative source of data for understanding historicity and meanings. I want to understand how people relate their memories of the socialist welfare state to the present advent of private property rights and how they envision a new economic ethos.

There are also important trade-offs between listening and seeing as sources of empirical data. As a matter of social fact and human nature, most people romanticize, conflate, and exaggerate their memories and life stories, and in their natural state of mind do not ordinarily reveal the totality of their true self. In my experience, a candid self-depiction is probably *not* more normal than occasional, situational, and habitual hiding and lying. It is hence unwarranted to rely purely on what people recount about their lives, what they claimed they had encountered, and what had been their endeavors. On the contrary, the actual behavior and practices of informants, consciously or inadvertently, provide rich data in tackling the issues of *what* and *how*—although not *why*. Still, the dilemma remains that informants are also actors who can ingeniously perform and pretend in their daily life as if they are sincere and innocent. In ethnographic studies, such contrasts and complementarities between *what is said* and *what is done* are an enduring empirical and theoretical concern. For instance, Edmund Leach (1976) has noted the tension between "structuralist-rationalist" anthropologists—who maintain that the social reality "exists" in the verbal statements of informants, and the "functionalist-empiricists"—who focus on people's acting out of the customary conventions and dismiss the structure of ideas as a second order, unobservable, abstraction invented by theoreticians; but he nonetheless considers them complementary and that one is a transformation of the other. With a view to bridging the gaps, I set out to contrast the narratives of housing evictees and investors (chapters 2 and 4) with their actual encounters and interactions (chapters 3 and 5). I consider such a narration–action divide a productive organizational device. There is also this peril of ethnographers' forcing representation of action on agents, as forewarned of by Pierre Bourdieu (1977). Hence for the benefit of different vantage points, I approach the analysis of actions in chapters 3 and 5 through the nonrepresentational theories of "practice" and "affect," in juxtaposition to the discussion of right in relation to the representational entities of "need," "desire," and "risk."

Throughout my research, I have been assisted principally by three student assistants. They are, respectively, Ran Xueyu, an MPhil student in English Literature (Chongqing University); Gao Minyi, a senior undergraduate student in Real Estate Construction (Chongqing University); and Yang Ling, an MPhil student in Sociology (Southwest University); all of them are fluent in Chongqing dialects. During many weekends, they took turns accompanying me on some of the more important visits. Their participation was mainly out of curiosity, as I did not pay them any fee, except for a transport subsidy and eating out. Before they started, I briefed them on the objective and methodology of ethnography, and asked them to try out participant observation. My assistants provided three substantive types of support: first, simultaneous interpretation: most Chongqingers converse with Putonghua, but many elderly people speak in a dialect or with a heavy accent. Second, rapport building: their companionship substantially facilitates the trust of evictee residents. Third, note-taking and transcription: I verified the content by comparing them with my own notes; in the case of any doubt, the contents were discarded. Subsequent translation into English was conducted entirely by me.

In the demolition field, very often several informants all talked at once. Their random interruptions and cross-cutting dialogues rendered note-taking exhaustingly difficult; even when tape recording was allowed, subsequent transcriptions could be ineffective and confusing, and when evictees agreed to one-on-one discussions, most of them refused tape recording and a great many of them became hesitant once they saw me pulling out my notebook to write. Ethnographers can never run a control experiment to test how informants would respond differently, with and without a researcher taking notes. With this in mind, the gifted competence of local students in note-taking, memorizing, and dictating has become imperatively helpful; otherwise a great deal of the precious data, and even their very accuracy, would have been lost or in grave doubt. Conventional ethnographic practices deem it the norm for ethnographers to perform competently and independently all the tasks of participant observation, interviewing, note-taking, and transcription. In reality, however, this may not be the best arrangement for three reasons.

First, the richness and authenticity of data are predicated on the depth of dialogue between the interviewers and interviewees as two "equals," with give-and-take from both sides. It is rarely the case that a candid and fruitful account is attained in a unidirectional question-and-answer fashion. The experience, skills, knowledge, and attitude of the ethnographer are also crucial. In my experience, I could concentrate on participating in the conversation much more effectively when my assistants were present. This is no mere trivial division of labor but a recognition of intersubjectivity's important bearing on the social process of knowledge production and a methodological enhancement which allows for better research quality, echoing Saraswati Haider's (1998) remark that authentic, reality-revealing, flesh-and-blood data is perhaps only obtainable when one is intimately, subjectively, and personally involved with one's subjects.

Second, every researcher has distinct comparative strengths and weaknesses. Anthropologists are generally candid concerning how their research plan is affected by the unpredictability of field work, and ethnographers are now more open to reflexive evaluation of their emotions encountered in the field. But it is less common for field workers to explicitly discuss how their specific inexperience, immaturity, or lack of skills might severely compromise the outcome and value of the whole project, particularly in the case of young doctorate students, many of whom have not even worked a single day in the non-academic, real world away from home. In my case, my fading short-term memory faculty and difficulty in commanding a new dialect constitute particular handicaps. Relying only on myself, I find it necessary to return and repeat the questions. But with the striking effectiveness provided by my assistants, I could conduct follow-up inquiries with better thoroughness. On the other hand, my own comparative strength is my shrewdness in people observation and broad knowledge on China that enables engaged conversations, which should be employed rigorously to improve the effectiveness of field work.

Third, as most of the more important transcripts were completed within several days to several weeks with the help of my assistants, I could relate the transcripts to the context of conversations more productively and in a timely manner. This procedure is of immense importance for ascertaining the "authenticity" of data interpretation, compared with the more common practice of waiting up to many months before the transcribing of recordings and field notes is complete. Here, I do not mean the authenticity of informants' meaning or behaviors per se, but the authenticity of ethnographers' own representation of such, subject to their inevitable reinvention of the authenticity of the context, content, and connotations in their reports. Dimitrios Theodossopoulos (2013) says authenticity consists of blurred, context-specific, often undefined semantic boundaries, indicative of its dynamic and flexible nature. This is no less valid regarding ethnographers' own analyses, for there could be multiple versions of authenticity depending on how accurately reality is recorded and portrayed. With this caveat in mind, I am anxious to minimize contamination by the element of time, while also realizing the process may not conform strictly to the conventional way of conducting ethnographic work.

Nonetheless, I consider that richness, accuracy, and authenticity of data are always at stake in ethnographic works. Borrowing statistical jargons, my deeper concern is to avoid a *type II error* or a false negative, which is to say the avoidance of taking my informants inaccurately or out of context concerning their true representations or meanings. It is perhaps a pity if an ethnographer misses certain significant data because of oversight or doubt, which is analogous to a statistical *type I error* or a false positive. But the damage of such an error in terms of research integrity and data authenticity is far less serious compared with that of a type II error. It is my view that overly confident ethnographers are particularly vulnerable to committing type II errors inadvertently. I could not emphasize more that this is a generic methodological risk of all ethnographic inquiries, rather than a questioning of the competence or integrity of a particular anthropologist. Strathern (1999) reminds us that the follow-up work after field research is an "imaginative re-creation" by way of engaging the fields of observation and analysis simultaneously. She calls the effect of such engaging the *ethnographic moment* that "works as an example of a relation which joins the understood (what is analyzed at the moment of observation) to the need to understand (what is observed at the moment of analysis)." In this regard, my attempt is to underscore the less problematic idea of what is *understood* at the moment of analyzing (*to understand*), and hence minimizing the risk of accessing "contaminated" data in the first instance. By employing certain technical amendments, I am convinced I have created a minor, but valid methodological innovation committed to mitigating both my specific shortcomings and an inherent, generic risk of ethnographic research.

In a recent article, Townsend Middleton and Jason Cons (2014) point out that in the history of ethnography, we know research assistants have played a central role in the field, but they have suffered considerable omission and elision along the way, and more often than not, discussions of research assistants are limited to footnotes or formal acknowledgments, etc. Middleton and Cons candidly attribute this phenomenon to the academic norms of proficiency and authorship, wherein the existence of research assistants necessarily "problematizes" these norms of scholastic autonomy. Such is the assumption, expectation, and rule of game in the academic world, one that I personally have grave doubt about its practicality, efficacy, and value in actual practice. It is thus my intention to spell out the academic myth of flawless ethnographic practices and a heroic individuated ethnographic self, and present my own humble, practical case of remedy.

Bibliography

Adam, Barbara, and Joost van Loon. 2000. "Introduction. Repositioning Risk: The Challenge for Social Theory." In *The Risk Society and Beyond: Critical Issues for Social Theory*, edited by Barbara Adam, Ulrich Beck, and Joost van Loon, 1–32. London: Sage.

Agarwal, Bina. 1997. "'Bargaining' and Gender Relations: Within and Beyond the Household." *Feminist Economics* 3: 1–51.

Ahmed, Sara. 2004. "Affective Economies." *Social Text* 22: 117–139.

Alchian, Armen. 2008. "Property Rights." *The Concise Encyclopedia of Economics*. www.econlib.org/library/Enc/PropertyRights.html (accessed May 1, 2013).

Ames, Roger, and Henry Rosemont, Jr. 2011. "Were the Early Confucians Virtuous?" In *Ethics in Early China: An Anthology*, edited by Chris Fraser, Dan Robins, and Timothy O'Leary, 17–40. Hong Kong: Hong Kong University Press.

Amnesty International. 2012. *Standing Their Ground: Thousands Face Forced Eviction in China*. London: Amnesty International Ltd.

Anderson, Ben. 2012. "Affect and Biopower: Towards a Politics of Life." *Transactions of the Institute of British Geographers* 37: 28–43.

Angle, Stephen. 2002. *Human Rights and Chinese Thought: A Cross-Cultural Inquiry*. Cambridge: Cambridge University Press.

Angle, Stephen, and Michael Slote, eds. 2013a. *Virtue Ethics and Confucianism*. New York: Routledge.

———. 2013b. "Introduction." In *Virtue Ethics and Confucianism*, edited by Stephen Angle and Michael Slote, 1–12. New York: Routledge.

Angle, Stephen, and Marina Svensson, eds. 2001. *The Chinese Human Rights Reader: Documents and Commentary 1900–2000*. Armonk, NY: M.E. Sharpe.

Appadurai, Arjun. 1986. "Introduction: Commodities and the Politics of Value." In *The Social Life of Things: Commodities in Cultural Perspective*, edited by Arjun Appadurai, 3–63. Cambridge: Cambridge University Press.

Bach, Jonathan. 2010. "'They Come in Peasants and Leave Citizens': Urban Villages and the Making of Shenzhen, China." *Cultural Anthropology* 25: 421–458.

Barreto, José-Manuel. 2011. "Rorty and Human Rights: Contingency, Emotions and How to Defend Human Rights Telling Stories." *Utrecht Law Review* 7: 93–112.

Bauman, Zygmunt. 1991. *Modernity and Ambivalence*. Cambridge: Polity Press.

BBC. 2014. "Zhou Yongkang: China Investigates Ex-Security Chief." July 29. www.bbc.com/news/world-asia-28544428 (accessed July 29, 2014).

Beck, Ulrich. 1992. *Risk Society: Towards a New Modernity*. London: Sage.

———. 2002. "The Terrorist Threat: World Risk Society Revisited." *Theory, Culture & Society* 19: 39–55.

Beitz, Charles. 2009. *The Idea of Human Rights*. Oxford: Oxford University Press.

Bell, Duran. 2008a. "Marriage Payments: A Fundamental Reconsideration." *Structure and Dynamics* 3 (1). http://escholarship.org/uc/item/6mv253zb#page-1 (accessed May 1, 2013).

———. 2008b. *China's New Confucianism: Politics and Everyday Life in a Changing Society*. Princeton, NJ: Princeton University Press.

Berard, Tim. 2005. Rethinking Practices and Structures. *Philosophy of the Social Sciences* 35: 196–230.

Berdahl, Daphne. 2000. "Introduction: An Anthropology of Postsocialism." In *Altering States: Ethnographies of Transition in Eastern Europe and the Former Soviet Union*, edited by Daphne Berdahl, Matti Bunzl, and Martha Lampland, 1–13. Ann Arbor, MI: University of Michigan Press.

Berdahl, Daphne, Matti Bunzl, and Martha Lampland, eds. 2000. *Altering States: Ethnographies of Transition in Eastern Europe and the Former Soviet Union*. Ann Arbor, MI: University of Michigan Press.

Bi Xiangyang (毕向阳). 2006. 从"草民"到"公民"— 当代北京都市运动 (From "Subject" to "Citizen": Urban Movements in Contemporary Beijing). 清华大学社会学系博士学位论文 (PhD dissertation, Department of Sociology, Tsinghua University).

Birge, Bettine. 2002. *Women, Property, and Confucian Reaction in Sung and Yüan China (960–1368)*. Cambridge: Cambridge University Press.

Boholm, Åsa. 2003. "The Cultural Nature of Risk: Can There be an Anthropology of Uncertainty?" *Ethnos* 68: 159–178.

Bourdieu, Pierre. 1977. *Outline of a Theory of Practice*. Translated by Richard Nice. Cambridge: Cambridge University Press.

———. 1984. *Distinction: A Social Critique of the Judgment of Taste*. Translated by Richard Nice. Cambridge, MA: Harvard University Press.

———. 1990. *The Logic of Practice*. Translated by Richard Nice. Stanford, CA: Stanford University Press.

———. 2005. *The Social Structures of Economy*. Translated by Chris Turner. Cambridge: Polity Press.

Boyer, Dominic. 2010. "Why Not Neosocialism?" *Savageminds.org*. http://savageminds.org/2010/02/16/why-not-neosocialism/ (accessed May 6, 2013).

Braybrooke, David. 2005. "Where does the Moral Force of the Concept of Needs Reside and When?" *The Philosophy of Need* 57: 209–228.

Bridger, Sue, and Frances Pine, eds. 1998. *Surviving Post-Socialism: Local Strategies and Regional Response in Eastern Europe and the Former Soviet Union*. London: Routledge.

Buckley, Chris. 2012. "In China's Chongqing, Dismay over Downfall of Bo Xilai." *Reuters* March 16. http://reuters.com/article/2012/03/16/us-china-chongqing-idUSBRE82F0H120120316 (accessed October 4, 2012).

Buckley, Chris, and Ben Blanchard. 2012. "China's Wen Rebukes Key Leadership Contender." *Reuters* March 14. http://reuters.com/article/2012/03/14/us-china-npc-wen-chongqing-idUSBRE82D0GS20120314 (accessed October 4, 2012).

Buoye, Thomas. 2000. *Manslaughter, Markets, and Moral Economy: Violent Disputes over Property Rights in Eighteenth-Century China*. Cambridge: Cambridge University Press.

Burawoy, Michael, and Katherine Verdery, eds. 1999. *Uncertain Transition: Ethnographies of Change in the Postsocialist World*. Lanham, MD: Rowman & Littlefield.

Butler, Judith. 1987. *Subjects of Desire: Hegelian Reflections in Twentieth-Century France*. New York: Columbia University Press.

Cao, Nanlai. 2010. *Constructing China's Jerusalem: Christians, Power, and Place in Contemporary Wenzhou*. Stanford, CA: Stanford University Press.

Caskie, Paul. 2000. "Back to Basics: Household Food Production in Russia." *Journal of Agricultural Economics* 51 (2): 196–209.

Chang Ping. 2011. "A House Divided." *South China Morning Post* August 30. http://scmp.com/article/977569/house-divided (accessed August 30, 2011).

Chau, Adam. 2008. "An Awful Mark: Symbolic Violence and Urban Renewal in Reform-Era China." *Visual Studies* 23: 195–210.

Chen Guangjin (陈光金). 2012. 迈向全面建成小康社会的新阶段 (Approaching the New Stage of Accomplishing Relative Affluence of Society in All Aspects). In陆学艺 李培林 陈光金 主编2013年中国社会形势分析与预测 (Analysis and Forecasts on Society of China 2013, edited by Lu Xueyi, Li Peilin, and Chen Guangjin), 1–18. 北京：社会科学文献出版社 (Beijing: Social Sciences Academic Press).

Chen, Joshui (陈弱水). 2006. 公共意识与中国文化 (*Public Consciousness and Chinese Culture*). 北京：新星出版社 (Beijing: New Star Press).

Chen Peng (陈鹏). 2010. 当代中国城市业主的法权抗争 (Urban Homeowners' Legal Rights Activism in Contemporary China). 社会学研究 (*Sociological Studies*) 25 (1): 34–63.

Cheung, Chi-Pui. 2012. "The Paradox of China's Urban-Rural Integration: The *hukou* System, Rural Policy, and Rural Land Development." *Urban Anthropology* 41: 293–328.

Cheung, Steven. 1982. *Will China Go "Capitalist"?: An Economic Analysis of Property Rights and Institutional Change*. London: The Institute of Economic Affairs.

Chibnik, Michael. 2011. *Anthropology, Economics, and Choice*. Austin, TX: University of Texas Press.

Ch'ien Mu (钱穆). 1979 从中国历史来看中国民族性及中国文化 (The Nature of Chinese Nationality and the Chinese Culture from the Perspective of Chinese History). 香港: 中文大學出版社 (Hong Kong: The Chinese University Press).

China Index Academy (中国指数研究院). 2014. 中国房地产指数系统百城价格指数报告 (*China Real Estate 100 City Price Index Report*) January 1. http://fdc.fang.com/report/7508.htm (accessed March 10, 2014).

Chongqing Daily Editorial (重庆日报社论). 2012. 科学发展,富民兴渝 (Scientific Development for the Prosperity of the People and Chongqing). 重庆日报 (*Chongqing Daily*) June 23, p. 2.

Chongqing Morning Post (重庆晨报). 2011. 坚定不移走共同富裕道路 (Following the Road of Common Prosperity resolutely). July 25, p. A02.

Chongqing Times (重庆时报). 2011. 最高法院：强拆遇自杀等极端行为应停止执行 (The Supreme Court: Forced Demolition Should Be Aborted When Encountered by Extreme Acts Like Suicides). September 10, p. 2.

Clough, Patricia. 2007. "Introduction." In *The Affective Turn: Theorizing the Social*, edited by Patricia Clough and Jean Halley, 1–33. Durham, NC: Duke University Press.

———. 2010. "The Affective Turn: Political Economy, Biomedia, and Bodies." In *The Affect Theory Reader*, edited by Melissa Gregg and Gregory Seigworth, 206–225. Durham, NC: Duke University Press.

Cowan, Jane. 2006. "Culture and Rights after *Culture and Rights*." *American Anthropologist* 108: 9–24.

Cowan, Jane, Marie-Bénédicte Dembour, and Richard Wilson. 2001. "Introduction." In *Culture and Rights: Anthropological Perspectives*, edited by Jane Cowan, Marie-Bénédicte Dembour, and Richard Wilson, 1–26. Cambridge: Cambridge University Press.

Cui Zhiyuan (崔之元). 2011. 重庆实验的三个理论视角：乔治、米德与葛兰西 (The Three Theoretical Vantage Points in the Chongqing Experiment: George, Meade, and Gramsci). 开放时代 (*Open Times* 30). http://opentimes.cn/bencandy.php?fid=312&aid=1389 (accessed August 4, 2013).

Davis, Deborah. 1995. "Introduction: Urban China." In *Urban Spaces in Contemporary China: The Potential for Autonomy and Community in Post-Mao China*, edited by Deborah Davis, Richard Kraus, Barry Naughton, and Elizabeth Perry, 1–22. Cambridge: Cambridge University Press.

Davis, Deborah, and Wang Feng. 2009. "Poverty and Wealth in Postsocialist China: An Overview." In *Creating Wealth and Poverty in Postsocialist China*, edited by Deborah Davis and Wang Feng, 3–19. Stanford, CA: Stanford University Press.

de Bary, William. 1998a. "Preface." In *Confucianism and Human Rights*, edited by William de Bary and Tu Weiming, ix–xx. New York: Columbia University Press.

———. 1998b. "Introduction." In *Confucianism and Human Rights*, edited by William de Bary and Tu Weiming, 1–26. New York: Columbia University Press.

Dikötter, Frank. 2010. *Mao's Great Famine: The History of China's Most Devastating Catastrophe 1958–1962*. New York: Walker & Co.

Du Yu (杜宇). 2012. 住房城乡建设部有关负责人谈棚户区改造 (An Official from the Ministry of Housing and Urban-Rural Development Comments on Shanty Town Redevelopment). 新华社 (*Xinhua News Agency*) November 29. http://cusdn.org.cn/news_detail.php?id=218434 (accessed January 20, 2013).

Duckett, Jane. 2011. *The Chinese State's Retreat from Health: Policy and the Politics of Retrenchment*. London: Routledge.

The Economist. 2007. "Ideology in China: Confucius Makes a Comeback." May 17. http://economist.com/node/9202957 (accessed June, 10, 2013).

Eiss, Paul, and David Pedersen. 2002. "Introduction: Values of Value." *Cultural Anthropology* 17: 283–290.

Engels, Friedrich. (1872) 1979. *The Housing Question*. Moscow: Progress Publishers.

Englund, Harri. 2006. *Prisoners of Freedom: Human Rights and the African Poor*. Berkeley, CA: University of California Press.

———. 2013. "Reclaiming the Anthropology of Claim-making." *Journal of the Royal Anthropological Institute* 19: 248–249.

Englund, Harri, and James Leach. 2000. "Ethnography and the Meta-Narratives of Modernity." *Current Anthropology* 41: 225–248.

Erie, Matthew. 2012. "Property Rights, Legal Consciousness and the New Media in China: The Hard Case of the Toughest Nail-House in History." *China Information* 26: 35–59.

Fang Yaomei, and Wang Bingtuan (方耀楣 王兵团). 2006. 城市拆迁的社会学思考 (A Sociological Thought on Urban Demolition and Relocation). 中共福建省委党校学报(*Journal of Fujian Party School*) 309 (9): 53–57.

Fei Xiaotong. (1947) 1992. *From the Soil: The Foundations of Chinese Society*, translated by Gary Hamilton and Wang Zheng. Berkeley, CA: University of California Press.

Feng Yujun (冯玉军). 2004. 权力、权利和利益的博弈—我国当前城市房屋拆迁问题的法律与经济分析 (A Game Between Power, Rights, and Interests). 中国法学 (*China Legal Science*) 19 (4): 40–81.

Fisher, Irving. 1930. *The Theory of Interest as Determined by Impatience to Spend Income and Opportunity to Invest It*. New York: The Macmillan Company.

Fleischer, Friederike. 2005. "Housing China's Emerging Classes." PhD dissertation, Graduate Faculty in Anthropology, The City University of New York.

———. 2010. *Suburban Beijing: Housing Consumption in Contemporary China*. Minneapolis, MN: University of Minnesota Press.

Fong, Vanessa. 2006. *Only Hope: Coming of Age Under China's One-child Policy*. Stanford, CA: Stanford University Press.

Foucault, Michel, and Gilles Deleuze. 1977. "Intellectuals and Power: A Conversation between Michel Foucault and Gilles Deleuze." In *Language, Counter-Memory, Practice: Selected Essays and Interviews by Michel Foucault*, edited by Donald Bouchard, 205–217. Ithaca, NY: Cornell University Press.

Fraser, Nancy. 1989. *Unruly Practices: Power, Discourse and Gender in Contemporary Social Theory*. Cambridge: Polity Press.

Garnsey, Peter. 2007. *Thinking about Property: From Antiquity to the Age of Revolution*. Cambridge: Cambridge University Press.

Gates, Hill. 1996. *China's Motor: A Thousand Years of Petty Capitalism*. Ithaca, NY: Cornell University Press.

Geisler, Charles. 2006. "Ownership in Stateless Places." In *Changing Properties of Property*, edited by Franz von Benda-Beckman, Keebet von Benda-Beckman, and Melanie Wiber, 40–57. New York: Berghahn Books.

Giddens, Anthony. 1979. *Central Problems in Social Theory*. Berkeley: University of California Press.

Gledhill, John. 2004. "Neoliberalism." In *A Companion to the Anthropology of Politics*, edited by David Nugent and Joan Vincent, 332–349. Malden, MA: Blackwell.

Gluckman, Max. 1940. "Analysis of a Social Situation in Modern Zululand." *Bantu Studies* 14: 1–30.

———. 1954. *Rituals of Rebellion in South East Africa*. Manchester: Manchester University Press.

Goffman, Erving. 1958. *The Presentation of Self in Everyday Life*. Edinburg: Bateman.
Goodale, Mark. 2009. *Surrendering to Utopia: An Anthropology of Human Rights*. Stanford, CA: Stanford University Press.
Goody, Jack. 1973. "Bridewealth and Dowry in Africa and Eurasia." In *Bridewealth and Dowry*, edited by Jack Goody and Stanley Tambiah, 1–58. Cambridge: Cambridge University Press.
———. 1998. "Dowry and the Rights of Women to Property." In *Property Relations: Renewing the Anthropological Tradition*, edited by Chris Hann, 201–213. Cambridge: Cambridge University Press.
Gough, Janet. 1988. "Risk and Uncertainty." Information paper no. 10, Centre for Resource Management, University of Canterbury and Lincoln College.
Graeber, David. 2001. *Toward an Anthropological Theory of Value: The False Coin of Our Own Dreams*. New York: Palgrave.
Grammaticas, Damian. 2012. "Bo Xilai Scandal: Litmus Test for China?" *BBC* April 20. http://bbc.co.uk/news/world-asia-china-17793949 (accessed October 4, 2012).
Greenhalgh, Susan. 2008. *Just One Child: Science and Policy in Deng's China*. Berkeley, CA: University of California Press.
Guan Bing (管兵). 2010. 维权行动和基层民主参与:以B市商品房业主为例 (Rights Protecting Actions and Grassroots Democratic Participation: The Case of Homeowners in City B). 社会 (*Society*) 30: 46–74.
Guo, Xiaolin. 1999. "The Role of Local Government in Creating Property Rights." In *Property Rights and Economic Reform in China*, edited by Jean Oi and Andrew Walder, 71–94. Stanford, CA: Stanford University Press.
Guo Yuhua, and Shen Yuan (郭于华 沈原). 2012. 居住的政治: B市业主维权与社区建设的实证研究 (The Politics of Living: Empirical Research on the Rights Defense and Community Building of Beijing). 开放时代 (*Open Times*) 31 (2). http://opentimes.cn/bencandy.php?fid=331&aid=1573 (accessed October 16, 2012).
Guo Zhongxiao (咼中校). 2012. 广东改革新路径汪洋要突破利益集团压力 (The New Reform Path of Guangdong and Wang Yang's Breakthrough in Countering the Vested Interest Groups). 亚洲周刊 (*Yazhou Zhoukan*) May 25. http://yzzk.com/cfm/Content_Archive.cfm?Channel=ae&Path=2428180342/22ae1a.cfm (accessed July 4, 2012).
Guyer, Jane. 2009. "Composites, Fictions, and Risk: Toward an Ethnography of Price." In *Market and Society: The Great Transformation Today*, edited by Chris Hann and Keith Hart, 203–220. Cambridge: Cambridge University Press.
Handelman, Don. 2006. "The Extended Case: Interactional Foundations and Prospective Dimensions." In *The Manchester School: Practice and Ethnographic Praxis in Anthropology*, edited by Terry Evens and Don Handelman, 94–117. New York: Berghahn.
Haney, Lynne. 1999. "'But We are Still Mothers': Gender, the State, and the Construction of Need in Postsocialist Hungary." In *Uncertain Transition: Ethnographies of Change in the Post Socialist World*, edited by Michael Burawoy and Katherine Verdery, 151–187. Lanham, MD: Rowman & Littlefield.
Hann, Chris. 1998. "Introduction: The Embeddedness of Property." In *Property Relations: Renewing the Anthropological Tradition*, edited by Chris Hann, 1–47 Cambridge: Cambridge University Press.
———, ed. 2002. *Postsocialism: Ideals, Ideologies and Practices in Eurasia*. London: Routledge.
Hann, Chris, and Keith Hart. 2011. *Economic Anthropology*. Cambridge: Polity Press.
Hardt, Michael. 2007. "Foreword: What Affects are Good for." In *The Affective Turn: Theorizing the Social*, edited by Patricia Clough and Jean Halley, ix–xiii. Durham, NC: Duke University Press.
Harms, Erik. 2013. "Eviction Time in the New Saigon: Temporalities of Displacement in the Rubble of Development." *Cultural Anthropology* 28: 344–368.
Hart, Keith. 2000. *Memory Bank: Money in an Unequal World*. London: Profile Books.
Harvey, David. 2005. *A Brief History of Neoliberalism*. Oxford: Oxford University Press.

Heimer, Maria. 2006. "The Cadre Responsibility System and the Changing Needs of the Party." In *The Communist Party in Reform*, edited by Kjeld Brodsgaard and Zheng Yongnian, 122–138. New York: Routledge.
Heller, Agnes. 1974. *The Theory of Need in Marx*. London: Allison & Busby.
Hess, Steve. 2010. "Nail-Houses, Land Rights, and Frames of Injustice on China's Protest Landscape." *Asian Survey* 50: 908–926.
Hirsch, Eric. 2010. "Property and Persons: New Forms and Contests in the Era of Neoliberalism." *Annual Review of Anthropology* 36: 347–360.
Hirschman, Albert. 1977. *The Passions and the Interests*. Princeton, NJ: Princeton University Press.
Ho, Karen. 2009. *Liquidated: An Ethnography of Wall Street*. Durham, NC: Duke University Press.
Ho, Peter. 2001. "Who Owns China's Land? Policies, Property Rights and Deliberate Institutional Ambiguity." *The China Quarterly* 166: 387–414.
Hoffman, Lisa. 2010. *Patriotic Professionalism in Urban China: Fostering Talent*. Philadelphia, PA: Temple University Press.
Holston, James. 2008. *Insurgent Citizenship; Disjunctions of Democracy and Modernity in Brazil*. Princeton, NJ: Princeton University Press.
Hong, Haolan, and Steve Jiang. 2011. "Outrage in China after Toddler Run Over, Ignored." *CNN* October 18. http://edition.cnn.com/2011/10/17/world/asia/china-toddler-hit-and-run / index.html?hpt=wo_bn4 (accessed June 10, 2013).
Hsing, You-tien. 2010. *The Great Urban Transformation: Politics of Land and Property in China*. Oxford: Oxford University Press.
Hsu, Carolyn. 2007. *Creating Market Socialism: How Ordinary People are Shaping Class and Status in China*. Durham, NC: Duke University Press.
Huang, Yasheng. 2008. *Capitalism with Chinese Characteristics: Entrepreneurship and the State*. Cambridge: Cambridge University Press.
Huang, Youqin. 2004. "The Road to Homeownership: A Longitudinal Analysis of Tenure Transition in Urban China (1949–94)." *International Journal of Urban and Regional Research* 28 (4): 774–795.
Huang, Youqin, and Chengdong Yi. 2011. "Second Home Ownership in Transitional Urban China." *Housing Studies* 26 (3): 423–447.
Huang Zongzhi (黄宗智). 2011. 重庆："第三只手"推动的公平发展？(Chongqing: is the 'Third Hand' Promoting Equality in Development?). 开放时代 (*Open Times*) 30 (9). http://opentimes.cn/bencandy.php?fid=312&aid=1387 (accessed October 4, 2012).
Hubbert, Jennifer. 2014. "Ambiguous State: Confucius Institutes and Chinese Soft Power in the U.S. Classroom." *Political and Legal Anthropology Review* 37: 329–349.
Hudson, Michael. 2012. *The Bubble and Beyond: Fictitious Capital, Debt Deflation and Global Crisis*. Dresden: ISLET.
Humphrey, Caroline. 2002. "Does the Category 'Postsocialist' Still Make Sense? In *Postsocialism: Ideals, Ideologies and Practices in Eurasia*, edited by Chris Hann, 12–14. London: Routledge.
———. 2007. "New Subjects and Situated Interdependence: After Privatisation in Ulan-Ude." In *Urban Life in Post-Soviet Asia*, edited by Catherine Alexander, Victor Buchli, and Caroline Humphrey, 175–207. London: UCL Press.
Humphrey, Caroline, and Ruth Mandel. 2002. "The Market in Everyday Life: Ethnographies of Postsocialism." In *Markets and Moralities: Ethnographies of Postsocialism*, edited by Ruth Mandel and Caroline Humphrey, 1–16. Oxford: Berg.
Humphrey, Caroline, and Katherine Verdery. 2004. "Introduction: Raising Questions About Property." In *Property in Question: Value Transformation in the Global Economy*, edited by Caroline Humphrey and Katherine Verdery, 1–25. Oxford: Berg.
Hunt, Lynn. 2007. *Inventing Human Rights: A History*. New York: W.W. Norton.
Ignatieff, Michael. 2001. *Human Rights as Politics and Idolatry*. Princeton, NJ: Princeton University Press.
Isin, Engin. 2008. "Theorizing Acts of Citizenship." In *Acts of Citizenship*, edited by Engin Isin and Greg Nielsen, 15–43. London: Zed Books.

Jacobs, Andrew. 2011. "Confucius Statue Vanishes Near Tiananmen Square." *New York Times* April 22. www.nytimes.com/2011/04/23/world/asia/23confucius.html?_r=0 (accessed June 10, 2013).

Jankowiak, William 2004. "Market Reforms, Nationalism, and the Expansion of Urban China's Moral Horizon." *Urban Anthropology* 33: 167–210.

———. 2009. "Wellbeing, Cultural Pathology, and Personal Rejuvenation in a Chinese City, 1981–2005." In *Pursuits of Happiness: Wellbeing in Anthropological Perspective*, edited by Gordon Mathews and Carolina Izquierdo, 147–166. New York: Berghahn.

Jenne, Erin. 2006. *Ethnic Bargaining: The Paradox of Minority Empowerment*. Ithaca, NY: Cornell University Press.

Ji Shiming (纪硕鸣). 2009. 重庆模式创中国经济反攻新路径 (The Chongqing Model Creates a New Path for the Chinese Economic Counter Offensive). 亚洲周刊 (*Yazhou Zhoukan*) February 15. http://yzzk.com/cfm/Content_Archive.cfm?Channel=ae&Path=3157217821/06ae1a.cfm (accessed May 4, 2012).

Jiang, Yihong. 2013. "Altering the Rules: Chinese Homeowners' Participation in Policymaking." *Journal of Current Chinese Affairs* 42: 124–148.

Joyce, Michael, David Miles, Andrew Scott, and Dimitri Vayanos. 2012. "Quantitative Easing and Unconventional Monetary Policy—An Introduction." *The Economic Journal* 122: F271–F288.

Juris, Jeffrey. 2012. "Reflections on #Occupy Everywhere: Social Media, Public Space, and Emerging Logics of Aggregation." *American Ethnologist* 39: 259–279.

Kaneff, Deema. 2002. "The Shame and Pride of Market Activity: Morality, Identity and Trading in Postsocialist Rural Bulgaria." In *Markets and Moralities: Ethnographies of Postsocialism*, edited by Ruth Mandel and Caroline Humphrey, 33–51. Oxford: Berg.

Kendzior, Sarah. 2011. "Digital Distrust: Uzbek Cynicism and Solidarity in the Internet Age." *American Ethnologist* 38: 559–575.

Kingston-Mann, Esther. 2006. "The Romance of Privatisation and Its Unheralded Challenges: Case Studies from English, Russian, Soviet and Post-Soviet History." In *Changing Properties of Property*, edited by Frank von Benda-Beckman, Keebet von Benda-Beckman, and Melanie Wiber, 58–83. New York: Berghahn Books.

Kipnis, Andrew. 2007. "Neoliberalism Reified: *Suzhi* Discourse and Tropes of Neoliberalism in the PRC." *Journal of the Royal Anthropological Institute* 13: 383–399.

———. 2008. *China and Postsocialist Anthropology: Theorizing Power and Society After Communism*. Norwalk, CT: EastBridge.

Kleinman, Arthur, Yunxiang Yan, Jing Jun, Sing Lee, Everett Zhang, Pan Tianshu, Wu Fei, and Guo Jinhua 2011. *Deep China: The Moral Life of the Person*. Berkeley, CA: University of California Press.

Knight, Frank. (1921) 2009. *Risk, Uncertainty and Profit*. Kissimmee, FL: Signalman Publishing.

Kolb, Deborah, and Judith Williams. 2003. *Everyday Negotiation: Navigating the Hidden Agendas in Bargaining*. San Francisco, CA: Jossey-Bass.

Kotz, David. 2000. "Lessons from Economic Transition in Russia and China." In *Political Economy and Contemporary Capitalism*, edited by Ron Baiman, Heather Boushey, and Dawn Saunders, 210–217. Armonk, NY: M. Sharpe.

Kui Yingtao (隗瀛涛). 1991. 近代重庆城市史研究 (Urban History Study of Modern Chongqing). 近代史研究 (*Modern Chinese History Studies*) 4: 69–98.

Ladwig, Patrice. 2008. "From Revolution to Reform: Ethics, Gift Giving and Sangha-State Relationship in Lao Buddhism." PhD dissertation, Department of Social Anthropology, University of Cambridge.

Laidlaw, James. 2002. "For an Anthropology of Ethics and Freedom." *Journal of the Royal Anthropological Institute* 8: 311–332.

———. 2013. *The Subject of Virtue: An Anthropology of Ethics and Freedom*. Cambridge: Cambridge University Press.

Lampland, Martha. 2000. "Afterword." In *Altering States: Ethnographies of Transition in Eastern Europe and the Former Soviet Union*, edited by Daphne Berdahl, Matti Bunzl, and Martha Lampland, 209–218. Ann Arbor, MI: University of Michigan Press.

Lazar, Sian. 2010. "Citizenship." In *The Routledge Encyclopedia of Social and Cultural Anthropology*, second edition, edited by Alan Barnard and Jonathan Spencer, 120–122. Oxon: Routledge.

Leach, Edmund. 1976. *Culture and Communication: The Logic by Which Symbols Are Connected*. Cambridge: Cambridge University Press.

Lee, Ching Kwan. 2009. "From Inequality to Inequity: Popular Conceptions of Social (In)Justice in Beijing." In *Creating Wealth and Poverty in Postsocialist China*, edited by Deborah Davis and Wang Feng, 213–231. Stanford, CA: Stanford University Press.

Lee Ming-huei. 2013. "Confucianism, Kant, and Virtue Ethics." In *Virtue Ethics and Confucianism*, edited by Stephen Angle and Michael Slote, 47–55. New York: Routledge.

Liang Qian, and Wang Zheng (梁倩 王政). 2013. 上半年重点城市卖地收入爆发式增长 (Explosive Growth in Major Cities' Land Sales Income in the First Half Year). 人民日报(*The People's Daily*) July 2. http://politics.people.com.cn/n/2013/0702/c1001-22039804.html (accessed July 3, 2013).

Lin Chengxi (林成西) 1994. 清代乾嘉之际四川商业重心的东移 (The shift of Sichuan's commercial centre to the east in the Qianlong–Jiaqing era of the Qing Dynasty). 清史研究 (*Studies in Qing History*) 3, 62–69.

Liu Xin. 2009. "Institutional Basis of Social Stratification in Transitional China." In *Creating Wealth and Poverty in Postsocialist China*, edited by Deborah Davis and Wang Feng, 85–96. Stanford, CA: Stanford University Press.

Liu Zhonghe, and Zhou Ke, eds (刘忠和 周珂 主编). 2012. 学习雷锋好榜样 (*Learn from Lei Feng*). 北京：人民日报出版社 (Beijing: People's Daily Press).

Lynteris, Christos. 2012. *The Spirit of Selflessness in Maoist China: Socialist Medicine and the New Man*. Hampshire: Palgrave Macmillan.

Ma, Shu-Yun. 2010. *Shareholding System Reform in China: Privatizing by Groping Stones*. Cheltenham: Edward Elgar.

Macfarlane, Alan. 1998. "The Mystery of Property: Inheritance and Industrialization in England and Japan." In *Property Relations: Renewing the Anthropological Tradition*, edited by Chris Hann, 104–123. Cambridge: Cambridge University Press.

Mains, Daniel. 2012. "Blackouts and Progress: Privatization, Infrastructure, and a Developmentalist State in Jimma, Ethiopia." *Cultural Anthropology* 27: 3–27.

Mak, Stephen, Lennon Choy, and Winky Ho. 2007. Privatization, Housing Conditions and Affordability in the People's Republic of China. *Habitat International* 31: 117–192.

Makeham, John. 2008. *Lost Soul: "Confucianism" in Contemporary Chinese Academic Discourse*. Cambridge, MA: Harvard University Asia Center.

Mandel, Ruth, and Caroline Humphrey, eds. 2002. *Markets and Moralities: Ethnographies of Postsocialism*. Oxford: Berg.

Marshall, John. 2009. "The Financial Crisis in the US: Key Events, Causes and Responses." The House of Commons Library Research Paper 09/34. http://www.voltairenet.org/IMG/pdf/US_Financial_Crisis.pdf (accessed July 1, 2013).

Marx, Karl, and Friedrich Engels. (1848) 2005. "The Communist Manifesto." In *The Communist Manifesto: A Road Map to History's Most Important Political Document*, edited by Phil Gasper, 37–90. Chicago, IL: Haymarket Books.

Massumi, Brian. 1995. "The Autonomy of Affect." *Cultural Critique* 31: 83–109.

Maurer, Bill, and Gabriele Schwab. 2006. "Introduction: the Political and Psychic Economies of Accelerating Possession." In *Accelerating Possession: Global Futures of Property and Personhood*, edited by Bill Maurer & Gabriele Schwab, 1–17. New York: Columbia University Press.

Mauss, Marcel. (1950) 1990. *The Gift: The Form and Reason for Exchange in Archaic Societies*, translated by Wilfred Halls. New York: Norton.

Merrifield, Caroline, Erik Harms, Ryan Jobson, and Sayd Randle. 2013. "Modernity of This Century: Four Ethnographic Perspectives." *Anthropology of This Century* 8. http://aotcpress.com/articles/modernity-century-ethnographic-perspectives/ (accessed July 1, 2014).

Merry, Sally. 2006. *Human Rights and Gender Violence: Translating International Law into Local Justice*. Chicago, IL: The University of Chicago.

Messer, Ellen. 1993. "Anthropology and Human Rights." *Annual Review of Anthropology* 22: 221–249.
Middleton, Townsend, and Jason Cons. 2014. "Coming to Terms: Reinserting Research Assistants into Ethnography's Past and Present." *Ethnography* 15: 279–290.
Ministry of Finance, PRC (中华人民共和国财政部). 2013. 2013 年各省（区,市）财政预算报告会编 (A Compilation of Budget Reports of the Various Provincial Governments 2013). www.mof.gov.cn/zhuantihuigu/2013ssyshb/ (accessed October 15, 2013).
Mitchell, Clyde. (1956) 2006. "Case and Situation Analysis." In *The Manchester School: Practice and Ethnographic Praxis in Anthropology*, edited by Terry Evens and Don Handelman, 23–44. New York: Berghahn Books.
Miyazaki, Hirokazu. 2013. *Arbitraging Japan: Dreams of Capitalism at the End of Finance*. Berkeley, CA: University of California Press.
Moore, Henrietta. 2011. *Still Life: Hopes, Desires and Satisfactions*. Cambridge: Polity.
Morgan, Lewis H. (1877) 2006. "Ethnical Periods." In *Readings for a History of Anthropological Theory*, edited by Paul Erickson and Liam Murphy, 42–50. Toronto: Higher Education University of Toronto Press.
Mosko, Mark. 2000. "Inalienable Ethnography: Keeping-While-Giving and the Trobriand Case." *Journal of the Royal Anthropological Institute* 6: 377–396.
Mukhija, Vinit. 2003. *Squatters as Developers?: Slum Demolition and Redevelopment in Mumbai, India*. Hampshire: Ashgate Publishing.
Muthoo, Abhinay. 1999. *Bargaining Theory with Applications*. Cambridge: Cambridge University Press.
Navaro-Yashin, Yael. 2009. "Affective Spaces, Melancholic Objects: Ruination and the Production of Anthropological Knowledge." *Journal of the Royal Anthropological Institute* 15: 1–18.
Negri, Antonio. 1999. "Value and Affect", translated by Michale Hardt. *Boundary* 2 (26): 77–88.
News.163.com. 2007. 男子称扶摔倒老太反被告 被判赔4万 (A Man Who Said He Had Helped an Old Woman was Fined Forty Thousand Yuan). September 6. http://news.163.com/07/0906/05/3NMDBNR600011229.html# (accessed June 10, 2013).
Nonini, Donald. 2008. "Is China Becoming Neoliberal?" *Critique of Anthropology* 28: 145–176.
OECD. 2007. *Chongqing Municipality's Development Strategy: Some Reflections from the International Experience of the Territorial Development Policy Committee of the OECD*. http://oecd.org/dataoecd/14/13/40061625.pdf (accessed July 20, 2012).
Ong, Aihwa. 2006. *Neoliberalism as Exception: Mutations in Citizenship and Sovereignty*. Durham, NC: Duke University Press.
Ong, Aihwa, and Li Zhang. 2008. "Privatizing China: Powers of the Self, Socialism from Afar." In *Privatizing China: Socialism from Afar*, edited by Li Zhang and Aihwa Ong, 1–20. New York: Cornell University Press.
Opler, Morris. 1968. "Tylor's Application of Evolutionary Theory to Public Issues of His Day." *Anthropological Quarterly* 4: 1–8.
Ortiz, Horacio. 2013. "Financial Value: Economic, Moral, Political, Global." *HAU: Journal of Ethnographic Theory* 3: 64–79.
Ortner, Sherry. 2006. *Anthropology and Social Theory: Culture, Power, and the Acting Subject*. Durham, NC: Duke University Press.
Osburg, John. 2013. *Anxious Wealth: Money, and Morality among China's New Rich*. Stanford, CA: Stanford University Press.
Ouroussoff, Alexandra. 2010. *Wall Street at War: The Secret Struggle for the Global Economy*. Cambridge: Polity Press.
Parry, Jonathan, and Maurice Bloch. 1989. "Introduction: Money and the Morality of Exchange." In *Money and Morality of Exchange*, edited by Jonathan Parry and Maurice Bloch, 1–32. Cambridge: Cambridge University Press.
Peerenboom, Randall. 1995. "Rights, Interests, and the Interests in Rights in China." *Stanford Journal of International Law* 31: 359–386.

———. 1998. "Confucian Harmony and Freedom of Thought." In *Confucianism and Human Rights*, edited by William de Bary, and Tu Weiming, 234–260. New York: Columbia University Press.

Peng Xiaobing, and Zheng Rongjuan (彭小兵 郑荣娟). 2010. 利益博弈, 制度公正与城市拆迁纠纷化解机制 (The Game of Interests, Institutional Justice, and the Mechanism of Resolving Urban Demolition Conflicts). 重庆大学学报 (*Journal of Chongqing University*) 16 (1): 39–46.

People's Daily Commentator (人民日报评论员). 2012. 坚决拥护党中央的正确决定 (In Resolute Support of the Right Decision of CPC Central Committee). 人民网 (*People's Daily Online)* April 11. http://opinion.people.com.cn/GB/17621326.html (accessed October 4, 2012).

People's Daily Online. 2012. "Bo Xilai Expelled from CPC, Public Office." September 28. http://english.people.com.cn/90785/7965161.html (accessed October 4, 2012).

———. 2013. "Bo Xilai Sentenced to Life Imprisonment." September 22. http://english.peopledaily.com.cn/90785/8406360.html (accessed September 23, 2013).

Perry, Elizabeth. 2008. "Chinese Conceptions of 'Rights': From Mencius to Mao—and Now." *Perspectives on Politics* 6: 37–50.

Pieke, Frank. 1996. *The Ordinary and the Extraordinary: An Anthropological Study of Chinese Reform and the 1989 People's Movement*. London: Kegan Paul.

———. 2009. *The Good Communist: Elite Training and State Building in Today's China*. Cambridge: Cambridge University Press.

Pine, Frances, and Sue Bridger. 1998. "Introduction: Transition to Post-Socialism and Cultures of Survival." In *Surviving Post-Socialism: Local Strategies and Regional Responses in Eastern Europe and the Former Soviet Union*, edited by Sue Bridger and Frances Pine, 1–15. Oxon: Routledge.

Platz, Stephanie. 2000. "The Shape of National Time: Daily Life, History, and Identity During Armenia's Transition to Independence, 1991–1994." In *Altering States: Ethnographies of Transition in Eastern Europe and the Former Soviet Union*, edited by Daphne Berdahl, Matti Bunzl, and Martha Lampland, 114–138. Ann Arbor, MI: University of Michigan Press.

Postill, John. 2010. "Introduction: Theorising Media and Practice." In *Theorising Media and Practice*, edited by Birgit Bräuchler and John Postill, 1–23. Oxford: Berghahn.

Read, Benjamin. 2003. "Democratizing the Neighbourhood? New Private Housing and Homeowner Self-Organization in Urban China." *The China Journal* 49: 31–59.

———. 2008. "Property Rights and Homeowner Activism in New Neighborhoods." In *Privatizing China: Socialism from Afar*, edited by Li Zhang and Aihwa Ong, 41–56. New York: Cornell University Press.

———. 2012. *Roots of the State: Neighborhood Organization and Social Networks in Beijing and Taipei*. Stanford, CA: Stanford University Press.

Rehm, Gebhard, and Hinrich Julius. 2009. "The New Chinese Property Rights Law: An Evaluation from a Continental European Perspective." *Columbia Journal of Asian Law* 22: 177–234.

Ren, Hai. 2010. "The Neoliberal State and Risk Society: The Chinese State and the Middle Class." *TELOS* 151: 105–128.

Ren, Xuefei. 2013. *Urban China*. Cambridge: Polity Press.

Ren Hong, and Wang Lin (任宏 王林). 2008.中国房地产泡沫研究 (*Research on China's Real Estate Bubbles*). 重庆:重庆大学出版社 (Chongqing: Chongqing University Press).

Ribet, Steven. 2011. "Confucius Statue Erected in Tiananmen Square." *Press TV*, January 14. www.youtube.com/watch?v=oLKdrt0zoDU (accessed June 10, 2013).

Richard, Analiese, and Daromir Rudnyckyj. 2009. Economies of Affect. *Journal of the Royal Anthropological Institute* 15: 57–77.

Riles, Annelise. 2006. "Introduction: In Response." In *Documents: Artifacts of Modern Knowledge*, edited by Annelise Riles, 1–40. Ann Arbor, MI: University of Michigan Press.

———. 2011. *Collateral Knowledge: Legal Reasoning in the Global Financial Markets*. Chicago, IL: University of Chicago Press.

Rofel, Lisa. 2007. *Desiring China: Experiments in Neoliberalism, Sexuality, and Public Culture*. Durham, NC: Durham University Press.

Rorty, Richard. 1998. "Human Rights, Rationality and Sentimentality." In *Truth and Progress*, edited by Richad Rorty 167–185. Cambridge: Cambridge University Press.

Rosemont, Henry Jr. 1998. "Human Rights: A Bill of Worries." In *Confucianism and Human Rights*, edited by William de Bary and Tu Weiming, 54–66. New York: Columbia University Press.

Rosen, Lawrence. 1984. *Bargaining for Reality: The Construction of Social Relations in a Muslim Community*. Chicago, IL: The University of Chicago Press.

Rothbard, Murray. 1998. *The Ethics of Liberty*. New York: New York University Press.

Rouse, Joseph. 2007. "Practice Theory." In *Handbook of the Philosophy of Science: Philosophy of Anthropology and Sociology*, edited by Stephen Turner and Mark Risjord, 639–681. Amsterdam: Elsevier.

Ruo Li (若离). 2014. 土地财政巅峰？地方政府2013年土地出让金收入创历史之最 (The Peak of Land Finance? Local Governments' 2013 Land Sales Income Hit a New High). 华尔街见闻 (*wallstreetcn.com*) July 14. http://wallstreetcn.com/node/99091 (accessed August 10, 2014).

Saad, Reem. 2012. "The Egyptian Revolution: A Triumph of Poetry." *American Ethnologist* 39: 63–66.

Sahlins, Marshall. 1976. *Culture and Practical Reason*. Chicago, IL: The University of Chicago Press.

———. 2013. "On the Culture of Material Value and the Cosmography of Riches". Paper presented at the History and Anthropology Seminars, King's College, University of Cambridge.

Schatzki, Theodore. 1997. "Practices and Actions: A Wittgensteinian Critique of Bourdieu and Giddens." *Philosophy of the Social Sciences* 27: 283–308.

Schwenkel, Christina. 2013. "Post/Socialist Affect: Ruination and Reconstruction of the Nation in Urban Vietnam." *Cultural Anthropology* 28: 252–277.

Seigel, Jerrold. 1983. "Books Review: The Problem of Human Needs and the Critique of Civilisation." *The Journal of Modern History* 55: 513–515.

Seigworth, Gregory, and Melissa Gregg. 2010. "An Inventory of Shimmers." In *The Affect Theory Reader*, edited by Melissa Gregg and Gregory Seigworth, 1–28. Durham, NC: Duke University Press.

Shao, Qin. 2008. "Bridge Under Water: The Dilemma of the Chinese Petition System." *China Currents* 7 (1). http://chinacenter.net/bridge-under-water-the-dilemma-of-the-chinese-petition-system/ (accessed December 12, 2012).

———. 2013. *Shanghai Gone: Domicide and Defiance in a Chinese Megacity*. Lanham, MD: Rowman & Littlefield.

Shi Yunqing (施云卿). 2007. 机会空间的营造: 以B市彼拆迁居民集团行政诉讼 (The Construction of Opportunity Space: A Case Study on Collective Lawsuit in City B). 社会学研究 (*Sociological Studies*) 22 (2): 80–110.

Smart, Alan. 2001. "Unruly Places: Urban Governance and the Persistence of Illegality in Hong Kong's Urban Squatter Areas." *American Anthropologist* 103: 30–44.

Smart, Barry. 1999. *Facing Modernity: Ambivalence, Reflexivity and Morality*. London: SAGE.

Smith, Karl. 2012. "From Dividual and Individual Selves to Porous Subjects." *The Australian Journal of Anthropology* 23: 50–64.

Sneath, David. 2004. "Proprietary Regimes and Sociotechnical Systems: Rights Over Land in Mongolia's 'Age of the Market.'" In *Property in Question: Value Transformation in the Global Economy*, edited by Katherine Verdery and Caroline Humphrey, 161–184. Oxford: Berghahn Books.

Solinger, Dorothy. 1999. *Contesting Citizenship in Urban China: Peasant Migrants, the State, and the Logic of the Market*. Berkeley, CA: University of California Press.

Springborg, Patricia. 1981. *The Problems of Human Needs and Critique of Civilization*. London: Allen & Unwin.

Stewart, Kathleen. 2007. *Ordinary Affects*. Durham, NC: Duke University Press.

Strathern, Marilyn. 1988. *The Gender of the Gift: Problems with Women and Problems with Society in Melanesia*. Berkeley, CA: University of California Press.

———. 1999. *Property, Substance and Effect: Anthropological Essays on Persons and Things*. London: Athlone Press.

——— 2004. “Transactions: An Analytical Foray.” In *Transactions and Creations: Property Debates and the Stimulus of Melanesia*, edited by Eric Hirsch and Marilyn Strathern, 85–109. New York: Berghahn.

———. 2006. “Divided Origins and the Arithmetic of Ownership.” In *Accelerating Possession: Global Futures of Property and Personhood*, edited by Bill Maurer and Gabriele Schwab, 135–173. New York: Columbia University Press.

Strathern, Marilyn, and Eric Hirsch. 2004. “Introduction.” In *Transactions and Creations: Property Debates and the Stimulus of Melanesia*, edited by Eric Hirsch and Marilyn Strathern, 1–20. Oxford: Berghahn.

Su Wei (苏伟). 2010. 薄熙来新政与重庆模式 (The New Deal of Bo Xilai and the Chongqing Model). 凤凰财经网 (*Fenghuang Finance*) June 9. http://finance.ifeng.com/opinion/ fhzl/20100609/2294597.shtml (accessed October 4, 2012).

Su Wei, Yang Fan, and Liu Shiwen (苏伟 杨帆 刘士文). 2011. 重庆模式 (The Chongqing Model). 北京：中国经济出版社 (Beijing: China Economic Publishing House).

Sun Liping (孙立平). 2013. 社会需要稳定,”权力维稳模式”必须清算 (Society Needs Stability, the “Model of *weiwen* by Power” Must be Redressed). *sohu.com* April 24. http://sunliping.blog.sohu.com/261989579.html (accessed June 4, 2013).

Szelényi, Ivan (伊万·塞勒尼). 2011. 诸种第三条道路 (The Variants of the Third Way). 开放时代 (*Open Times*) 30 (9). http://opentimes.cn/bencandy.php?fid=312&aid=1391 (accessed November 9, 2012).

Terjesen, Andrew. 2013. “Is Empathy the ‘One Thread’ Running through Confucianism?” In *Virtue Ethics and Confucianism*, edited by Stephen Angle and Michael Slote, 201–208. New York: Routledge.

Tett, Gillian. 2009. *Fool’s Gold: How the Bold Dream of a Small Tribe at J.P. Morgan was Corrupted by Wall Street Greed and Unleashed a Catastrophe*. New York: Free Press.

———. 2013. “Three Meetings, Many Partings.” March 9, p. 78.

Theodossopoulos, Dimitrios. 2013. “Laying Claim to Authenticity: Five Anthropological Dilemmas.” *Anthropological Quarterly* 86: 337–360.

Thomassen, Bjørn. 2012. “ Anthropology and Its Many Modernities: When Concepts Matter.” *Journal of the Royal Anthropological Institute* 18: 160–178.

Thomson, Garrett. 1987. *Needs*. London: Routledge & Kegan Paul.

Tomba, Luigi. 2005. “Residential Space and Collective Interest Formation in Beijing’s Housing Disputes.” *The China Quarterly* 184: 934–951.

Tsai, Lily. 2007. *Accountability Without Democracy: Solidarity Groups and Public Good Provision in Rural China*. Cambridge: Cambridge University Press.

Tu Wei-Ming. 1985. *Confucian Thought: Selfhood as Creative Transformation*. Albany, NY: State University of New York Press.

———. 1998. “Epilogue: Human Rights as a Confucian Moral Discourse.” In *Confucianism and Human Rights*, edited by William de Bary and Tu Weiming, 297–307. New York: Columbia University Press.

Valentine, Seán. 2006. “The modernisation of China and the Chinese critique of Modernity.” *Revista HMiC* IV: 7–22.

Verdery, Katherine. 1991. “Theorizing Socialism, a Prologue to the Transition.” *American Ethnologist* 18: 419–439.

———. 1996. *What was Socialism, and What Comes Next?* Princeton, NJ: Princeton University Press.

———. 1999. “Fuzzy Property: Rights, Power, and Identity in Transylvania’s Decollectivization.” In *Uncertain Transition: Ethnographies of Change in the Postsocialist World*, edited by Michael Burawoy and Katherine Verdery, 53–81. Lanham, MD: Rowman & Littlefield.

———. 2004. “After Socialism.” In *A Companion to the Anthropology of Politics*, edited by David Nugent and Joan Vincent, 21–34. Malden, MA: Blackwell.

Visser, Oane. 2006. "Property, Labor Relations and Social Obligations in Russia's Privatized Farm Enterprises." In *Changing Properties of Property*, edited by Frank von Benda-Beckman, Keebet von Benda-Beckman, and Melanie Wiber, 126–146. New York: Berghahn.

von Benda-Beckman, Frank, Keebet von Benda-Beckman, and Melaine Wiber. 2006. "The properties of property." In *Changing Properties of Property*, edited by Frank von Benda-Beckman, Keebet von Benda-Beckman, and Melanie Wiber, 1–39. New York: Berghahn.

Wang, Fei-Ling. 2010. "Conflict, Resistance and the Transformation of the *hukou* System." In *Chinese Society: Change, Conflict and Resistance*, edited by Elizabeth Perry and Mark Selden, 80–100. London: Routledge.

Wang Jianxin, Cui Jia, and Liu Zhiqiang (王建新 崔佳 刘志强). 2012. 重庆探索共同富裕 (Chongqing's Search for Common Prosperity). 人民日报 (*People's Daily*) January 9, p. 1.

Wang, Qingbin, and Qin Zhou. 2010. "China's Divorce and Remarriage Rates: Trends and Regional Disparities." *Journal of Divorce and Remarriage* 51: 257–267.

Wang, Shaoguang. 1995. "The Politics of Private Time: Changing Leisure Patterns in Urban China." In *Urban Spaces in Contemporary China*, edited by Deborah Davis, Richard Kraus, Barry Naughton, and Elizabeth Perry, 149–172. Cambridge: Cambridge University Press.

Wang Wei (王炜). 2012. 告别蜗居 照亮生活 (Farewell to Cramped Dwellings, Lighting Up Life). 人民日报 (*People's Daily*) September 25, p. 1.

Wang, Ya Ping, Lei Shao, Alan Murie, and Jianhua Cheng. 2012. "The Maturation of the Neo-Liberal Housing Market in Urban China." *Housing Studies* 27: 343–359.

Wang Yu, and Li Jing (汪瑜 黎静). 2011. 新婚姻法房屋如何依法登记 房产归属被明确 (How to Register Real Estate Under the New Marriage Law). *www.focus.cn* August 24. http://house.focus.cn/news/2011-08-24/1449247.html (accessed August 24, 2011).

Wang, Zhengxu, Long Sun, Liuqing Xu, and Dragan Pavlićević. 2013. "Leadership in China's Urban Middle Class Protest: The Movement to Protect Homeowners' Rights in Beijing." *The China Quarterly* 214: 411–431.

Watson, Ruby. 1991. "Afterword: Marriage and Gender Inequality." In *Marriage and Inequality in Chinese Society*, edited by Ruby Watson and Patricia Ebrey, 347–368. Berkeley, CA: University of California Press.

Weinstein, Liza, and Xuefei Ren. 2009. "The Changing Right to the City: Urban Renewal and Housing Rights in Globalizing Shanghai and Mumbai." *City & Community* 8: 407–432.

Weller, Robert. 1999. *Alternate Civilities: Democracy and Culture in China and Taiwan*. Oxford: Westview.

Whyte, Martin, and William Parish 1984. *Urban Life in Contemporary China*. Chicago, IL: The University of Chicago Press.

Wilson, Richard. 2006. "Afterword to 'Anthropology and Human Rights in a New Key': The Social Life of Human Rights." *American Anthropologist* 108: 77–83.

Wirth, Louis. 1938. "Urbanism as a Way of Life." *The American Journal of Sociology* 44: 1–24.

Wong, John, and Zheng Yongnian, eds. 2001. *Thenanxun Legacy and China's Development in the Post-Deng Era*. Singapore: Singapore University Press.

World Bank. 1996. *World Development Report 1996: From Plan to Market*. New York: Oxford University Press.

Wringe, Bill. 2005. "Needs, Rights, and Collective Obligations." In *The Philosophy of Need*, edited by Soran Reader, 187–207. Royal Institute of Philosophy Supplement. Cambridge: Cambridge University Press.

www.sina.com.cn. 2011. 专访中国最年轻博士: 要父母全款在北京买房 (An Interview With China's Youngest PhD: Demanding Parents to Buy House in Beijing in Full Payment). October 17. http://news.sina.com.cn/s/sd/2011-10-17/102423314883.shtml (accessed April 28, 2013).

Xinhua News. 2006. "China Publishes 'Harmonious Society' Resolution." October 19. http://china.org.cn/english/2006/Oct/184810.htm (accessed June 10, 2013).

———. 2007. "Road to Happiness." December 18. http://english.people.com.cn/90001/90776/90882/6322902.html (accessed June 2, 2013).

———. 2012. "Curbing Property Speculation a Long-Term Task: Premier Wen." July 7. http://news.xinhuanet.com/english/china/2012-07/07/c_131700984.htm (accessed July 10, 2012).

———. 2013a. "CPC Announces Decision on Comprehensive Reform." November 12. http://news.xinhuanet.com/english/china/2013-11/12/c_132882325.htm (accessed November 14, 2013).
———. 2013b. "China to Ease One-Child Policy." November 15. http://news.xinhuanet.com/english/china/2013-11/15/c_132891920.htm (accessed November 15, 2013).
———. 2014a. "Xi Stresses Core Socialist Values." February 25. http://news.xinhuanet.com/english/china/2014-02/25/c_126190257.htm (accessed July 15, 2014).
———. 2014b. "CPC Set New Blueprint for Rule of Law." October 23. http://news.xinhuanet.com/english/china/2014-10/23/c_133737845.htm (accessed January 25, 2015).
———. 2015. "Xi Asks Party Organs to Support Independent Judicial System." January 20. http://news.xinhuanet.com/english/china/2015-01/20/c_133933467.htm (accessed January 25, 2015).
Xu Mingyue, and Huang Dongbin (许明月 黄东斌). 2010. 城市房屋从"拆迁"到"征收"的跨越与私有财产保护制度的完善 (The Leap from "Demolition" to "Expropriation" of Urban Houses and the Institutional Advancement of Private Property Protection). 西南民族大学学报 (*Journal of Southwest University for Nationalities*) 31 (12): 90–95.
Yan, Alice. 2012. "Selfish Mainland Chinese Society Needs Good Samaritan Laws, Critics Say." *South China Morning Post* August 27. www.scmp.com/news/china/article/1023010/selfish-mainland-chinese-society-needs-good-samaritan-laws-critics-say (accessed November 12, 2013).
Yan, Yunxiang. 1996. *The Flow of Gifts: Reciprocity and Social Networks in a Chinese Village*. Stanford, CA: Stanford University Press.
———. 2009a. "The Good Samaritan's New Trouble: A Study of the Changing Moral Landscape in Contemporary China." *Cultural Anthropology* 17: 9–24.
———. 2009b. *The Individualization of Chinese Society*. Oxford: Berg.
———. 2011. "The Changing Moral Landscape." In *Deep China: The Moral Life of the Person*, edited by Arthur Kleinman, Yunxiang Yan, Jing Jun, Sing Lee, Everett Zhang, Pan Tianshu, Wu Fei, and Guo Jinhua, 1–35. Berkeley, CA: University of California Press.
Yang, Mayfair. 1989. "The Gift Economy and State Power in China." *Comparative Studies in Society and History* 31: 25–54.
———. 1994. *Gifts, Favors, and Banquets: The Art of Social Relationships in China*. New York: Cornell University Press.
———. 2002. "The Resilience of *guanxi* and Its New Deployments: A Critique of Some New *guanxi* Scholarship." *The China Quarterly* 170: 459–476.
Yazhou Zhoukan (亚洲周刊). 2013. 國五條打壓房產市場 為避稅中國爆發離婚潮 (The State Council's Five Policies of Combating the Property Market Triggered Divorces for Tax Avoidance). March 17. www.yzzk.com/cfm/Content_Archive.cfm?Channel=bc&Path=386015171/11bca.cfm (accessed March 18, 2013).
Ye, Juliet, and Emma Ashbum. 2010. "Fighting Eviction: The Videogame." *China Real Time Report* September 16. http://blogs.wsj.com/chinarealtime/2010/09/16/fighting-eviction-the-videogame/ (accessed December 21, 2012).
Yessenova, Saulesh. 2010. "Borrowed Places: Eviction Wars and Property Rights Formalization in Kazakhstan." *Research in Economic Anthropology* 30: 11–45.
Yu Guangyuan (于光远). 1978. 谈谈社会主义公有制和按劳分配问题 (*A Discussion on the Socialist Public Ownership System and the Problem of Distribution According to Work*). 上海：人民出版社 (Shanghai: People's Press).
Yurchak, Alexei. 2006. *Everything was Forever, Until It was No More: The Last Soviet Generation*. Princeton, NJ: Princeton University Press.
Zaloom, Caitlin. 2006. *Out of the Pits: Traders and Technology from Chicago to London*. Chicago, IL: The University of Chicago Press.
Zhang, Li. 2001. *Strangers in the City: Reconfigurations of Space, Power, and Social Networks Within China's Floating Population*. Stanford, CA: Stanford University Press.
———. 2004. "Forced from Home: Property Rights, Civic Activism, and the Politics of Relocation in China." *Urban Anthropology* 33: 247–281.

———. 2006. "Contesting Spatial Modernity in Late-Socialist China." *Current Anthropology* 47: 461–484.

———. 2010. *In Search of Paradise: Middle Class Living in a Chinese Metropolis*. New York: Cornell University Press.

Zhang Lei (张磊). 2005. 业主维权运动:对北京市几个小区个案的考查 (Beijing Homeowners' Rights Defense Movement). 社会学研究 (*Sociological Studies*) 20 (6): 1–39.

Zhang Zhanpeng (张展鹏). 2013. 防不胜"房"—"中国式离婚"如何收场? (How Would "China- Style Divorces" End Up?). *www.news.cn* April 18. http://news.xinhuanet.com/fortune/2013-04/18/c_115443362.htm (accessed April 28, 2013).

Zhao, Jianhua. 2014. "Shame and Discipline: The Practice and Discourse of a 'Confucian Model' of Management in a Family Firm in China." *Critique of Anthropology* 34: 129–152.

Zheng, Tiantian. 2009. *Red Lights: The Lives of Sex Workers in Postsocialist China*. Minneapolis, MN: University of Minnesota Press.

Zhou Tao (周滔). 2010. 房地产领域腐败的形成及对策 (The Causes and Solutions of Corruption in the Real Estate Arena). 经济体制改革 (*Reform of Economic Structure*) 4: 166–169.

Zhou, Xueguang. 2004. *The State and Life Chances in Urban China: Redistribution and Stratification, 1949–1994*. Cambridge: Cambridge University Press.

Zhou Xueguang (周雪光). 2005. 关系产权：产权制度的一个社会学解析释 (Property Rights as a Relational Concept: A Sociological Approach). 社会学研究 (*Sociological Studies*) 20 (2): 1–31.

Zhou Yong (周勇). 1989. 近代重庆经济中心的初步形成 (The Early Development of Chongqing As an Economic Center in the Modern Era). 社会科学研究 (*Social Science Research*) 5: 100–108.

Zhou Yongming. 2006. *Historicizing Online Politics: Telegraphy, the Internet, and Political Participation in China*. Stanford, CA: Stanford University Press.

Zhu Jiangang (朱健刚). 2011. 以理抗争:都市集体行动的策略—以广州南园的业主维权为例 (Confrontation by Rightness: Strategy in Urban Collective Actions—The Case of Guangzhou Nanyuan Owners' Rights Defense). 社会 (*Society*) 31: 24–41.

Zhuang Wenjia (庄文嘉). 2011. 跨越国家赋予的权利？对广州市业主抗争的个案研究 (Beyond State-Conferred Rights? A Case Study on Homeowners' Confrontation in Guangzhou). 社会 (*Society*) 31: 88–113.

Zigon, Jarrett. 2013. "Human Rights as Moral Progress? A Critique." *Cultural Anthropology* 25: 716–736.

Index

About the Author

Ho Cheuk-Yuet is adjunct assistant professor of anthropology at the Chinese University of Hong Kong. He received his doctoral degree from the University of Cambridge. Prior to studying anthropology, he was a finance professional and economic researcher in Asia for more than twenty years. His research interests include property rights, human rights, anthropology of finance, and political economy.

www.ingramcontent.com/pod-product-compliance
Lightning Source LLC
Chambersburg PA
CBHW031414220926
51612CB00004B/24
* 9 7 8 1 4 9 8 5 0 6 8 3 0 *